THE SIX
PERFECTIONS

THE SIX PERFECTIONS

BUDDHISM AND THE CULTIVATION OF CHARACTER

DALE S. WRIGHT

OXFORD
UNIVERSITY PRESS

OXFORD
UNIVERSITY PRESS

Oxford University Press, Inc., publishes works that further
Oxford University's objective of excellence
in research, scholarship, and education.

Oxford   New York
Auckland   Cape Town   Dar es Salaam   Hong Kong   Karachi
Kuala Lumpur   Madrid   Melbourne   Mexico City   Nairobi
New Delhi   Shanghai   Taipei   Toronto

With offices in
Argentina   Austria   Brazil   Chile   Czech Republic   France   Greece
Guatemala   Hungary   Italy   Japan   Poland   Portugal   Singapore
South Korea   Switzerland   Thailand   Turkey   Ukraine   Vietnam

Copyright © 2009 by Oxford University Press, Inc.

Published by Oxford University Press, Inc.
198 Madison Avenue, New York, New York 10016
www.oup.com

First issued as an Oxford University Press paperback, 2011.

Oxford is a registered trademark of Oxford University Press

Library of Congress Cataloging-in-Publication Data
Wright, Dale Stuart.
The six perfections : Buddhism and the cultivation
of character / by Dale S. Wright.
p. cm.
Includes bibliographical references and index.
ISBN 978-0-19-538201-3 (hardcover); 978-0-19-989579-3
1. Paramitas (Buddhism). 2. Buddhist ethics.
I. Title. II. Title: 6 perceptions.
BQ4336.W75   2009
294.3'422—dc22   2009002661

Printed in the United States of America
on acid-free paper

CONTENTS

THE SIX
PERFECTIONS

INTRODUCTION

The question my life presses upon me, whether I face it directly or not, is "How shall I live?" "As what kind of person?" All of us face the task of constructing a life for ourselves, of shaping ourselves into certain kinds of people who will live lives of one kind or another, for better or worse. Some people undertake this task deliberately; they make choices in life in view of an image of the kind of person they would hope to become. From the early beginnings of their tradition, Buddhists have maintained that nothing is more important than developing the freedom implied in their activity of self-cultivation—of deliberately shaping the kind of life you will live. For Buddhists, this is the primary responsibility and opportunity that human beings have. It is, they claim, our singular freedom, a freedom available to no other beings in the universe. And although circumstances beyond anyone's control will make very different possibilities available for different people, Buddhists have always recognized that the difference between those who assume the task of self-sculpting with imagination, integrity, and courage, and those who do not is enormous, constituting in Buddhism the difference between enlightened ways of being in the world and unenlightened ways.

This book adopts a Buddhist point of departure on these crucial issues in order to develop a philosophy of self-cultivation. The primary purpose of such a philosophy is practical, that is, to guide life practice. That has certainly been the goal of Buddhists who for over two millennia have spoken and written profoundly on the methods, goals, and significance of the pursuit of enlightenment. At the center of this long-standing Buddhist practice has been a list of "perfections," understood as particular ideals of human character that guide self-cultivation. The perfections provide a concrete image of the human qualities that Buddhists consider truly admirable. An early Buddhist list of "faculties" requiring perfection names five: faith, energy, mindfulness, meditation, and insight.[1] The *Jātaka Tales* about the Buddha's own previous lives list ten perfections, as do late Mahayana texts, although these two lists differ. But the most

frequently named group of perfections, and to my mind the most interesting, is the six perfections, found throughout the early Mahayana sutras
and then beyond in many strands of the Buddhist tradition. These six
qualities of enlightened character are the basis of this book's meditations
on self-cultivation. One sutra introduces the six perfections by having a
disciple ask the Buddha: "How many bases for training are there for
those seeking enlightenment?" The Buddha responds: "There are six:
generosity, morality, tolerance, energy, meditation, and wisdom."[2]

This sutra claims that the six perfections are "bases for training." This
means that they constitute a series of practices or "trainings" that guide
Buddhist practitioners toward the goal of enlightenment or awakening.
These six "trainings" are the means or methods to that all-important end.
But the perfections are much more than techniques. They are also the
most fundamental dimensions of the goal of enlightenment. Enlightenment is defined in terms of these six qualities of human character;
together they constitute the essential qualities of that ideal human state.
The perfections, therefore, are the ideal, not just the means to it. Being
generous, morally aware, tolerant, energetic, meditative, and wise is
what it means for a Buddhist to be enlightened. If perfection in these
six dimensions of human character is the goal, then enlightenment,
understood in this Buddhist sense, would also be closely correlated to
these particular practices. Recognizing this, one sutra says: "Enlightenment just is the path and the path is enlightenment."[3] To be moving along
the path of self-cultivation by developing the six perfections is the very
meaning of "enlightenment."

The six perfections, therefore, provide a concrete image of the Buddhist goal or ideal end. This end, which in classical Greek philosophy is
called the "idea of the good," or the "ideal of a good life," is in Buddhism
called the "thought of enlightenment." For Buddhists, the "thought of
enlightenment" is the ideal image that gives purpose and direction to
human lives—it guides decisions, provides reasons for acting, and shapes
the will. There is an important sense in which almost everyone has a
"thought of enlightenment"—some "idea of the good." We all imagine
better lives than what we have managed so far—better ways to do what
we are doing, better relationships with others, better character, and so on.
For most people, though, this idea or thought is underdeveloped and
immature. It has not been systematically cultivated to become the driving
force behind deliberate change. More a daydream than a well-honed
understanding, an immature "thought of enlightenment" will have little

capacity to guide a life and very little power to shape deliberations on how we might best live our lives.

For those who do cultivate ideals for the purpose of self-sculpting, there are still a number of difficulties to overcome. One common mistake is to project an idea of the good for your life that does not inspire, an image of life that is so bland and ordinary that it hardly amounts to an aspiration. When we lack imagination for what we might do with our lives, little movement is empowered. When the goals that guide a life are entirely conventional, they fail to provide the exhilaration and energy sufficient to generate movement and inspired effort. The opposite mistake is to project a "thought of enlightenment" that is simply unattainable, a goal that no human being could ever accomplish. In cultivating a "thought of enlightenment," not just any concept will do. Worthy ideals are not the products of fantasy. If we take as our "thought of enlightenment" some flatteringly divine image, that image will be unable to guide us in shaping our lives because it is out of accord with the reality of our situation. An authentic "thought of enlightenment" would be one that fits our actual possibilities and that can be revised as our situation in life changes. It would be a conception of an ideal for our lives that accords with possibilities that are both really our own and truly ideal. To find it, we ask ourselves: What can we reasonably and ideally aspire to be under the circumstances that we now face?

Now in any particular form of Buddhism, of course, this image of the ideal is given to participants. It is given in the form of images of enlightened saints in sacred stories and texts, in the ideals that the tradition provides to participants for admiration and emulation. But when we stand back to examine these traditions over large stretches of historical time and geographical space, we see that these ideal images are multiple and various. Different Buddhist teachers in different Buddhist cultures at different times have conceived the "thought of enlightenment" in somewhat different ways; they engage in different practices and lead intriguingly different kinds of enlightened lives. Although initially troubling, this complexity and diversity in Buddhism is enormously beneficial, a gift to Buddhists and in the long run to the world. "Enlightenment" has not been and cannot be static and unchangeable if human beings are not. It cannot be a single human possibility set for all time, even if some Buddhists have naïvely assumed that it is. The human ideal varies in accordance with the circumstances in which particular people find themselves, and it evolves as human history unfolds.

If Buddhism offered only one option, a single form of human excellence, then it would be useful only to people in situations just like the original circumstances in which the ideal was formed. Fortunately, Buddhism and its "thought of enlightenment" have histories—complex responses to the issue of human excellence derived from a variety of circumstances over long stretches of time—and many of these are available as models for consideration in crafting an image of the human ideal that best suits contemporary circumstances. Along with the "thought of enlightenment," of which each of the six is a part, the perfections evolve in the minds of Buddhist practitioners. Our understanding of excellence in all spheres of life grows as we develop and move toward it. We learn to extend our image of excellence in sports and music, for example, every time we see or hear the greatest performers. Encountering their brilliance, we revise and enlarge the image of what perfection in that domain might be.

Similarly, in the realm of ethics or human character, we learn what enlightened life is by encountering images of greatness. We extend our understanding of admirable generosity, for example, when we learn about Mother Teresa or other people who embody that particular excellence of human character. Where do we encounter these images of human excellence? Occasionally in person, but more commonly in outstanding cultural achievement—in literature, philosophy, and the arts, where some vision of the ideal or anti-ideal is set out before us. Buddhist literature and culture abound in vivid examples of human excellence, concrete images that function to show us what greatness of character might look like.

The Sanskrit word traditionally translated as "perfection" is *pāramitā*. This is an ancient word whose origins are obscure. On one account, *pāramitā* derives from *pāram*, meaning "the other side" plus the past participle *itā*, meaning "gone." From this perspective, something is perfected when it has "gone to the other side," that is, when it has fully transcended what it would be in ordinary lives. Others, however, link *pāramitā* to the term *parama,* which means "excellent," or "supreme," such that something is perfected when it arrives at the state of excellence or supremacy. But whatever its etymology, the word *pāramitā* soon became a technical term in Buddhist ethics naming the dimensions of human character that are most important in the state of enlightenment.

As a central term in ethics, however, the English word "perfection" is far from perfect. The most troubling implication in the word "perfection" is the suggestion that at some point there would be an end to human striving and self-cultivation, a final point of completion beyond which no further enlightenment would be possible. In this picture, enlightenment is imagined as the finish line in a race, a particular threshold that, once crossed, ends the activities of human imagination and enlargement. Moreover, if there is such a fixed and final goal for human beings, "perfection" would mean that this final state is the same for all people in all situations and all times. Neither of these implications is credible on Buddhist grounds because, understood in this way, both "enlightenment" and human life lose their depth, becoming static, one dimensional, and lacking all evolutionary potential.

No doubt, many Buddhists have assumed that the "perfections" and "enlightenment" are permanent and fixed in this way. Buddhist wisdom, however, makes a specific target of this common assumption. It suggests, instead, that all things change in complex ways, that nothing is fixed or static, and that, like everything else, the path of enlightenment is open and ongoing, without end. The quest for enlightenment is ongoing, not because we never attain greater insight or comprehension but because in ascending to a higher level we become capable of envisioning something even greater beyond where we currently stand. To travel far is to develop the capacity to see more, not less, and movement in this direction enlarges the space within which ongoing exploration can take place. The truth is that as long as we are human, we will always be perfecting multiple dimensions of our lives and the world. In a healthy spiritual tradition, authentic achievements transform and enrich the "thought of enlightenment" that guides practice, making possible both greater insight and greater freedom.

What is it that we are perfecting in the six perfections? The best word in English for that would be our *character.* It is through resources of character that we undertake enlightening practices, and it is our character that is enlightened. The English word "character" is derived from ancient Greek words meaning to "stamp" or "engrave," activities that leave a "characteristic" mark or impression on something. But this image will be misleading if we take it to mean all of the marks that have been stamped upon us by generative forces in our world—the genetics of our birth inheritance, or the impact of parents, family, neighbors, friends, teachers, and others upon us. All of these forces and many more do make an enormous contribution to the shaping of our identity, but they do not define character. I reserve the word "character" for that part of our overall identity that is shaped by the choices that we ourselves make.

Your character, therefore, is defined by your own acts of self-construction. Unlike other dimensions of your overall identity, character is neither given to you at birth nor imprinted upon you by environment. Many unique developments will shape you into a particular kind of person, often without your being aware of them, but none of these forces will individuate you more than the development of character through a lifetime of deliberate choices. The more character you have developed, the greater the role it will play in defining your overall identity.

Character is a disposition to engage in the world in view of a chosen end, a tendency to impress a "thought of enlightenment" upon all acts and choices. When you act in view of your own vision of the good, your acts will be shaped by that vision, and through that shaping, your character will be gradually formed. Cultivating character in this way presupposes conceiving of yourself as both free and responsible, free to choose what you do and responsible for the outcome of those actions. It also implies the capacity to cultivate the desires that motivate your action and the depth of character to take responsibility for the kind of person your desires will create. Since, as we have seen, the six perfections define and give content to the "thought of enlightenment" in Buddhism, taken together they provide concrete guidance for the construction of character.

Some Buddhist texts maintain that the greatest "awakening" in life is the first one, a point in life when we awaken to the fact that we are both free and responsible to engage in enlightening self-transformation. They refer to this initial breakthrough as "generating of the thought of enlightenment," the moment when we realize that there is a wide variety of human destinies possible for us and that deliberately actualizing one of them depends in part on what we do and how we live. Prior to this awakening, our identity is largely fortuitous—our lives are shaped by things that simply happen to us, without reference to our own deliberations and choices. Generating a "thought of enlightenment" awakens us from this default condition and gets the creative part of our lives under way.

The Buddhist teachings on the six perfections imply a kind of ethics that focuses directly on daily life. Instead of a set of principles to help solve occasional moral quandaries, ethics of this sort permeates everyday activity. Its actions are an integral part of what we do from moment to moment. In this sense, the six perfections are less like a set of principles or rules and more like a system of training. The aim of these six regimes of training is to put into practice a certain manner or quality of spiritual life, and this is accomplished through the daily practice of shaping character. A good analogy for this would be training in physical fitness. Practicing the six perfections, one engages in training to become more generous, moral, tolerant, energetic, meditative, and wise. To train, one must practice on a regular basis, shaping one's life around the various aspects of the training regimen. Just as a physical training program would prepare you to engage in an athletic event, an ethical training program like the six perfections trains practitioners to engage in these basic dimensions of life in deeper and more enlightening ways.

For the kinds of Buddhist ethical practices suggested by the six perfections, more important than the application of rules and adherence to duty is the appreciation and admiration of human lives that embody the kinds of excellence of character contained in the perfections as ideals. Admirable lives, in Buddhism as in other traditions, serve as models to follow and emulate in one's own life practice. In the sutra traditions surrounding the six perfections, these models are called *bodhisattvas*, "enlightened beings" whose practice of the perfections is most highly accomplished. Images of bodhisattvas serve as models of spiritual excellence available for anyone to contemplate and imitate in constructing their own lives.

There are dangers to heed in the activity of emulating paradigmatic lives, however. One danger is that since no previous life has ever arisen in a context exactly like yours, and no prior human being has ever been exactly like you, there will be no perfect model for the kind of life that you ought to live. Your own individual life must be shaped out of circumstances that are precisely your own, out of experiences, personal relationships, and histories that are unique. Drawing on previous, admirable lives as models, therefore, we will need to consider the adaptability of the personal excellences we see in other lives to our own settings, and decide which of these will adequately correlate with our own context and which will either be inapplicable or require adjustments and alterations.

Fortunately, traditions as voluminous and comprehensive as Buddhism offer a wide repertoire of options, some of which, but not all, will be worth considering in our own lives. To make use of these models, we need as much self-knowledge and imagination as we need outward appreciation and imitation of these other lives. The danger is that we might feel obligated by ideal images of human excellence to copy their actions when those might not be suitable for us. Furthermore, we make a mistake in self-cultivation if our admiration of these figures puts us in a slavish or servile relationship in which we are bound and overwhelmed by them. It is therefore essential to maintain enough freedom from models, especially religious models, to avoid subservience and to maintain wise, critical thinking. It is also important to realize that, whatever others have done in the past, it is we who must now make admirable lives for ourselves and we can only do that in a position of freedom and self-respect.

This point leads to a second danger entailed in the emulation of models of greatness. In Buddhism as in other religious traditions, the image of religious exemplars tends over time to ascend to incredible levels of elevation. The stories about saints and prophets accumulate elevation over time through repeated telling, even to the point where they tend to rise above the human realm altogether. This is certainly the case with the literature surrounding bodhisattvas, enlightened beings in Buddhism who represent the ideals of the tradition at the highest levels. In their literary forms, bodhisattvas are imagined to attain the most perfect forms that can be conceived by human authors, including capacities of knowing and accomplishment that rise above the constraints of finitude. Bodhisattvas of this kind are magical and supernatural beings. Wherever this heightened level of transcendence appears in Buddhist literature, the images that they offer are the most exalted forms of life that their authors can imagine without facing the constraints of human finitude. But in that form they are no longer human and are therefore not helpful models for human beings to emulate in deciding how to live their lives.

So, whereas Buddhist bodhisattvas have historically served two functions, only one of these is applicable to the practice of the six perfections. Where bodhisattvas are models of truly admirable human lives, they are substantial resources for our efforts at self-cultivation. On the other hand, wherever bodhisattvas are objects of devotion projected out beyond the human realm into the sphere of the divine, they are removed from the domain of spiritual self-cultivation and placed in the setting of confessional or devotional religious practice. In this sphere, the human role is one of worship and devotion rather than admiration and inspiration.

The more images of excellence we have before us, the more breadth there is to our understanding of the perfections and to our "thought of enlightenment." All of us are born into particular cultural contexts that offer models of excellent human character. But as we encounter more and more of the world, we come to realize that the possibilities presented to us by the immediate context of our family, religious heritage, and education are limited, and that we now have access to an even richer set of possibilities by virtue of an emerging global cultural awareness. The cultivation of breadth of cultural awareness enlarges our ethical imagination by acquainting us with images of greatness that derive from very different settings. Seeing this in travel and in cross-cultural education, we come to realize that the conventional possibilities for life available to us are really only a small subset of the global possibilities into which we may now tap. The global citizen of the future will understand him or herself as inheriting all traditions of human excellence and as responsible for creative, thoughtful arbitration between them.

One common criticism in our time to the entire topic of self-cultivation is the critical point that the extent of focus on the self that self-cultivation implies is itself inappropriate, even delusory, and that it fails to acknowledge the more fundamental communal or social dimension of human life. This is an important point, and one that Buddhists have faced as directly and as responsibly as anyone in other traditions. The overall Buddhist response to this critique entails two primary points. First, and most important, Buddhists maintain that the beneficiary of your practice of self-cultivation is not just you but others around you and, ultimately, the whole of humanity. Early in the career of Mahayana Buddhists who are serious about practicing the perfections, a vow is taken—the bodhisattva vow—in which practitioners vow to seek enlightenment not just for themselves but on behalf of everyone equally. It is the whole of society that needs to be enlightened, not just certain individuals, even if individuals are the catalyst through which such enlightenment might become a reality. In effect, the vow is just to seek enlightenment, at whatever level and to whatever degree that can be accomplished, and not be possessive about it—enlightenment not simply for oneself but on behalf of greater vision for everyone and everything.

The second point follows from the first. We have no choice but to begin the quest wherever we happen to be. If, like most people, we attend primarily to our own well-being, then our interest in enlightenment or the six perfections or anything else extends only so far as the good we think it will do for us as individuals. If the range of our interest and concern does not extend far beyond our own lives, then that is where we must begin, imagining the perfections and enlightenment as beneficial for us as individuals, which, of course, they are. Nevertheless, as we will see shortly, each of the six perfections functions as a system of training to overcome the narrow and myopic sense of self that we all have in immature stages of development. As we progress through the perfections—even if we began for essentially selfish reasons—the practices themselves undermine that sense of self, gradually showing us its superficiality and opening us to a more comprehensive vision. The general criticism of self-cultivation as being too individualistic fails to recognize that we are unable to be of service to others until we have undergone enough self-transformation to begin to see larger realities beyond the importance of our own personal well-being.

So we might say, paraphrasing a Buddhist point on this matter, that all of us need self-cultivation up to a certain point of maturity, but that beyond this point there is very little point in calling it *self*-cultivation because our concerns have broadened dramatically to the point where we are just cultivating enlightenment. This enlightenment is not intended as the property of anyone in particular but as the common good. Making the shift from the primacy of one's own personal development to a broader concern for the well-being and development of all beings is the overarching intention of the six perfections. From a Buddhist point of view, we are always in the process of shaping ourselves to be more attentive to the needs of everyone, even when, at an advanced point of development, we no longer think of it primarily as a process of shaping ourselves. There is no end to the need to open ourselves to the world.

Like many others, I came to the study of Buddhist philosophy in pursuit of truths that would wake me up, providing the kinds of transformation that I could see in images of bodhisattvas and other figures of greatness. I assumed that a close encounter with Buddhist styles of contemplation would change not just what I thought but who I am. I assumed that the primary point of this study was personal transformation, a transformation of mind and character far-reaching enough that it would open me to the world in new ways. I was, at that point, naïve enough to be surprised when it became clear that graduate programs in philosophy and religion at our universities are not organized in accordance with these assumptions. I learned, early on, that academic professionalization required a separation between personal quests for self-transformation, on the one hand, and sophisticated study of world culture, on the other. I was taught that studying different cultures' answers to important religious and philosophical questions need not have a bearing on the kind of person you are, and that the quest for knowledge and the quest for self-transformation are best left to separate parts of oneself, on separate occasions.

Eager to engage in the cultivation of knowledge for what it might contribute to the global enlightenment of character, I made the adjustments necessary to be a full participant in the world of higher knowledge. My original orientation to these matters did not shift decisively, however. I was not persuaded by the dichotomy that separated these forms of self-cultivation. I still sought to be fundamentally reoriented in my own life by means of what I studied. I burden you with this one autobiographical segment only to make the simple point that this book is the result of my ongoing effort to cultivate and extend this initial motive for study. In studying the six perfections and in engaging in the "thought of enlightenment" implied in them, I unapologetically place knowledge in the service of practical wisdom, and strive to make the effects of this search profoundly transformative both to me as writer and to you as reader. What matters most, from my point of view, is not so much what we know as who we become in the process of learning. On this issue, I have learned a great deal from the mainstream of the Buddhist tradition. Throughout its history, Buddhist philosophy has been placed in the service of enlightenment, defined as a profound transformation of human character that encompasses within it the development of knowledge.

Given that particular orientation in its composition, this book is addressed to particular kinds of readers—to many readers, I hope, but certainly not all. This book, like others, is written in a particular style, at a particular level of conceptual difficulty. To whom, then, is it addressed?

- To all those who feel themselves to be faced with the question: How shall we live our lives? To all those who are aware that living passively—simply inheriting the form of their lives without question— is an inadequate, weak response to the obligations and opportunities of life. To all those who already sense that sculpting a worthy life for themselves and others will require disciplines aimed in a practical but long-term way to cultivate a variety of essential human powers, from generosity to wisdom. For all readers of this sort, I have written this book as a guide to reflection and life practice. My aim is to serve as a pathfinder for those who will soon be finding their own, or who are already on the way.
- To young readers, especially, those just now realizing that an intellectual, spiritual, and practical pursuit of this kind is a real option— those, perhaps, just now beginning to see its possible value. My hope is to awaken them to the importance of this task for their future and

for the future of human culture. These are the readers who in
principle have the most to gain from the practice of philosophical
reflection on ideals in human life and from practices of intentional
self-cultivation. Although having struggled along this path myself, I
aspire to serve as their guide on this early stretch of the journey, my
hope is that the forms of excellence that they might one day attain
would extend out beyond my comprehension.

- To readers who may or may not be educated experts in these
  intellectual fields—ethics, philosophy, religious studies, Buddhist
  studies. I therefore write without presupposing technical philosophical language, or Buddhist terms. The few Buddhist concepts
  for which there is no adequate English translation I explain as
  clearly as I can. That does not mean, however, that this book will be
  easy to read. It will require of you both a willingness and an ability to
  think hard about issues that are so close to our lives that they are
  difficult to see. Philosophy that is easy to read and simple to conceive
  is not really philosophy. I urge you to challenge yourself, or take the
  challenge from me, to expand your capacities of imagination and
  conception in the very act of reading in a meditative way. In order to
  avoid any distraction from this task of thinking, I have kept the
  academic etiquette of references and endnotes to a minimum. The
  spirit of the book is exploratory and experimental, an exercise in
  reflective meditation on human ideals. I invite all readers to think
  critically along with me, to disagree, and taking off from what I have
  said, to ask themselves how to go beyond what they have found here.
  Engagement in that critical practice is the point of the book.

- To those who are Buddhists, I offer a reflective meditation on central
  values in your tradition. In doing so, I hope to provoke Buddhists, to
  challenge them to recognize and to use the enormously profound
  resources in their own tradition to confront contemporary life in
  insightful and innovative ways. It is my belief that if Buddhists
  overcome the comforting temptations of traditional orthodoxy that
  simply hold to past ideas and norms in spite of their lack of fit with
  current circumstances, they will find an incredible range and depth
  of cultural resources capable of having an enlightening impact on
  the contemporary world. This is not a call to discard tradition. On
  the contrary, it is a challenge to make innovative use of traditional
  resources in a way that offers wise and compassionate leadership in a
  struggling world. As the great Buddhist texts make clear, although

the first step is a reverent absorption of the tradition, the second step is to guard against attachment, literalism, and other unskillful ways in which a tradition can do as much harm as good. The best way to show gratitude to your tradition is to extend it further and improve it, and that is the challenge that I put to you.

- To those who are not Buddhists, I offer this opportunity to explore Buddhist resources for the purpose of reflection on issues that are of fundamental concern to all human beings. Throughout these chapters, I claim that Buddhism makes available to everyone in our global culture a set of concepts and practices that are extraordinary in their applicability to the task of constructing wise and admirable lives. It is my belief that these Buddhist resources can make a valuable contribution to the development of an ethical consciousness suitable for the global culture of the twenty-first century. In order to clarify and identify specifically Buddhist ideas, I have divided each chapter into two segments. The shorter opening segment of each chapter provides an overview of traditional Buddhist views of the topic of that chapter, describing what the most important Buddhist sutras and other texts have said about each of the six perfections. The second, longer section in each chapter takes that descriptive account up into contemporary reflection. In this more substantial segment—the heart of the book— I aspire to provide for contemporary Buddhism a basic theory for the practices of the six perfections. This section is constructive, not descriptive. Rather than describe what Buddhists have thought on these matters so far, it attempts to build on that foundation, to think further. It raises questions that have not been addressed in Buddhist texts because these questions are crafted in a new era and from the perspective of a culture that is not historically Buddhist. Using Buddhist resources, this book aspires to make a creative contribution to contemporary thinking. It poses the question of how today we would need to conceive of these dimensions of enlightenment in order to regard them as truly "enlightening." It asks what the six perfections of generosity, morality, tolerance, energy, meditation, and wisdom would need to mean today for them to be the admirable ideals that they are intended to be.

Is this book primarily practical or theoretical? It is both, from beginning to end, because it entails the practice of Buddhist theory—the practice of philosophy—insofar as this theory aims at the transformation of everyday life. The same is true throughout the history of Buddhist philosophy—by altering the way you understand the world you alter the way you live and participate in it. It is instructive to note, as we will see in the chapter on the perfection of meditation, that the practice of philosophy in the Buddhist tradition is positioned as a subcategory within the overarching context of meditation. Meditation as contemplation or thoughtfulness is simply one form of meditation practice aimed at transforming the way you live in the world. So, when these chapters engage in philosophical meditation, they are to be understood as a form of "practice," and their aim is the transformation of our daily life—what we do in the world and how. The ultimate goal of this book, as it is for Buddhist philosophy, is practical wisdom.

If this book is exploratory, as claimed, and if there is no end to the ways that human ideals can be extended in our evolutionary future, then it will have failed miserably if, arrogantly, it purports to be a definitive account of these issues. A definitive account of something, as we can see in the root word *fin* or end, puts an end to discussion. This book intends the opposite. It seeks to be exploratory, to open up new paths for reflection in contemporary ethics. While it offers possible answers to many questions that arise in the course of these meditations, the best answers are those that open paths previously unknown and that lead to lines of question and answer that we cannot even imagine now. If this book is successful, it will have evoked new thinking and new meditation, rather than settling matters once and for all. It aspires to enrich and deepen the quality of questions that we are able to pursue.

Is this book primarily philosophical or religious? The aim of the book is to develop a philosophy of spiritual self-cultivation. For thousands of years, many Buddhists (although certainly not all) have undertaken the quest for authentic spiritual life without reference to questions that seem essentially religious from a Western point of view—questions about God or the existence of deity. Without taking a position on the existence or nonexistence of divine beings, Buddhists have placed primary emphasis on the task of self-shaping and the quest for enlightenment, kinds of training wherein we consciously seek to awaken to a broader sense of freedom and responsibility. It is best, I think, not to delay embarking on such a quest until traditional religious questions have been settled. Once you are seriously engaged in enlightening practice, the kinds of questions that seem important will already be in the process of change.

And finally, it is worth our asking: Is this book Buddhist, or not? Yes it is, in certain important respects at least. It considers basic teachings of Buddhist spiritual practice and does so from points of view that include many forms of traditional Buddhism. But something about this question misses the point—that is not what the book is really about. This book, based on Buddhist ideas and written from a point of view that has been shaped by both Buddhist and non-Buddhist resources, is about ideals and the cultivation of character. Drawing on the most insightful resources available, wherever they can be found, it sets a stage upon which you, the reader, will be challenged to ask: How shall we live? From an authentic Buddhist point of view, it matters little whether something can be identified as "Buddhist" or not. What matters is whether what it says is transformative and whether the transformation it offers will enlighten and awaken our lives.

The traditional Buddhist sources for studying the six perfections are enormous. Many of the great texts of this tradition discuss the perfections at length. For the purposes of this study, the classic Mahayana sutras constitute the primary source, especially those known as the *Perfection of Wisdom Sutras,* for example, the *Diamond Sutra*, the *Large Sutra on Perfect Wisdom*, and the *Perfection of Wisdom in Eight Thousand Lines*. In addition, I have drawn resources from the *Vimalakīrti Sūtra*, the *Samdhinirmocana Sūtra*, and especially revealing accounts of the perfections found in the *Pāramitāsamāsa* by Ārya-Śūra, and Śāntideva's *Bodhicaryāvatāra*. Other sources of inspiration, both within and beyond the Buddhist tradition—those without which I could not have even begun to write this book—are listed as "references" at the end of the book.

1

THE PERFECTION OF
GENEROSITY

TRADITIONAL BUDDHIST IMAGES OF
THE PERFECTION OF GENEROSITY
(*DĀNAPĀRAMITĀ*)

Mahayana Buddhist sutras maintain that the most admirable human beings, bodhisattvas at the highest level, are characterized by a profound, universal compassion, compassion so far-reaching that their daily actions demonstrate as much concern for the well-being of others as for themselves. In order to pursue the Buddhist ideal of compassion at this exalted level, practitioners train themselves in the perfection of generosity. Generosity of spirit—the capacity to give of oneself in a wide range of creative ways—has been an important dimension of Buddhist self-cultivation throughout the long history of this tradition.

How, then, does generosity emerge as a topic of self-cultivation in early Mahayana sutras? Although in some sense the first step up a progressively more difficult ladder of Buddhist virtues, generosity is also closely tied to the ultimate goal—enlightenment. Buddhas and enlightened bodhisattvas are imagined to be generous above all else, practicing the broader virtue of compassion toward all sentient beings. The *Perfection of Wisdom Sutras* praise the virtue of generosity and challenge all prospective bodhisattvas to train relentlessly in this capacity as the all-important first step through the six perfections.

The *Perfection of Wisdom Sutras* divide the practice of giving into two types, following the lead of the earlier Buddhist tradition. At the most basic level is the gift of material goods of various kinds, especially those goods necessary for life itself, and at the higher level is the gift of the *dharma*, the teachings, the very possibility of a spiritually significant life. But the teachings are powerless if hunger and poverty stand in the way. So the sutras teach compassion for all levels of human suffering and demand that material generosity be the first order of business for an authentic Buddhist. Therefore the *Large Sutra on Perfect Wisdom* asserts: "Do give gifts! For poverty is a painful thing. One is unable, when poor, to accomplish one's own welfare, much less that of others!"[1]

This sutra heads the list of material objects to be given by saying that the Buddha "gives food to the hungry."[2] But food is just the beginning, and the list goes on to add drink, clothing, shelter, land—the most essential material conditions of life. Nor is that the end of giving. The sutra recommends giving a wide variety of gifts, including what we would consider luxury items such as gold, jewels, perfumes, and so on. Why are these gifts thought to be important in a religion of material renunciation? Two reasons. First, the division of two kinds of giving corresponded in the early Buddhist social world to a division between monks or nuns and lay people. Monks and nuns, because of their vows of poverty, had no material objects to give, not even food. So this list of material objects to give applied more to lay people than to monks, and precisely because Buddhism was a religion of renunciation, even for the laity, radical acts of giving were possible spiritual practices for a devout lay bodhisattva.

The second reason for the inclusion of these luxury gifts was that the sutras in which they are found were meditation manuals as much as they were instructions for actual living. In meditation, anyone, whether they owned material objects or not, could work through the imaginary mental exercises of giving. Visualizing and contemplating acts of giving in meditation, Buddhists hoped to inculcate profound feelings of generosity which in the future would give rise to compassionate, charitable acts on behalf of the well-being of others. Therefore, because it was a mental exercise, the list of items given goes even further, to what would seem to be outrageous extremes. A bodhisattva would meditate on the act of giving away (that is, renouncing) his own family members or, the final material object one could give, his or her own bodily life. These meditative extremes symbolized spiritual renunciation at the highest level, the final surrendering of the self. Thus the *Perfection of Wisdom Sutras* include admonitions like: "A Bodhisattva must cast away even his body, and he must renounce all that is necessary to life."[3]

Meditating on the act of giving away even one's own body, bodhisattvas cultivated what Buddhists considered the most noble motive for all generosity—that the welfare of others be placed on a par with one's own. Recall that the bodhisattva vows compassion in the form of postponing his or her own enlightenment so that others might also have such an opportunity. The bodhisattva vows to achieve a selfless state of compassion in which the enlightenment of others is as important as his or her own and strives toward that goal by training the mind to respond to others in a spirit of open generosity. This training constitutes the early contemplative life of the bodhisattva, and its intention is to effect fundamental change in actual life attitude and behavior.

Beyond material gifts—the first level of generosity—is the gift of the *dharma*—teachings aimed at the elevation of human life to an enlightened level. This second type of giving was thought to be most appropriate for monks and nuns, whose very lifestyle prohibited material giving and who were therefore, by that very act of renunciation, fit to give teachings of spiritual renunciation. Ordinary people were most often pictured as donating the material livelihood of the monastery, while the monks reciprocated with spiritual gifts made possible by the generosity of the laity. But Mahayana Buddhists also realized that anyone—monk, nun, or layperson—might rise to the ideal level of compassion and wisdom pictured in the image of the perfected bodhisattva. Images of lay bodhisattvas, like the wealthy householder Vimalakīrti, emphasized the value of enlightened generosity.

That material generosity, while important, is less exalted than spiritual generosity is a point made frequently in early Mahayana sutras. Picturing human life as most importantly a spiritual quest, the kind of generosity that the sutras most fervently proposed was the gift of visionary life and human excellence, not material objects, and it is in this vein that they were written. Thus the *Sandhinirmocana Sūtra* says: "When Bodhisattvas benefit sentient beings by means of the perfections, if they are satisfied merely by providing benefits to beings through giving material goods and do not establish them on virtuous states after having raised them up from non-virtuous states, this is not skillful."[4] The principal reason for giving material gifts is that human beings might be solidified in their lives and elevated to the point where a spiritual life of wisdom and compassion becomes possible. So, no matter how much material well-being is imagined, the possibility of an authentic spiritual practice goes far beyond it. Therefore the *Diamond Sutra* makes this point firmly: "If someone were to offer an immeasurable quantity of the seven treasures to fill the worlds as infinite as space as an act of generosity, the happiness resulting from that virtuous act would not equal the happiness resulting from a son or daughter of good family who gives rise to the awakened mind and reads, recites, accepts, and puts into practice the sutra, and explains it to others, even if only a *gatha* of four lines."[5]

Upon whom should the bodhisattva bestow his or her generosity? Although answers to this question in the early Mahayana sutras occasionally vary, for the most part they prescribe universal giving. Although in practical circumstances it may be necessary to target those who are most needy, what the sutras want to cultivate is the desire to be generous with everyone. The virtues of nondiscrimination and impartiality are given high praise. Although there was a theory in circulation during the early years of Mahayana Buddhism that the value or merit of a gift is proportional to the worthiness or spiritual merit of the recipient, many texts speak directly against this idea. In this spirit, the *Large Sutra on Perfect Wisdom* describes the true bodhisattva as "having given gifts without differentiating.... But if a Bodhisattva, when faced with a living being ... who does not seem worthy of gifts, should produce a thought to the effect that 'a fully enlightened Buddha is worthy of my gifts, but not this [one],' then he does not have the *dharma* of a Bodhisattva."[6]

Furthermore, the attitude of the giver and the spirit of the gift are essential to the practice of generosity. Calm and even-minded, the enlightened donor is not moved by anything but the welfare of human beings and the openness of heart entailed in noble giving. Therefore, no thought is given to the rewards or "fruit" that inevitably flow back to the donor from a genuine act of generosity. Although there will be rewards that are a natural consequence of an act of giving, focus on those "fruits" demean and undercut the act. The higher and more selfless the conception of the gift, the greater is the perfection of giving. Thus the *Large Sutra* ends a section on the perfection of generosity by warning that the bodhisattva "does not aspire for any fruit of his giving which he could enjoy in Samsāra, and it is only for the purpose of protecting beings, of liberating them, that he courses [i.e., trains] in the perfection of giving."[7]

Indeed, any attitude of self-congratulation on the part of the practitioner of giving is disdained. Self-satisfaction in a good deed displays the weakness of that act of generosity; it demonstrates that the motive and self-conception behind it are still immature. Coveting neither reward nor honor nor gratitude, the bodhisattva gives simply because a need exists. He gives anything, including himself, for the sake of others and in so doing meditates on the idea that "what is my very own this is yours."[8] The difference between generosity grounded in an ingrained sense of ownership and giving that is free of any claim about what is "mine" is developed very clearly into a conception of two distinct kinds of giving. Although both kinds of generosity are beneficial and therefore worthy of cultivation, nevertheless, the "perfection of generosity" is fully defined only in one of these practices.

The first of these two kinds of generosity is "worldly giving." Worldly giving encompasses a wide range of generous acts, from a grudging, stingy gift given for essentially selfish motives all the way to magnanimous gifts of enormous generosity. In fact, one may give everything away, including one's life, and still be within the domain of worldly giving. So what constitutes its worldliness? The answer is: the conception that structures the act itself. Worldly generosity occurs when, having given, the bodhisattva thinks: "I give, that one receives, this is the gift."[9] Even if the bodhisattva also goes so far as to think: "I renounce all that I have without any niggardliness; I act as the Buddha commands. I practice the perfection of giving. I, having made this gift into the common property of all beings, dedicate it to supreme enlightenment, and that without basing myself on anything. By means of this gift and its fruit, may all beings in this very life be at their ease, and may they without any further clinging enter final Nirvana."[10]

Even that is still worldly giving, due to the character of the understanding out of which it arises. According to the *Large Sutra*, the problem with this way of being generous is: "The notion of self, the notion of others, the notion of a gift. To give a gift tied by these three ties, that is called worldly giving."[11] By contrast, the sutra describes the perfection of an act of generosity by way of a "threefold purity": "Here a Bodhisattva gives a gift, and he does not apprehend a self, a recipient, or a gift; also no reward of his giving. He surrenders that gift to all beings, but does not apprehend those beings, or himself either. And, although he dedicates that gift to supreme enlightenment, he does not apprehend any enlightenment. This is called the supermundane perfection of giving."[12]

The distinction between these two levels of the practice of generosity is essential to the *Perfection of Wisdom Sutras*, even though both levels are admired and advocated. On the worldly level we find bodhisattvas giving generously, acting out of a highly cultivated compassion on behalf of all suffering beings without discrimination. The benefits of this kind of giving are described in detail. Bodhisattvas who practice in this way really do help people, suffering is alleviated to some extent, and the teachings of enlightenment are perpetuated. Moreover, bodhisattvas achieve a higher state of enlightenment—they overcome greed and insecurity, the fear of losing possessions. They become more unselfish than they were before and attain a significant peace of mind and happiness. These results are far from inconsequential. Therefore, even though there is a greater perfection of generosity to be taught, all genuine acts of giving are applauded.

The question remains, though: How should we understand the higher form of generosity—"perfect giving"? The answer can be found throughout the *Perfection of Wisdom Sutras*, because wisdom is precisely what is needed to perfect generosity. Wisdom is the sixth perfection, the most perfect of the perfections, and the essential ingredient in all the others. Therefore it will need to be considered here in order to complete our understanding of the ideal of perfect generosity.

Perfect wisdom, whether related to generosity or any other dimension of life, consists in the realization of "emptiness," and it is this teaching that the sutras promulgate from beginning to end. Although emptiness (*śūnyatā*) was an infrequently used word in the earliest layers of Buddhist literature, when it did make its appearance as the central concept in Mahayana sutras, it was defined in terms that were already familiar in the Pali sutras. To say that something is "empty" is to say that it is subject to continual change, that its existence is wholly dependent on factors outside of itself, and that it has no unchanging core or permanent essence. Making that claim, Mahayana Buddhists invoked the basic Buddhist teachings of impermanence, dependent arising, and no-self. All things are "empty" of their own self-established permanent essence because they are always subject to alteration and revision and because they are composed and defined in terms of what lies outside of them.

The "perfection" of giving incorporates the wisdom of "emptiness" to transform the perspective from which acts of giving occur. When the impermanence, dependence, and insubstantiality of all things are absorbed into one's worldview down to the level of daily comportment, everything changes. A new, nonself-centered identity gradually emerges, one that entails reciprocity with everything that previously seemed to be other than oneself. This identity dissolves previous habits of self-protection and self-aggrandizement, opening the "self" to others in a connection of compassionate identification. To see how the vision of "emptiness" transforms thinking about generosity or giving, we look closely at passages in the sutras.

Instructing his disciple, Subhuti, in the perfection of generosity, the *Large Sutra* has the Buddha say: "Do not imagine that the gift is one thing, its fruit another, the donor another, and the recipient another. . . . And why? Because this gift is empty of a gift, its fruit empty of a fruit, and also the donor is empty of a donor and the recipient empty of a recipient. For in emptiness no gift can be apprehended nor its fruit, no donor, and no recipient. And why? Because absolutely those dharmas are empty in their own-being."[13]

The Buddha says, "Do not imagine." Imagine what? Do not imagine that the world is divided up into separate self-subsistent entities, the way we ordinarily assume it to be. Do not imagine yourself as one of these isolated entities. Why not? Because all of these seemingly separate "things" are what they are only in connection to other things that make them what they are. Nothing stands on its own, and that is what it means to be "empty" of "own-being." Applied to the act of giving, we see that the gift is not a gift without a donor and a recipient. Likewise, without the gift, there is no donor, no recipient. Each depends on the others, and when one changes, so do the others.

Moreover, when "I" give, there is far more than *me* making this possible. My giving depends on many factors behind and beyond me. It depends on my having something to give as well as the capacity to do that. To a great extent that depends on my parents, my family, my friends, my teachers, my upbringing, my employers, and much, much more. Without my parents shaping me the way they did, without my family providing so well for me, without teachers preparing me, employers paying me, farmers and grocers feeding me, and a broader culture teaching me to value generosity, "I" would not be giving. And that is just the beginning of the analysis of dependency. Without oxygen, gravity, sunshine, and an endless list of other essentials, there would certainly be no gift, because no donor and no recipient. Because my generosity is made possible by this enormous background of interdependent factors, it's not simply *my* generosity. Understanding that truth transforms and opens up the act of giving. Now consider the recipient of the gift. How many factors have come to shape this particular person to be exactly who he or she is? Billions—everything that has ever shaped his or her life. Everything depends, and the scope of this basic interdependency is enormous.

Why does this matter when it comes to giving? Because, as everyone already knows, both giving and receiving vary greatly in quality, and this variation in quality depends on the level of understanding from which it has derived. Although all forms of generosity are good in some sense, rarely do acts of giving reveal ideal levels of generosity because they are limited by the boundaries of the donor's self-understanding. Those who give are most often still encircled by themselves. Although able to give, self-concern retains its primacy, and this is evidenced in the way giving occurs. When first learning to give, it is hard not to give for self-centered reasons, because those are the only kinds of reasons we have. Enveloped in limited self-understanding, it is perfectly natural to give for ulterior motives and to be proud of one's generosity. It is inevitable that, at least to some extent, we are condescending toward those who are receiving rather than giving, and that we selfishly hold back much more than is given.

Therefore, over and over, the sutras recommend that "when the Bodhisattva is faced with a beggar, he should produce a thought thus: he who gives, he to whom he gives, what he gives," in all of these "the own-being cannot be apprehended."[14] The Bodhisattvas' "own-being" "cannot be apprehended" because they have no "own-being." Their being—what they are—depends to a great extent on other beings, and they change over time. Nothing is self-established; nothing stands on its own. All of us who fail to understand this will, as donors, tend to be more self-concerned in giving than concerned about the other. Understanding ourselves and others as isolated entities, each on our own, in the act of giving we will likely be as much or more self-promoting as truly generous.

The gift may still be a good thing. The beggar will, for example, still get the food he so desperately needs. But he will not get the sense of human dignity and equality that he may need to recover his standing in the world, nor a glimpse of the open-hearted human love and concern that we all need to live well. Moreover, the one who gives will not get these either, and the deep sense of well-being that might have come in the act of giving is stifled, replaced tragically by more isolation, pride, and arrogance, and hence more future suffering for both the giver and others.

Unless we as donors can see clearly and unflinchingly that who we are as donors—secure in wealth and health—is completely dependent on numerous turns of good fortune, on the care and help of others, and on opportunities not available to everyone, our acts of giving will be less than fully generous. These acts will therefore not have the liberating effects that they might otherwise have had. When we are able to see that the homeless person's parents did not do for him what ours did for us, that his teachers did not do for him what ours did for us, then we begin to understand the contingency of our fortune, and, looking more deeply, the thorough interdependency of all reality.

Recall that Buddhist teachings from the very beginning suggest that practitioners meditate on the idea that there is "no-self," that there is no

permanent essential core that is "me." Contemplating all of the elements
that have come together in the creation of each person, all the influences that have shaped us to make us exactly who we are, Buddhists hoped
to mitigate distortions of perspective that give rise to relentless acts of self-
promotion and self-securing. From this Buddhist point of view, our
"normal" self-absorption ends up looking like a harmful consequence
of shallow misunderstanding. One later version of this early Buddhist
teaching is the Mahayana realization that we are collectively interdependent, that we are all in this life together rather than struggling along on
our own. This, in fact, is what "Mahāyāna" means: that the "vehicle"
(yāna) on which we progress in life—Buddhism—is "large" (mahā)
because it always includes everyone from the most enlightened donor to
the most dependent recipients. Therefore, when the sutras teach generosity, they seek a variety of ways to convince us that our sense of isolation
is an illusion and that we will not be truly generous until we see that
truth.

Thus, a sutra has the Buddha say: "When the Bodhisattva, who
courses [i.e., trains] in perfect wisdom, gives gifts, then, taken hold of
by perfect wisdom, he is not one who perceives duality in that."[15] Free
from the false image of independence, the bodhisattva does not dwell on
the "duality" between himself as generous donor and the other as unworthy beggar, and, on account of that, is "free of craving and ignorance."[16]

Overcoming negative consequences of any "duality" between themselves and others, donors and recipients, bodhisattvas are empowered to
give and to be generous in an attitude and a spirit previously impossible.
Therefore, the Large Sutra claims, the bodhisattva "should give gifts after
he has reflected that 'what is my very own that is yours.'"[17] Thinking that
thought, we are more able to give, and the mental state out of which we
give becomes less hesitant, less self-absorbed, and less condescending. But
nonduality works both ways. So the sutra instructs the bodhisattva to
realize that the welfare of a gift is for both donor and recipient to
share—"do not think that this benefit is theirs and not ours."[18] The gift
is for everyone, because everyone is enveloped within the interdependent
whole, whether they can see that truth or not.

Exactly how a gift benefits the donor can be considered from a number
of perspectives, but the most common treatment in the history of Buddhism employs the image of spiritual "merit" (punya). When a donor gives
or performs any kind of moral act, that act merits a reward of a spiritual
kind. The reward can be conceived very generally as a share in the

well-being of the society as a whole, or as our slightly enhanced personal capacity to give in the future. Or it can be conceived through imagery much like a savings account in the bank, where positive merit-flows are stored for personal uses in the future, including a better rebirth in the next life.

No matter what the form of the conception, though, the bodhisattva is taught to "dedicate" that merit to the enlightenment of all beings, to "turn it over" to others for their spiritual use. The concept of "dedication" or "turning over" (*parinamana*) is one of the cornerstones of Mahayana practice, in that bodhisattvas have vowed to seek enlightenment not simply for themselves but on behalf of all beings equally. This idea works forcefully against the practice of spiritual selfishness, a form of religious self-absorption. Whatever the bodhisattva is able to accomplish in the realm of generosity and compassion is "turned over" to others so that pride and arrogance do not undercut the good that was generated in giving. The bodhisattva is to give all the way and not stop short by hoarding the good that follows from it. "Stopping short" of complete generosity, bodhisattvas would limit the extent to which acts of generosity could be enlightening, for themselves and for others.

One interesting facet of the picture of the perfection of generosity developed in early Mahayana texts is that they tend to treat "giving" primarily as meditation, as a mental exercise more than directly as an act in the world. The bodhisattva who "courses" in the perfection of generosity is undergoing a process of mental training through which views and sentiments conducive to generosity are being cultivated. Thus Śāntideva claims that "perfection" resides in "the mental attitude itself."[19]

Bodhisattvas were thus envisioned as "in training," and the discussion seems to have focused primarily on this preparatory dimension of practice. The operative theory of training seems to have been that habituation to certain ways of viewing life situations establishes the basis on which spontaneous acts of generosity would one day unfold. Self-centeredness was thought to be pervasive initially, even within spiritual practice, and very difficult to root out. The bodhisattva could do this, however, by daily meditation through which new ways to conceiving of "self and others" would gradually replace earlier tendencies to exclusive self-concern.

So, if we ask how the Buddhist ideal of generosity is presented to practitioners in the sutras, we find that it is not in the form of a set of rules to follow when giving. It is not a demand placed on what one must do or how one must do it, because it is assumed that if the ideal is exalted at all, this is precisely what most of us cannot do. We cannot do it because the contours and shape of our current character do not allow us to identify with and to understand such an ideal, much less to practice it. Therefore, in place of a set of rules or demands placed on people's actual behavior, the ideal of generosity is given in the form of mediations or trainings through which practitioners might gradually transform themselves into kinds of people who would both understand why this ideal is truly ideal, and be able to act in accordance with it. One's character, Buddhists claimed, is not fixed or static. It is always malleable, always in motion, and always in a position to admire and strive for some higher ideal than it currently follows.

One of the best ways to do this, according to early Mahayana Buddhists, is to place the ideal—the image of perfection itself—out before the practitioner's mind so that it would gradually take root there. Consequently, we find the sutras featuring meditations on how to picture purified forms of generosity, both as conceptual training practices and as descriptive images of ideal bodhisattvas in the act of giving. Selecting one of these, we conclude this description of the way early Mahayana texts have imagined "perfect" generosity with a summary of that ideal from the *Vimalakīrti Sūtra*: "Vimalakīrti said, 'The giver who makes gifts to the lowliest poor of the city, considering them as worthy of offering as the Tathāgata himself, the giver who gives without any discrimination, impartially, with no expectation of reward, and with great love—this giver, I say, totally fulfills'" the perfection of generosity.[20]

CRITICAL ASSESSMENT:
A CONTEMPORARY PERFECTION
OF GENEROSITY

Our goal now is to assess this traditional Buddhist account of generosity for current plausibility. If the perfection of generosity is still an admirable ideal today, what would that look like for us in our current circumstances? What would a contemporary practice of generosity entail, and how might we understand the place of that practice within the overarching framework of our lives? To take the challenge of these questions, we will need to go beyond our sources, raising specific issues that have not been addressed in traditional Buddhist texts. We will want to ask critical questions and to frame these matters in somewhat different terms. But if we do this with rigor, we will begin to discover the wealth of insight suggested by these extraordinary Buddhist resources and begin the process of putting them to contemporary use.

The Foundations of Generosity

One thing that Mahayana Buddhist authors realized, and that is worth our recognizing, is that generosity is best understood as an achievement of a whole society and not simply of individuals within that society, even though it is most often within the lives of admirable individuals that the culture's achievement can be seen. Individuals are enabled to prize generosity, to admire it, to cultivate and practice it, only to the extent that the society's history and language have made that possible. A profoundly generous person does not simply emerge in a culture suddenly and without preparatory historical development. Human beings refined to this extent are the outcome of lengthy social development, the formation of a culture through many generations, and are therefore treasured historical products, people of whom the entire culture can be genuinely proud.

Mahayana Buddhists allude to this communal realization in the image of the "Mahayana" as the "large vehicle," the vehicle on which all members of the society move toward some form of enlightenment together, even when the disparity between the most highly developed and the least capable is immense. The achievement of individuals always requires this larger cultural framework as a foundation that makes their particular excellence possible. Truly generous people, like Buddhist bodhisattvas, elevate and ennoble the society through their extraordinary acts of giving, but both they and their generous acts have been made possible by the development of a culture of generosity. For this reason, failure to recognize that "my" achievements are grounded in the achievements of others in my society—and failure to acknowledge that dependence widely—is a sign of considerable shortsightedness, an indication that the spirit of generosity and the vision that must accompany it are still in early stages of development.

It is important to note, as well, that among both individuals and societies the distinction between those who are generous and those who do not give is not at all a distinction between rich and poor. It is entirely a matter of the development of generosity of character, whether among the wealthy or least privileged. Profound generosity of spirit is rare, but when we do see it, it is at least as likely to be found among the poor as it is among those blessed with substantial resources. Both history and common experience attest to this egalitarian fact.

The culmination of Buddhist practices of generosity can be seen in their ideal form, the bodhisattva who gives unselfishly out of a deep compassion for all living beings. Compassion is the ultimate aim of these practices. But that culmination is the result of a long process of self-cultivation. For the most part, compassion is something we *learn* to feel. It is not innate, not a "natural" feeling. For these reasons, we cannot feel compassion simply by deciding to feel it, or by telling ourselves that it is our responsibility to feel it. We do, however, have the capacity to develop compassion by cultivating our thoughts and emotions in ways that enable it. This is the function of the "practice" of giving. Making generosity of character an explicit aim of self-cultivation, we sculpt our thoughts, emotions, and dispositions in the direction of a particular form of human excellence.

Most of us, most of the time, have a weak capacity for generosity. Admiring this element of character and deciding to emulate it does not make us able to give. But it does initiate momentum in the direction of generosity and gets us moving. At first, our motivations to give are not primarily compassion for those we want to help. More frequent, and a motivation more in correspondence with our initial state of character, is the desire to be a certain sort of person, someone who is magnanimous and compassionate. Self-concern, in other words, is what we practice overall, so it is not surprising that motivations toward generosity are initially constructed out of that inclination of character. When we give, we do so for reasons, and these tend to be reasons related to our own self-enhancement in one form or another. We give so that we may receive in exchange. We give in order to be accepted in a community, to be admired, to be honored or praised. We give in order to think well of ourselves, to actually *be* good and therefore deserving. Except at relatively high levels of generosity, the motivation for giving tends to be the good that it will return to us more than or as much as the good of the other. But this inauthenticity at the outset need not be condemned. It need not be criticized, because the movement from selfishness to selfless generosity is less a leap than a gradual movement and maturation. It takes time, and everyone begins wherever they happen to be.

The long-term point of this first perfection, the practice of generosity, is the cultivation of compassion and the ability to be guided by its power. Therefore, beginning at whatever level is appropriate, the practices of generosity train us to reach out to others and away from ourselves. We all give according to our understanding of the separation between ourselves and others, our sense of connection to or isolation from others. The extent to which that line of separation is firm and definitive is the extent to which generosity may make little sense to us. The more an understanding of community and interdependence dissolve that line of separation, the more capable we will be of giving. Buddhists define enlightened beings in terms of depth of self-understanding, a state in which hard barriers of separation between ourselves and others have been softened. As we develop deeper and more nuanced understanding of who we are and how we fit into the larger world, generosity becomes a more natural act, eventually one that requires little motivation beyond the fact that others are in need or there is good to be accomplished.

This realization directs us to the connection between the ideal of generosity and the Buddhist concept of "no-self." The most radical forms of generosity are closely linked to the most radical forms of selflessness in the same way that lack of generosity is correlated to selfishness. The practices of generosity produce feelings of compassion precisely insofar as they are able to transform the kinds of self-understanding and self-concern that structure our lives. The new sense of self gradually generated is based on a recognition that my own good as a person is closely bound up with the good of others. From this perspective, egocentric people are always those whose lives are based on a misconception, a mistaken or immature understanding about how the world of human beings is structured. Living in that state of human character, we tragically see ourselves as independent and alone in the world, and our actions, therefore, as isolating, protecting, and securing ourselves.

The practices of generosity—acts of giving, whether in meditation or in the social world—function to develop a more mature and expansive sense of self, one that naturally gives rise to a greater capacity for opening ourselves to others. Indeed, the kind of transformation that Buddhists envision—the movement from ignorance to enlightenment—requires an understanding of the "self" that is to some extent malleable or flexible, capable of becoming something different from what it used to be. Such a change in human lives happens gradually through purposeful effort— the result of practices, meditations of various kinds—upon which enlightened life depends.

All practices of giving take place in view of an ideal, a mental model of admirable beings who demonstrate what a life of generosity would be like. Buddhists call this mental model the "thought of enlightenment" (*bodhicitta*). In the most general sense, this is an initial idea, hope, or sense that superior forms of human life are possible and that "I" can gradually transform myself toward these freer forms of life. As soon as this ideal is firmly in mind to the point that it begins to influence and change what one desires, then the discipline is already under way. To begin the process, one works toward habituating oneself in the performance of certain actions, both mental and physical. Images of the goal—generosity at the most mature level imaginable—serve to provide reasons to act and motivation to undergo the discipline of practice.

In the process of explicit practice, we construct a character capable of authentic giving. Because we are self-consciously pursuing a more generous, magnanimous way of living, the variety of practices that we perform—the occasions in which we "practice" generosity—are not seen as isolated, separate acts, but rather as acts that form a larger pattern of behavior that permeates our whole life. They are acts of self-sculpting through which we strive to enlighten both ourselves and others, hoping ultimately to fulfill a version of the bodhisattva's vow to live as though others are just as important and valuable as we are. Slowly constructing a certain quality of selfless character through practices of giving, we refashion our very desires, and out of transformed desires new habits of daily life begin to emerge. To have engaged the "thought of enlightenment" in the first place was to have taken responsibility for our actions, for the desires and images that motivate those actions, and for the kind of person we become as a result of them.

One significant consequence of this transformation is an exhilarating experience of freedom. To act generously is to awaken a certain kind of freedom, freedom from the stranglehold of self-concern, and freedom to choose a level of responsibility beyond the minimal charge most of us have for ourselves. To give and be generous is, momentarily, to be free of ourselves, free of greed and attachments, resentments and hatreds, habitual and isolating acts of self-protection. A generous person is on that occasion not a prisoner of self-imposed boundaries and insecurities. This momentary experience is exhilarating because it entails an expansion out beyond the compulsive anxieties of self-protection. In this sense, the practices of generosity are among the practices of freedom, and they carry with them all the joy and pleasure that are associated with liberation. This is one good reason for placing the perfection of generosity first on the Buddhist list of virtues—its pleasures and joys are both attractive and energizing. They fill us with the will to explore further, a sense that if one "perfection" provides this much exhilaration, how much more might be in store.

Effective Generosity: Skill-in-Means

If, engulfed in our own world of concerns, we do not even notice when someone near us needs help, we will not be able to practice generosity. Similarly, if we maintain a distant posture toward others that, in effect, prevents them from appealing to us for help, we will rarely find ourselves in a position to give. The first skill that is vital to an effective practice of generosity is receptivity, a sensitive openness to others that enables both our noting their need and our receptivity to their requests. Our physical and psychological presence sets this stage and communicates clearly the kind of relation to others that we maintain.

The traditional Mahayana image of perfection in the capacity for receptivity is the bodhisattva Avalokiteśvara (Guanyin), whose multiple arms are always extended in the gesture of generous outreach. The bodhisattva of compassion welcomes and invites all pleas for help. Other familiar forms of presence, other gestures, restrict the field of asking and giving; they are more or less closed rather than open to others. Arms folded tightly around ourselves communicate that we are self-contained, not open outwardly; arms raised in gestures of anger say even more about our relations to others. The extent to which we are sensitively open to others and the way in which we communicate that openness determine to a great extent what level of generosity we will be able to manifest. In sensitivity we open our minds to the very possibility that someone may need our assistance, and welcome their gestures toward us. Skillful generosity is attentive to these two basic conditions.

Furthermore, if we are both open to help and notice when help is needed, but are mistaken and ineffectual in how we go about it, then what we intend as an act of generosity may in fact just compound the difficulties. The feeling of generosity itself is not enough to make someone effectively generous. The skills required in the ideal of generosity are complex and varied; they cover a broad range of abilities from initial perception to effective follow-through, including the skill to know when to stop giving.

These skills are not as simple and straightforward as they may seem at first glance. Without practical skill and wisdom, giving may be counterproductive. Generosity can be misguided in a number of ways. For one, it can be based on a superficial understanding of the overall situation. Wisdom is the guide in the exercise of all virtues, but this is especially true of generosity. It is essential to understand who might benefit from your giving and how that giving might affect others beside the recipient. It is essential to know when to give, how much to give, and how to do it with integrity, for the well-being of both the recipient and others, including yourself. Wisdom is involved in knowing how different ways of giving might be received by others, and to what effect. There is also wisdom involved in asking how often to give and at what intervals. Intelligent giving is learned through practice, both as a meditation when we reflect on possible giving and as an activity in the world. But in practice it is crucial that we learn from our mistakes, which requires that we notice them, assess them, and consider what can be learned from them. Moreover, wisdom includes an attentiveness that is watchful for our deepest and most ingrained habits, most especially the intrusions of self-concern and the always-present manipulations of self-interest.

The "enlightened being" envisioned by Buddhists pursues complex practices of generosity in the spirit of wisdom motivated by compassionate concern for the well-being of others. In every setting, however, there are specific complications and complexities that need to be interpreted skillfully. As an example, consider one difficult bind faced by teachers. How is it possible for a teacher to be generous to students while being truthful and just at the same time? Honest appraisal of students' work may disappoint, deflate, and discourage some; such criticism can sometimes be deeply counterproductive. On the other hand, undeserved praise, generously allotted "good grades," and other welcome gestures on the part of the compassionate teacher may be notoriously bad teaching practice. Generous gestures of that kind may have the effect of telling some students that their practices of learning are good enough as they are, when in fact they are not. In this respect, a teacher's generosity may deter learning as much as provide it.

Skillful teachers are always aware of straddling this balance; they continuously strive to readjust their practices to suit the particular circumstances. This requires knowing something about the minds, talents, and backgrounds of each student, knowing when to apply pressure and just how much, knowing when to criticize and when to praise, knowing how much advice and correction a student can effectively accommodate, and which among the various ways of giving them will most likely improve learning. Skillfully applied, criticism is direction and encouragement, a gift of enormous importance. Ineffectively applied, criticism is destructive; it deflates and discourages. When wisely presented, criticism demonstrates without doubt the teacher's care and concern for the students' success; it tells them convincingly that they can succeed and that further self-discipline is all that is required to reach the highest level of understanding possible for them. Skillfully communicated criticism is received as if it were more like planning for the future, and the teacher who is both compassionate and wise knows how to present it so that students receive it in this light. Teaching, like any other sufficiently complex undertaking, involves facing new circumstances insightfully, while making adjustments to deal with them effectively. Generosity in every sphere of life is always to be balanced against other concerns and made perfectly appropriate to the configuration of each case.

Imperfections in the Practices of Generosity

Although one important effect of the practices of generosity is a transformation in the giver's self-understanding, as with everything else, there is a danger of going too far. "Servility" is the name for a kind of generosity that has become a vice rather than a virtue. It is based on an unenlightened form of "selflessness." Servile people serve others generously, but never expect anything in return. They view themselves as inferior and therefore undeserving of just or fair treatment from others. At first glance, this kind of selflessness may seem to be an appropriate description of the Buddhist goal of "no-self"—having so much concern for others that no self-concern remains. On closer examination, however, we can see how servility becomes destructive, not just to oneself but to others as well, because it upends the balance of communal relations. It is very important to sort out which forms of selflessness are admirable and which are not.

Servility, the habit of unrelenting service, fails to take reciprocity into account as an essential ingredient of enlightened social relations. Expecting nothing, servile people fail to understand that every person in a community needs to be treated with respect and equal rights—even themselves. Always to set one's own rights aside and thus to dismiss issues of self-respect allows others to proceed as though equality and respect are not important. Under certain circumstances, denying oneself may set the stage for the denial of others. Most important, it gives the impression that injustice is acceptable. Although admirable people will certainly on occasion ignore or suspend their own rights out of generosity to the community as a whole, always to do so even when good reasons to do it are lacking is clearly a weakness in generosity, indicating perhaps a lack of courage or self-respect. Not expecting justice for oneself is a form of not expecting justice at all, and on that account, servility constitutes imperfect generosity and a weakness of character.

The dangers of servility—a kind of contempt for oneself—are perhaps not as great as contempt for those to whom we are being generous. Such contempt can take a variety of forms or levels of severity: pity, blame, judgment, and disdain. Skillful giving is not contemptuous; it is compassionate precisely in that it is based on an understanding of the equality of human beings and the contingency of the differences that separate us. The compassion behind authentic generosity is fueled by a profound sense that, although responsibility for the quality of one's own life is an essential ingredient of a mature human life, all of us need some assistance to get ourselves there. Many of us have had that assistance in childhood and beyond, without our even knowing or acknowledging it. Others who have not had that kind of support are less to blame for their situation in life than, in our pride, we generally concede. They need exactly what we got—thoughtful, nurturing care, not our condescension or contempt. One way to begin to do that is, instead of pitying their weakness, bolster their strength. Find ways to show them powers they already possess.

Even when we do not indulge in servility, it is still possible that we might give too much, or give ineffectually, if within our daily practice we focus more on the good of our generosity than on the well-being of the one to whom we give. Our acts of generosity, while perhaps being good for our character, may not be good for the other. Our giving may, for example, weaken others' capacity to provide for themselves. We can all recognize how the parent of a disabled child may generously act on behalf of the child to such an extent that the child never learns to be independent, never acquires the skills in life through struggle and effort that we all need. Although this scenario is most visible in the case of a disabled child, it is also a danger for all children, or anyone in a position of substantial dependency. When we give too much we teach total dependence and fail to communicate the interdependence that helps liberate us all.

That realization leads us to see that the question of how much to give should be answered primarily in relation to its effects on the well-being of the recipient. How will further gifts aid or obstruct his or her life, in the short and long term? Specific prescriptions about generosity will never be codifiable. Each situation is complex and needs to be judged on its own terms. Seeing which factors are relevant in each specific situation takes wisdom, the skill to understand how best to proceed under current circumstances in order to contribute to the well-being of the other and not undermine it. Wisdom is also needed to see when generosity requires that giving cease, so that the benefit of the relationship not be undermined by a devastating paternalism.

The foregoing three dangers inherent in the practices of giving— servility, contempt, and poor judgment about the effects of giving—show us something important: they make clear that, although vital, "selfless-ness" is not all there is to the perfection of generosity. Being unselfish is certainly the most important condition for admirable forms of generosity; we should not underestimate its centrality. But beyond selflessness, there are other essential conditions that are not generally recognized in tradi-tional Buddhist texts. Perhaps this is understandable. Self-centeredness is so pervasive and so powerful an illusion that most energy and ethical strategy has gone into overcoming it. But if it is not the only illusion, then the possibility remains that, in the effort to overcome the pervasive illusions of selfishness, we fail to recognize other imperfections that stand in the way of authentic generosity.

In order to delve more deeply into the role of selflessness in ideal forms of generosity, it will be helpful to reflect on a famous Buddhist story about generosity. This story is found among the *Jātaka Tales*, ancient Indian folk tales about the former lives of the Buddha. In the final chapter of this composite text, the *Vessantara Jātaka*, which recounts the Buddha's last life before attaining enlightenment, the Buddha is a certain Prince Vessan-tara, heir of the Sanjaya kingdom, who lives in the palace with his wife Maddi and their two children. The prince, the future Buddha, is of course the paragon of virtue; his generosity and compassion for the people of the kingdom are renowned. The prince's beneficence is epitomized in his generous use of a magical elephant on behalf of the people, an act that virtually guarantees the well-being of the realm by ensuring that rainfall in the kingdom is perfect for agriculture. But the prince is so generous that when an emissary from another land asks to be given the magic elephant, the prince does so in a spontaneous gesture of selfless giving.

Things begin to go badly. The people in the prince's kingdom, fright-ened by the prospects of their lives and furious at this act of outrageous generosity, force the king to banish Prince Vessantara. In one last gesture of generosity, the banished prince gives away all his possessions and leaves penniless with his family. On the journey, when asked by a despicable old couple who desire servants for themselves, the prince gives them his children to serve in this capacity. Fearing that Vessantara might give away even his wife and be utterly alone, the gods descend disguised as a brahmin and ask for his wife. When the prince concedes, the gods immediately give her back. According to the rules of gift-giving at that time, now that she is his as a gift, he is no longer entitled to give her away. Meanwhile, the king, remorseful for having banished his beloved son, gets Vessantara's children back and invites the prince and princess to return. All of the royal family comes together in blissful reunion, and Vessantara eventually becomes the king who rules most compassionately.

This is an ancient story—even pre-Buddhist in origins—and in it we cannot help but notice many things, including that the position of "wife" and "children" are regarded as property in the social customs of ancient Indian patriarchy. Although these customs dissolved in the Buddhist era in India, the story remained intact, becoming the best known of the *Jātaka Tales* and serving as the ultimate standard for the development of the virtue of generosity, even if no longer interpreted literally.[21] This story, among others, led early Mahayana Buddhists in their choice of generosity as one of the cardinal virtues of the bodhisattva. It was clear to them that the practice and development of this virtue was the first step toward enlightenment.

But ancient patriarchal customs should not be the only difficulty we notice in the story. If we look more closely, we realize that, although all of the acts of generosity in the story are profoundly selfless, not all of them are admirable, nor constructive for the good of everyone affected by them. In fact, some of them evoke our criticism because they appear to cause serious injustice. Why, for example, did the prince give his children to the greedy couple who wanted servants? Because they asked, we are told, and being unselfish and profoundly generous, the prince holds nothing back. But what if this gift is bad for the kids, bad for the parents, even bad in cultivating the greed of the selfish couple? What if this act of unselfish generosity is bad for the society as a whole? Then we would conclude that, in this case, the perfection of generosity requires not-giving, and that the greatest gift that can be given is wise judgment and forbearance. Even better than open, selfless giving is discriminating giving empowered by compassion—generosity that asks critical questions about the overall long- and short-run wisdom of the proposed gift. Selflessness directed by wisdom is greater than selflessness alone.

As we saw in the early Mahayana sutras, virtuous giving was required to be "impartial" and "nondiscriminating." We can now see, however, that this criterion needs a more comprehensive definition. Had the prince been more discriminating and less impartial, thinking about the welfare of everyone affected by his gift before acting, his generosity would have been considerably more effective in advancing the well-being of all the people under his care. His generosity would, in other words, have been more beneficial and more enlightening.

What the sutras ought to mean by these two important criteria—impartiality and nondiscrimination—is that in giving we should not discriminate between recipients on the grounds of who among them will most likely benefit us in return. We should be impartial and nondiscriminating about everything that might otherwise serve our own egos and desires, but not about the need and the situation of the prospective recipients, nor about our capacity to be generous and helpful in the future. We notice, therefore, that authors of the sutras have been especially concerned to work against ever-present self-interest in the practices of generosity, for very good reasons. But in doing so, they have neglected to consider the kinds of discrimination and judgment that will be required for the gift to be truly beneficial to the recipient and others involved.

The other criterion of perfect giving that we saw featured frequently in the sutras was that the giver must not dwell on the "fruits" of the act of giving. But once again, because the authors' concern was so heavily focused on the intrusions of the self in giving, they have not seen how concern for the consequences of our actions is often crucial in determining whether giving is the right thing to do. Had the prince in the story thought about the long-term effects of these gifts, he would have abstained from giving some of them. So although it is indeed important not to dwell on the "fruits" of our actions, this concern is limited to the "fruits" *for us,* and cannot mean that we do not attend to the probable repercussions of our actions overall. If we want our gifts to bear fruit for those to whom we have given and to be fruitful for the society overall, then caring about possible outcomes will be a significant dimension in our choice of actions.

In the *Vessantara Jātaka,* therefore, the moral dimension of the concept of generosity is limited to the virtue of selflessness. It suggests that less self is all there is to the practice of generosity as an ideal. In truth, however, the ethical dimension of the practice of generosity is more comprehensive than that—concern for the unselfishness of the giver's self is one dimension of the practice, and concern for the other's well-being is another. They fit together in a well-balanced ethic, but one is not the same as the other. No doubt many Buddhists have, in fact, taken this into account in their ethical activities, even when their conceptual articulation of the matter did not. As Buddhist metaphysics developed in time, especially in the Mahayana tradition, awareness of the interdependence of all components of reality provided a conceptual image of self and other in correlation that grounds a more balanced and comprehensive account of moral relations.

We have just considered how generosity may be misguided when focus on one's own unselfishness results in insufficient concern for the effectiveness of the gift on the well-being of the other. Is it possible that there are dangers on the other side, when too much concern for the other leads to insufficient self-concern? Yes, and we have already considered one situation in which such problems arise—the condition of servility in which lack of self-respect gives rise to indiscriminate giving. But there is another interesting issue to ponder here. What if, without being servile at all, generous people give so selflessly and so compassionately that they seriously harm themselves? Are there limits to unselfishness when others really do need our help? An example will help us get this difficult question in view, this one another story from the *Jātaka Tales* that goes to an ethical extreme in attempting to make its point.

Many versions of *The Hungry Tigress* tale have circulated throughout Asian Buddhism, but here is a summarized version sufficient for the purposes of our question: When, in a former life, the Buddha, then a Brahmin of great religious distinction, wandered into the forest to engage in spiritual practice, he encountered a tigress with a litter of cubs, all on the verge of starvation. Deeply affected by the suffering of this family and supremely compassionate, the future Buddha freely gave his own body to feed the tigress and cubs. Unwilling to preserve his own life at the expense of others, the Buddha sacrificed himself so that they might live.

This story has been told countless times throughout Asia to illustrate the truth that generosity is grounded in the achievement of "no-self," although it is usually told with the added proviso that it is not necessary for others to go to the extremes of self-sacrifice exemplified by the Buddha. But why not? Once you have seen that generosity is authentic to the extent that it is unselfish, what would justify stopping short of full giving to preserve yourself when others are in dire need? Avoiding the force of this question on the grounds that the story's sacrifice was limited to the act of saving tigers rather than human beings is too easy an escape from its central issue. This is a folk tale, potent in its point if we are willing to improvise. At least some people somewhere will starve today, while you and I have food in the kitchen and money in the bank. Although we do give to charitable organizations that seek to address this global problem, why shouldn't we give everything, offering to sacrifice our lives so that others might live? I imagine that all of us have found ourselves asking this moral question at some point in our lives. But I suspect that, like me, you avoid it whenever possible in order not to risk the conclusion that you cannot in fact justify your continued existence, or your bank account.

We are all aware of stories in which sacrificing oneself on behalf of others is clearly, at least in retrospect, the right or most admirable thing to do. Mahatma Gandhi nearly died in fasts of protest on behalf of the liberation of the people of India and in opposition to violence, and in the end he did die in the service of others. The soldier who leaps upon the live hand grenade in order to save the lives of his fellow soldiers is a hero of mythic proportions, as admirable in the human excellence of selfless generosity as we can imagine. But both of these examples feature specific and highly unusual situations in which self-sacrifice emerges as a moral possibility where greater good might come from someone's dying than from their living.

Few exemplars of generosity follow this pattern, however. Historical accounts tell us that the actual historical Buddha lived a very long life, and that whatever starvation he encountered among humans or animals while wandering around northern India did not prevent him from eating in order to sustain himself. Clearly, his self-conception focused on the task of human enlightenment, which could not be advanced without his own health and well-being. His primary gift to us was not food but rather the possibility of awakening to a level of profundity in our lives that would not have been possible without his life's work. Mother Teresa, the modern paragon of generosity, also lived a long life, and we are thankful that she did. Had she sacrificed herself early in life in order to save a starving family, tens of thousands of others would not have been fed through her lifelong efforts to overcome hunger and starvation in India and elsewhere.

In both of these cases, the generous concern that the Buddha and Mother Teresa had for others was made possible by an appropriate amount of self-concern. How can we know how much that is? In these

two cases, the self-concern at stake is far more than the food that
sustained them physically. It included, in both cases, an enormous amount
of time spent in meditative self-cultivation and other forms of spiritual
practice. The ability to give, as we have seen, does not come from
nowhere; it arises dependent upon the achievement of excellence in
character—the perfections. In his public talks, the Buddhist master
Thich Nhat Hanh is very clear about the life he lives. Although he offers
himself to us for instruction, he says quite plainly that the only reason he
is able to do that is that he knows when to retreat into meditation in order
to maintain himself in a position where he will have something worthwhile to give. Without wise self-concern, our powers of concern for others
are diminished. Without that kind of wisdom, giving is embedded in
irony; it becomes part of a pattern of life that destroys one's future
capacity for generosity.

Moreover, the magnanimous giver must always know when to stop,
when to pull back in the present for the sake of the future. Having
exhausted your resources, you will be in no position to be generous another
day, when what is perhaps a more important occasion arises. To be truly
effective in giving, you must realize your own limitations and the limitations
of your resources. This is true whether the resources are your money or your
time and energy. Going too far, you diminish the extent of giving that will be
possible for you in the future, when needs may be great. Timing is crucial,
knowing when to advance and when to rest in order to prepare yourself
for a long succession of challenges. A subtle balance between helping others
and maintaining or cultivating your capacity to help is a high-level skill
of great significance. Other forms of balance are also important. The
moral dimension of our responsibility for others, while basic, is just one
dimension of our lives. We are fortunate to have many other reasons to
live and many forms of engagement. Similarly, generosity is only one of the
perfections. Admirable people often understand the art of balance with
uncanny perceptiveness.

The question—how much should I give, or at what point in the
diminishment of my own resources should I stop giving?—is a theoretical
question for most of us that has little bearing on our life practice. This is
so because we have not yet engaged in the practices of generosity to an
extent that selfless over-generosity might endanger us. But two things
have become clear—that generosity is an excellence of character that all of
us would benefit from cultivating, and that thoughtfulness as well as
selflessness are essential to that excellence.

These subtleties in the practice of generosity are not the most obvious dimensions in the practice of giving. But they can be learned from a variety of sources. More often than not, we come to understand them through our admiration of others, from role models who set the standard for generosity of character. Precisely at the point where we are able to notice strength of character in someone else and see the corresponding weakness in our own character, we are in a position to learn. This kind of learning is most direct and effective when guided by teachers in our own social world, but there are certainly other ways to get it. In traditional Buddhist societies, this most often took the form of stories circulating through Buddhist storytellers. But it can also be readily found in books, narratives about lives lived by people, whether fictional or historical, who represent the ideal or the anti-ideal of generosity.

Mahatma Gandhi and Mother Teresa are noteworthy twentieth-century exemplars of generosity, but we have many more, some created in novels and others told in historical narratives. From these we get a concrete glimpse of the ideal, and through creative analysis we can begin to determine what would be entailed in seeking greater generosity in our own lives. We study the great musicians in learning music, the great athletes in our own athletic pursuits, and there is every reason to do the same in our own quest to construct a character that best suits our ideals and our situation in life. Although we can see that the great saints are spontaneously moved to generosity simply by seeing the suffering of the world, we realize that they were not born with that compassion, and set out to establish a discipline that might move us toward a similarly enlightened capacity for giving.

Perhaps even more important than teachers are friends. Those seeking enlightenment do not undertake the practices of generosity alone. They always seek and make good friends to accompany them on the way. The ethical importance of friendship is well known to the Mahayana sutra writers, and they develop this theme skillfully. The bond of friendship is a bond among equals, where, at least in principle, all share and share alike. They construct a network of support and encouragement in traversing the difficulties of an arduous discipline, the discipline of questioning one's own standpoint in the pursuit of various forms of excellence. As Aristotle knew, too, friendship entails a shared recognition of and pursuit of an "idea of the good," a "thought of enlightenment," however skillfully the friends in any particular case are able to conceptualize that. They travel a path together and seek the well-being and success of the others along with their own. To make generosity in life a goal, part of a larger goal of enlightened character, is to set out on a path that has numerous destinations but no final end. On such a path, companionship and fellow travelers are absolutely essential.

The Gift: What Can Be Given?

No definitive rule or code for giving can be provided. Generosity is a creative act of freedom that is bound only by the ideals of wisdom and compassion and the cultural shape of the world it seeks to benefit. Therefore, the "what" of giving is always open in every situation. Stretching our minds to see the good that generosity might accomplish in any particular setting requires insightful freedom, or creativity. Only in this open light can we adequately ask: What can be given?

Money is the easiest and most effective commodity for giving, because recipients can cash it to pay for whatever is truly needed, relieving the donor of the responsibility to understand fully the complex and always changing needs that the gift hopes to address. Money is not just another thing; it is our symbol of things, and in that capacity has extraordinary contemporary prominence. Money symbolizes the power of abundance and the security of our relations to the larger world. To give it requires a clear sacrifice on our part. Giving money so that others might procure what they need, we sacrifice some of our capacity to have what we want. In holding our money, we possess power; in giving our money, we exercise that power.

But giving is not simply a practice for the wealthy; it is a practice in which anyone can engage. Giving is closely linked to our freedom and is a fundamental dimension of being human, a possibility we all share. We can only give to the extent that we are truly free, that is, not possessed by our possessions, or our money, or ourselves.

So what can be given by those who do not possess an abundance of material resources? Clearly, we can give of ourselves—our labor, our time, our concern. In fact, in our own economic world, when we give money, it is often labor, time, and concern that it buys, and it is in our power to give these directly by offering what we can of our own involvement. The gift of volunteer labor is an act of extraordinary generosity, and when we witness someone able to give this gift freely, we cannot help but admire it. When we give of ourselves in this way, we set self-concern aside in order to identify with some concern beyond the ordinary boundaries of our own lives. The corresponding feeling associated with this act of generosity is exhilaration, a sense, however large or small, of expansion out beyond ourselves. In giving we experience directly the feeling of unselfishness implied in the Buddhist idea of "no-self" in which the borders that conventionally define us are erased.

Some gifts are so light and insubstantial that they can be given to others on a daily basis. One such gift is simple recognition, an affirmation in speech, gesture, or action that someone else exists, and that they matter. Often we fail to grant this simple gift of recognition, and the more often we fail in that the more alienating our social world becomes. We all know, for example, what it feels like to be in a room where those who have not been introduced to each other avoid eye contact, awkwardly trying to carry on as though the others are not there. Worse, we have all experienced powerfully self-possessed people who take over a room of people without ever acknowledging the presence of someone in the room. When recognition is withheld from anyone by anyone, the bond of care and generosity that holds a community or a family together is undermined in some small way. That is why this gift is so significant—when we give the simple affirmation of others present, we act to create a certain kind of community, and in so doing we make it more possible for others to do the same.

There are times, moreover, when this gift of recognition is crucial. These are occasions of suffering when someone is overwhelmed by the pain of their own existence. Sometimes this pain has an overt cause—the death of a family member, a personal failure or disappointment, for example—and at other times the cause is latent or hidden, the raw pain of anxiety. In either case, the ability to register the other's pain and to communicate a sense of understanding and care, whether through providing personal contact or appropriate distance, is an important skill in the perfection of generosity. Those who are able to do this with sensitivity possess an excellence that we can emulate with transformative effect.

There are times when all we experience is someone's distance, their utter alienation, without seeing the suffering at its roots. In these cases, we often mistake the symptoms. We interpret someone's distance—their rude behavior, their inability to communicate or to participate—as disdain or lack of care, and in response we shun or secretly condemn them. Frequently, however, these and other forms of alienation are masked signs of suffering, hidden pain with an enormous range of causes, conditions, and manifestations. The ability not to react to another's distance

with a natural corresponding distance is a mark of extraordinary perception and will; it shows someone's freedom not to have one's own response
predetermined, the freedom not to be forced to reciprocate with a
similarly alienated reply. Few people possess the personal power to give
such a gift, but when this rare act does occur, its effects are extraordinary
in reversing the tide of alienation or suffering.

In all of these situations, the skill of generosity is the ability to
communicate courage, the power to stand up to and to address whatever
is painful in life. Courage, in the form of encouragement, is a gift always
potentially in our possession but actualizable only if we have cultivated it,
only if we have developed our powers of compassionate, sensitive giving
in other circumstances. The perfection of generosity consists primarily,
therefore, in a system of practices aimed at the development of these
capacities and these skills.

Personal acts of giving to those who suffer, whether in the form of
money or assistance or sympathetic concern, are always limited in their
capacity to solve the overall problem of suffering, which is monumental
in proportions. Helping one hungry or under-privileged child is a wonderful achievement, but it still leaves the overall problem of suffering
largely as it was—everywhere to be found. For every child in pain, we can
hear thousands of others crying out for similar attention. Therefore,
authentic generosity requires more than our individual acts on behalf of
those in pain. It requires, very clearly, that we give attention to the
political world in which such suffering continues to grow.

Although we must feed the poor, doing so may do nothing to alter the
injustices and systems of power that have given rise to the problems of
unemployment, deprivation, and hunger in the first place. Therefore, in
addition to our practices of aiding those who need our help, authentic
generosity requires the practice of politics. Indeed, there are times and
situations in which political acts are more efficacious in bringing an end
to suffering than acts of charitable giving. Communities can practice
generosity just as individuals can, and the effort to persuade one's society
to engage in appropriate forms of giving is a gift of great consequence.
This is a dimension of the perfection of giving that we are in a position to
cultivate even if traditional Buddhists were not.

This is not to say, of course, that collective generosity—giving on the
part of communities or governments—is always the most effective political course. There are lessons to be learned from those who instruct about
the dangers of institutionalized giving, the possibility that our acts of

generosity and care might undermine self-respect and individual capacities. But those dangers are present, as we have seen, in any act of giving.
Thoughtfulness, an attentiveness to how to give, when to give, how much
to give, and how all these will affect the recipient and the society are
always important. So that caution about collective attention to the welfare
of others should not be used as an excuse selfishly or self-righteously to
terminate collective care for those among us who are in need.
The perfection of generosity and the health of any society require that
we selflessly seek an end to pointless suffering, to undeserved suffering,
and to suffering that does nothing but destroy human beings. And in
many circumstances, it will be communities that have the power to do this
rather than individuals within those communities.

There are some in any society who will need assistance, but they do not
necessarily need your assistance, or mine, except insofar as we do our
share to support public service institutions. Volunteer giving is to be
greatly admired and very important, but communities should not rely
too heavily on it because that allows others, those who are not generous, to
ignore their responsibility and the plight of the less fortunate. Everyone in
a society should be expected to acknowledge their own dependence on the
society as a whole, especially those who benefit most from current
arrangements of power and distribution. Everyone benefits when extreme poverty is eliminated in a community, when those who are living
in pain and hopeless conditions are offered some degree of communal
care. Everyone should be expected to participate in this effort, therefore,
even those who, due to lack of understanding, are unable to acknowledge
the responsibility of all citizens to do their share for the common good.
Much of the pointless suffering in the world can be alleviated through
intelligent political action, and any contemporary account of the perfection of generosity will need to acknowledge this.

To alleviate suffering among one's own family and friends while leaving
untouched the larger world of suffering is to have fallen short in one's quest
for authentic generosity. The "perfection of generosity" demands that we
give our attention and our labor toward the creation of a human world in
which compassion and kindness are the human norm, a world in which the
diminishment of suffering and the extension of opportunities to everyone
are among our foremost goals. Practices of generosity, therefore, include
efforts to enhance human equality, efforts toward guaranteeing through
social and political action that all children begin their lives with an equal
chance for happiness and well-being and end it with some share of peace

and dignity. Those who give of themselves through personal and political means toward these ends are in this respect admirable exemplars of the perfection of generosity. Although traditional Buddhists were content to recommend that we avoid doing injustice ourselves, a contemporary perfection of generosity would need to go beyond this. It would suggest that we give our time and energy in a thoughtful effort to minimize the society's collective injustice in as many forms as it can be found.

To understand in more concrete terms the significance of this dimension, imagine three different compassionate benefactors, three profoundly admirable people, each with distinct characteristics. The first is deeply compassionate, generous always in giving to those who need help. An uncommon degree of unselfishness gives this person saintly, distinguishing characteristics. But this person, like Prince Vessantara, is sometimes effective in giving and sometimes not, even though always unselfish. This person has not cultivated the ability to articulate thoughtful ends—both short- and long-term—to pursue in the spirit of selflessness, nor effective means. There are stories about saints of this sort in all of the world's religions. They are extraordinary in their compassion and selflessness but lack some degree of worldly skill.

Second, imagine someone of equal compassion, someone just as generous. This person, however, has the skill to give not just selflessly but to give effectively as well. Like Mother Teresa, this person sees that only well-honed institutions of generosity can dent the magnitude of the problem of hunger and poverty and sets out diligently to construct such an organization. This second donor's generosity yields liberating results that extend far out into the world.

Finally, picture a third benefactor, one with both deep feelings of compassion and the wisdom to give effectively. In addition, however, this person asks what gives rise to poverty and desperate human conditions in the first place. While continuing to treat the symptoms of the problem—feeding the starving, for example—such a person also seeks to understand and treat the cause of scarcity. Recognizing that certain governments and certain socioeconomic conditions will produce starving people as fast or faster than any one person can remedy, this benefactor pursues political change. With both long- and short-term political goals in mind, such a person wants to provide society with the ideal and a concrete plan for a morally coherent community that truly leaves no one behind.

The point of describing these three is not to suggest that selflessness is not important. Truly, nothing is more important, and practices aimed at cultivating selfless openness to others are fundamental to any authentic ethics. Nevertheless, descriptions of these three help us see that, although essential, selflessness is not enough, and that if we are honestly attempting to conceptualize ideal forms of generosity, we will need to recognize that there are dimensions of this virtue beyond selflessness that are also important ingredients of the ideal. Insightful understanding of the social circumstances in which we live and the courage to act on behalf of a more elevated vision of human culture are among these additional conditions for the perfection of generosity.

What other gifts might be included in our understanding of generosity? Some of the foregoing claims will at some point strike us as stern and joyless, and it would be a mistake not to include the gift of lightness and laughter that some among us are so gifted at giving. These people teach us irony; they make us laugh at ourselves and release our strained seriousness for just a moment. The freedom provided by humor is among our most cherished experiences, and some have cultivated their capacity to give it with magnificent skill. The momentary release of self-seriousness that suddenly emerges in laughter borders on the ecstatic and provides us with some of our most exhilarating moments. The generous freedom of laugher, and those skilled at providing it when we most need it, are known and appreciated by all of us.

Another of the most difficult gifts to give is admiration, a gift grounded in the freedom of selfless humility. When we become aware of someone who has the powers of generosity, or wisdom, or any truly excellent trait that we may lack, it is difficult not to respond in envy or jealousy—that is what we would like to be. What we ought to give in response to such people is admiration, the most honest, forthright, and nonalienating reaction to excellence. Only in our rare and best moments do we break free of ourselves enough to admire and to open our minds in praise of something truly excellent. This gift of admiration is important for three reasons. First, strong and admirable people occasionally need our acknowledgment and recognition, too. Giving it, we empower them to extend their skill further, to everyone's benefit. Second, acts of admiration force us honestly to assess our own capacities and to ask ourselves where and how we have failed to live up to our own ideals. Third, an act of open admiration affects everyone who witnesses it. In an honest and effective gesture of admiration, we place what we value out in the open for others to see; we make a public statement about what we find to be truly excellent and admirable. In doing so, we place our "thought of enlightenment" out into view for critical scrutiny by others, making it available to them in refining their own sense of human excellence.

Apologies are also gifts of great significance, but in this case, gifts demanded by a sense of reciprocity. When we have been unjust, only very specific words of apology will overcome the rift that separates us from someone who we have harmed. An authentic apology is not a way to release ourselves from what we owe, or from guilt. On the contrary, sincere apologies are accompanied by a pledge to rebuild justice in the relationship; they must show a commitment on our part to do whatever is needed over time, so that in the long run the wrong we have done costs us and not the person we have wronged. When we give a true apology, we give justice by backing our words with actions aimed at correcting the imbalance we have caused. A true apology is not a way to get out of what we owe; on the contrary, an apology is a pledge to set things straight again. When we give it, we give much more than words; we give our word and back it with justice.

Sincere apologies given set the stage for possible gifts of forgiveness. The word "give" within the larger compound word "forgiveness" shows us that forgiveness is also something that we are capable of giving. But forgiveness is a very specific kind of gift, based on rather precise conditions. Forgiveness is possible only when a wrongdoing has been admitted, and when the one who has done it admits what true reciprocity would require. Forgiveness can only be given by the one against whom the wrong was committed, not by anyone else, even a judge. In that, forgiveness differs from what a judge or jury can give—leniency or clemency.

Moreover, forgiveness does not erase the wrong; it does not change the fact that an injustice has been done. Forgiveness is neither denying nor forgetting. The injustice done remains, as does the memory of the wrong. What is given in forgiveness is an end to the grudge we "hold," an end to antipathy, especially hatred. It entails a decision to let go of one's own resentment. Only the offended party holds this resentment in full proportion, and therefore only that party can surrender it in a gesture of forgiveness. In that respect, like generosity more broadly, forgiveness shows us our own human freedom. To give someone forgiveness is to express our freedom in a remarkable way. It demonstrates to ourselves and to others that we are not bound to resentment or possessed by hatred. It also shows others around us that they too need not be bound in this way, and that the community as a whole is free either to hold or to let go of what might otherwise compel our resentment or force our retaliation.

When freely and skillfully given, forgiveness demonstrates the perfection of generosity.

Compassion and the Depth of Generosity

To understand the relationship between generosity and compassion, it is helpful to examine their place in Mahayana Buddhist thought. Generosity is the first of six perfections, six dimensions of character that are amenable to development and that must be cultivated in order to begin to awaken from a life of self-centered delusion. Compassion is not one of the six because it stands at the end of the path as a fundamental dimension of the goal. In Mahayana Buddhism, the two most essential characteristics of enlightened character are wisdom and compassion, each partially defined in terms of the other and each requiring the other for full actualization. Generosity, therefore, is preparatory for wisdom and compassion, even though it, too, is a component of enlightened character.

The primary reason for generosity's subordination to compassion in the Buddhist hierarchy of values is that when compassion is fully present, a separate concern for generosity is unnecessary. We require the effort of generosity only when we lack the compassion to live the bodhisattva's vow—to live on behalf of others as much as we do on behalf of ourselves. When compassion is complete, we do not hesitate to give; it comes forth quite naturally. Only when our feelings toward others assume a substantial separation do we need the guidance of generosity. When we simply do not feel compassion for others, the teachings and practices of generosity are available to help inaugurate those feelings. Bodhisattvas work on behalf of the enlightenment of the world out of compassion when it is deeply felt, and out of generosity when that feeling is still in rudimentary stages. The role of generosity, therefore, as the first of the perfections, is to inaugurate the movement toward compassion, to begin to plant and cultivate its seeds in our minds and character.

Generous, compassionate treatment of others is an exalted injunction found in segments of all major religions, even if, for the vast majority of practitioners, it is far out of reach. We find it, for example, in the Christian Gospel of Matthew (7:12): "Always treat others as you would like them to treat you." In its more compassionate form, we find: "Love your neighbor as yourself" (Matthew 22:39; Leviticus 19). Nowhere in those scriptures, however, does it tell us how to do that—how can you love neighbor as yourself when in truth you just do not? From the B

perspective sketched out here, actually to experience that level of love
in your daily life would require a major transformation in the understanding that you have of yourself and others. The implication of the
Buddhist position is that unless there is a profound congruence between
the demands of the injunction to love others as yourself and the deepest
understanding that you have of yourself, then the standpoint required
for carrying out that demand is unavailable. We do not, in our current
state, love others as we love ourselves, given how we understand
ourselves and others. That level of love would only be possible through
a radical transformation of self-understanding, and that transformation
is the ideal aim of Buddhist practice.

In Buddhism, the primary category of practice responsible for this
transformation is, of course, meditation. In meditative exercises, the
basis for compassion can gradually be constructed. Compassion originates
in acts of imagination. In order to feel for or along with someone else,
you must be able to imagine their suffering, both as it actually is in their
lives and as it would be in yours if it were you in that condition. Empathy
and compassion are correlative. You cannot have one without the other.
Meditation expands the powers of imagination and empathy, and in so
doing, it expands our capacity for giving and for compassion.

Meditations meant to develop compassion ask the practitioner to
work through a situation of suffering in detail. Beyond the fact that
someone is homeless and without work or resources to take care of
himself, the meditator looks into the specific experiences and repercussions of the situation. What is it like to live without a home, sleeping out
on the street; what are the dangers that someone in that situation must
face—the threat of violence, the physical pain and discomfort, the humiliation, the decline of mental and physical capacities? What does it mean
to be without possibilities, without hope, and how will these mental
conditions lead to further suffering? Meditators give contemplative
thought to what might be done to alleviate this condition and ask
themselves how assistance could be generated. They imagine a variety
of conditions in which a solution might be constructed and picture
themselves setting these in motion. Throughout, meditators work
through the emotional reactions that might be occurring in the homeless
person, the dangers that whatever process they might undertake may
seem degrading and demeaning. Finally, they imagine themselves in
exactly the same condition and situation, considering how they might
respond to the efforts of others to help. Meditation begins to make

generosity possible through the imaginative extension of oneself into the position of the other.

This is just one form that meditation can take in the development of compassionate generosity. Many others are also effective. At the other end of the spectrum from meditating on the suffering of others are meditations focused on their joy, well-being, and good fortune. Early Buddhists prized feelings of "sympathetic joy" (*muditā*) that could be cultivated in meditation by practicing responses to the happiness and success of others. They sought the mental capacity to share in the joy of others, and in so doing, to extend and to radiate that feeling of well-being so that it could be felt by everyone. The capacity of character to share the joy experienced by others is grounded in specific mental and social conditions, and Buddhist meditation is structured to cultivate those conditions. The same is true of compassion and the response of generosity to the deeply felt needs of others. It "arises dependent" upon particular conditions, and in spiritual practice anyone can cultivate those conditions. Without the development of the conditions on which it is based, compassion is not possible.

"Emptiness," understood as the interdependence of all things, functions in meditation to provide the requisite conditions for compassionate generosity. Meditating on interdependence, we develop the realization that we share a collective destiny with others, especially those in our immediate community but ultimately all living beings. The more we contemplate it, the more we realize in a functional sense that we are in solidarity with others. Understanding all of the ways in which we share the same global reality provides grounds for sharing; understanding tends to make generosity possible. Contemplating this, I understand ever more profoundly that what is good for me cannot be antagonistic to the good of others. What is best for me must be something that is good for others as well, because the goodness that is at stake here is neither mine nor theirs—it is ours, a shared possibility for enhanced life. Realizing this, the grounds have been laid to share the gifts that we have received. Understanding our interdependence with others and the debt we inevitably owe to others, we are empowered to respond generously to others and to make better lives possible for them whenever we can. The extent of our generosity is always in congruence with the understanding we have of ourselves. When this understanding is weak and self-centered, so is our capacity to give. When this understanding is broad and profound, so are our acts of generosity on behalf of others and human community as a whole.

Finally, it is helpful to reflect on the connection between generosity, the ability to give gifts, and gratitude, the ability to give thanks. Gift-giving and thanks-giving are tightly linked together, and that is the way we find them in the *Perfection of Wisdom Sutras*. There even the mythological Buddhas offer thanks for what came before them and what made their liberation possible, the perfection of wisdom in which they trained and through which they came to enlightenment.[22] There and elsewhere we see that one's inability to give and to be generous is linked to an inability to thank and to be grateful. If you cannot see your own dependence and do not acknowledge the gifts that have sustained you, you will be less able to tolerate the dependence of others, and therefore less able to help them get what they need. People trapped within themselves enjoy receiving, certainly, but it is their enjoyment alone. None of the joy is returned or disseminated in the form of gratitude, and thus the circle of communal connection is broken.

Of all the religious realizations possible, none may be as transformative as the ability to see that your own life has come to you as a gift. Contemplating this insight gives rise to a profound gratitude, a deep appreciation for the very fact of life, no matter to whom or what the thankfulness is conceived to be due. It is clearly one of the strengths of theism, the religious acknowledgment of a creator god, that at some point this mode of understanding gives rise to the feeling of gratitude and the sense of one's life as a gift.

In nontheistic forms of Buddhism, however, this gratitude is no less important, even if more difficult to conceive. At its basis is the Buddhist concept of "dependent arising." Everything that comes to be does so dependent on what came before. Nothing gives rise to itself; nothing exists on its own through its own act of will or cause. Every coming to be is a gift from what came before, and every passing away gives the gift of openness on which the future depends. Such conditionality entails indebtedness. My life is possible only through forces and conditions not of my own making or determination. To live is therefore to owe one's life, to be in debt. Although common modes of thinking, even religious ones, tend to obscure this realization and its far-reaching implications, even one steady glimpse into its truth evokes profound gratitude and the joy that accompanies it. Enlightened beings are those who are able and willing to acknowledge everything they have, including their lives, as a gift that is ultimately undeserved. Empowered by that profound and life-changing realization, these magnanimous ones are able to give generously, and it is in the spirit of that giving and that realization that they practice the perfection of generosity.

2

THE PERFECTION OF
MORALITY

TRADITIONAL BUDDHIST IMAGES OF
THE PERFECTION OF MORALITY
(ŚILĀPĀRAMITĀ)

From the earliest periods of Buddhist history, morality (*śilā*) was understood to be fundamental to the practice, often interpreted as the starting point of the Buddhist path or as a prerequisite for it. The early Buddhist monastic community organized itself around a set of ten precepts and a much more detailed set of monastic rules (*vinaya*) that served to guide practitioners and establish them in a very specific form of life. These were broadened and adapted to the lives of lay followers in separate lists and codes of virtue specifically tailored to the circumstances of nonmonastic life. Regardless of these differences, however, morality was considered fundamental to Buddhist practice. Thus, one early threefold division of the Buddhist path lists morality, meditation, and wisdom as the full spectrum of Buddhist concern.

The most basic moral teaching for Buddhist monks and nuns, and therefore the one most committed to memory, is a list of ten precepts, the first five of which constitute the moral fundamentals of the laity. These require that a Buddhist refrain from (1) harming living creatures, (2) taking what has not been given, (3) inappropriate sexual activity, (4) false speech, (5) intoxicants that lead to carelessness, (6) eating after midday, (7) attending entertainment, (8) wearing jewelry or perfume, (9) sleeping on luxurious beds, and (10) handling money. These precepts are considered "paths of training" (*śikṣā-pada*) because they function not just to prohibit immoral behavior but also, more importantly, to transform the character of the practitioner. In fact, in all forms of Buddhism, morality is "perfected" when an enlightened motivation takes hold, a motivation in which moral rules are no longer the focus of attention. When nonattachment, compassion, and wisdom prevail in the mind, then morality is thought to function naturally without recourse to rules and prohibitions. The precepts are part of the path of training meant to inculcate states of mind from which moral action might one day flow naturally.

Buddhists also distinguished between rules that are moral in the primary sense that they affect the treatment of others and rules that protect the practitioner's own commitment to training, rather than the welfare of others. Thus, the prohibitions on injury, stealing, and lying are understood to be primary, and therefore not rescindable for anyone, while the prohibitions on forms of luxury like jewelry, perfumes, and beds were patterns of voluntary training rather than fundamental moral rules.

Another set of moral prohibitions that has been very influential throughout the history of Buddhism, especially in Mahayana Buddhism, lists ten virtuous acts (*daśakuśala*). The ten acts of virtue are applicable to all Buddhists, monastic and laity, and are typically taught in terms of restraints on body, speech, and mind. These include abstention from (1) killing, (2) stealing, (3) sexual misconduct, (4) lying, (5) slander, (6) harsh, derogatory speech, (7) frivolous speech, (8) covetousness, (9) anger and malice, and (10) false views. The first three recommend restraint for the body, the next four delimit speech, and the final three refer to states of mind.

Skill in moral life entails cultivating an understanding of the Buddhist concept of karma, patterns of moral causality that are thought to govern all human transformation. Although karma literally means "action," the principle of karma concerns the connection between the quality of an act and the nature of the consequences that follow from it. Actions of a particular quality give rise to consequences of a corresponding kind, and this is thought to be a law inherent in the nature of things. Much of the Indian vocabulary of karma evolved out of agricultural metaphors. Karma is conceived as a "seed" that "ripens" into a specific "fruit." A seed of one kind can only ripen as a fruit of that particular kind. Although this principle is basic to all forms of Buddhism, interpretations of it are diverse. For some, because an act embodies a particular mental state, what follows from the act is understood to be a deepening of that mental state. Thus what follows from an act of theft is a deepening of the greed and possessiveness that gave rise to theft in the first place. Others interpret the correspondence between act and outcome more specifically. Stealing, they claim, culminates in loss of wealth for the thief; lying causes the liar to be deceived; killing gives rise to an inevitably short life; and drunkenness culminates in insanity.

What remains constant across a wide variety of interpretations is the thought that all acts generate consequences that shape the character of the actor. Not all acts are thought to be productive of karma, however, because karma is restricted to those done with volition, intention, or purpose. Moreover, changes in human lives brought about by the karmic consequences of an intentional act are thought sometimes to follow immediately from the act and sometimes to arise over time. This idea is extended beyond the range of a person's present lifetime to the point that the quality of a person's acts governs the form that a future rebirth will take. Karma and rebirth are thoroughly intertwined in Buddhist thought, and the combination of these two teachings more than any other set of moral ideas serves as motivation for moral action. We will return to the idea of karma as we begin to raise questions about what the perfection of morality might possibly mean in contemporary contexts. For now it is enough to see how this principle constitutes the underlying structure of Buddhist morality and how thinking in terms of this basic concept shapes Buddhist lives of all kinds.

The fact that what becomes of a person is based on the qualities of actions undertaken makes moral decision making central to Buddhist practice. If the goal is to become something in particular—a wiser, more compassionate, more enlightened person—then the actions that have the power to generate that state will need to be skillfully chosen and enacted with a disciplined mind. Buddhist texts therefore frequently link mindfulness to the practices of morality, thereby connecting morality with meditation. Śāntideva, who goes so far as to say that "the perfection is the mental attitude itself," writes extensively on "guarding awareness," because only by diligently shaping one's mind will acts conducive to negative karma be eliminated.[1] So he writes: "If I let go of the vow to guard my mind, what will become of my many other vows?"[2] This rhetorical question seems to imply that without mindfulness other vows aimed at enlightenment will naturally be lost, since greed, aversion, and delusion enter into the vacuum of an otherwise unoccupied mind. Therefore monks, nuns, and some lay Buddhists meditated on their vows, on the precepts, and on the mechanisms of karma so that they would not find themselves mindlessly under the sway of mental states that quite naturally produce poor qualities of human action.

"Guarding awareness" in the realm of morality, while indispensable, also leads to certain problems. The most significant of these recognized in

Buddhist texts is attachment to rules and procedures themselves. "Grasping" the precepts too firmly and too rigidly was thought to prevent the development of more skillful forms of moral awareness. "Clinging" to rules for monks and nuns stands in the way of a deeper moral consciousness, just as craving and attachment cloud perceptions of the world generally. Moreover, attachment to moral rules often undermines the compassionate and liberating connection to other people that morality intends to cultivate in a society. Wherever rule-following becomes mechanical and self-serving, where there is only joyless guarding of one's own moral standing, there the "perfection" of morality is rendered impossible.

Another common moral problem recognized by Buddhists is the tendency to be moralistic or judgmental about the quality of others' actions while being inattentive to one's own. Early Buddhist meditation texts, aware of this widespread human tendency, encouraged monks and nuns to focus on their own moral development, thereby allowing others to do the same. Mahayana bodhisattvas, however, sought to avoid self-enclosure and aspired to attend to the awakening of others to the same extent that they cared about their own. In order to work against unhelpful involvement in the moral cultivation of others, therefore, Mahayana texts advocate that a temporal priority be given to one's own moral development, after which concern for others can follow more successfully.

Since morality is a necessary dimension of practice, a dimension of perfection that enlightenment will require, bodhisattvas vow to help others initiate the practice. But in order to do that effectively, they must have attained a profound enough moral standing themselves that they will not be hypocritical in their moral instructions to others. Therefore Ārya-Śūra's chapter on the perfection of morality begins with the sentence: "The one in whom has arisen the strong concern to grace people with the ornament of a complete Buddha's morality should first of all purify his own morality."[3] It is not possible to teach what you are unable to practice yourself, and the outcome of this resolution is that Mahayana bodhisattvas are expected to focus first on their own moral wisdom, carrying it through extensively before they will be in a position to instruct others.

It was also recognized in Mahayana sutras that morality, like any other sophisticated dimension of human culture, only arises under certain conditions. It is not possible, for example, to expect someone who is hungry to be concerned about moral self-cultivation or to care about how others are faring. Bodhisattvas, therefore, placed a good deal of attention on the background conditions that would have made the cultivation of enlightened morality possible. They understood that immorality arises "through the lack of necessary conditions."[4] Without those conditions the development of moral sensibility would not be possible. Bodhisattvas therefore focused on other preliminary forms of assistance, and on the basis of that compassionate attention to the basic needs of others hoped to instruct through example rather than through verbal teachings.

In their effort to establish a more comprehensive understanding of Buddhist morality, Mahayana sources frequently classify morality into three increasingly significant categories.[5] First is morality as restraint, which aligns with most concerns of early Buddhist moral precepts. Steadfast in renunciation of ordinary worldly desires, the bodhisattva observes the precepts with great care and exactitude and does this with no thought of reward. Second is morality as the cultivation of virtue. More comprehensive than following the Buddhist precepts, the second level of moral practice is grounded in meditation and its concern for mindfulness. Attentive to all of the ways in which enlightenment can be cultivated, the bodhisattva undertakes these regimes of training in order to prepare for the final stage. Third is morality as altruism. This dimension of morality shows the bodhisattva's overarching concern for the welfare and enlightenment of others. Moral action at this stage, therefore, entails loving service to others, which includes everything from teaching to care for the poor and the sick. In the final analysis, moral action is not individual but collective, and the bodhisattva engages in morality for the betterment and enlightenment of all.

Morality for Self and Society

This ultimately communal orientation in the pursuit of morality links the perfection of morality directly to the bodhisattva's vow, the vow to pursue awakening on behalf of all beings. The point of moral action is not just one's own purity or enlightenment but also the perfection of human society as a whole and its movement toward enlightenment. Indeed, one's own enlightenment is linked to that of others; the pursuit of one is the pursuit of the other. To seek the enlightenment of others is to enlighten yourself, and seeking your own enlightenment will help bring about the enlightenment of others. Nevertheless, because enlightenment is defined in terms of certain qualities of selflessness and because our uncultivated inclinations are already shaped toward self-seeking, Mahayana Buddhist texts orient most moral practice in the direction of compassionate concern for others rather than concern for one's own enlightenment.

Buddhists have recognized that all of us begin the cultivation of morality from within whatever quality of self-understanding we happen to have. That means, of course, that our initial motives for moral action will be predominantly self-centered. But as moral practice matures and the accompanying mental transformation progresses, practitioners gradually recognize how the perfection of morality is grounded in compassion and sincere concern for others. Therefore, in his chapter on the perfection of morality, Ārya-Śūra writes: "Morality is the method for the habituation of virtue; moreover all virtues are contained in the thought of complete enlightenment, and that is cultivated through the virtue of compassion. For this reason, one should constantly be disposed toward compassion."[6] Similarly, the *Sandhinirmocana sūtra* has the Buddha say: "The perfections arise from the cause of compassion. Their results are desirable fruits and benefits for sentient beings. Their great significance is the completion of great enlightenment."[7]

The contemplative mechanism most commonly employed to help bodhisattvas shift orientation from self to others is the mental act of "dedicating" or "turning over" (*parinamana*) the merit of positive acts to the well-being and enlightenment of others. This was true in the perfection of generosity, and we will see that it continues to be pertinent through the first three perfections. Having performed a virtuous act, an act generating good karma, the bodhisattva enters into a meditative rite in which that beneficial karma is "given" to others, either to someone in particular or simply to all living beings. Whatever a bodhisattva might believe about the workings of karma, whether interpreted literally or in another way, the effect of this mental exercise is meant to shift the mind's orientation. Every good act is given away. Every accumulation of karmic wealth is offered to others. Practicing this meditation regularly, perhaps numerous times each day, the mind is wrested away from "self" improvement and refocused on the well-being of others.

In addition, this mental exercise gradually shifts the focus in moral practice from the original "restraints" of moral practice—all of the things that one ought not do—to the positive practices that are inspired by love and compassion. For example, instead of dwelling on noninjury, at a

certain point in practice this negative prohibition ceases to take prominence, and emphasis turns toward positive expressions of friendliness and
compassion. Hostile thoughts and injurious motives have moved into the
background, and what replaces restraints on them in the practice of
morality are creative thoughts about how bodhisattvas might make
themselves productive forces on behalf of universal enlightenment.

The fact that the ideal motivation for moral action is selfless compassion toward others does not mean that other more worldly motives do not
play a significant role. Indeed, Mahayana sutras and other writings
sometimes appear to feature what might seem to be selfish motivations
for a moral life. It is true that moral life tends to bring many mundane
and worldly benefits—the respect, trust, and goodwill of other people,
worldly success and plentitude, enlightenment for oneself, to name just a
few—and these are not insignificant. The fact that these are just the
beginning of the "wealth" that morality confers on its practitioners does
not invalidate them. This is where the path begins and, given the fact that
the sutras are written to inspire initiating the journey, this is where they
often focus their attention. Thus the texts frequently point to the reward
of a good rebirth or the respect and fame that truly moral people receive.

Morality is to the benefit of the selfish and selfless alike. Very often,
though, the texts skillfully shift the orientation away from what you will
receive if you behave morally toward more encompassing spheres of
justification and less self-centered motivation. The self-centered motives
that might have attracted someone to the practices of morality in the first
place will gradually be replaced by others if the practice advances to any
degree of depth. Undermined by the transformative effects inherent in
moral action, old mental habituation begins to fade, replaced by new
thoughts and new motives that have altered the mental landscape behind
the practice. The bodhisattva encourages the practice of morality by
skillfully articulating the rewards that follow from the practice on whatever level that they can be meaningfully understood and motivationally
active.

To the extent possible, bodhisattvas are encouraged to eschew those
rewards in their own practice and to raise their minds to a more profound
grasp of what is at stake in moral life. This is the crucial point in
"perfecting" moral practice. Perfection, in all six dimensions of human
character, consists in the application of wisdom. Recall that wisdom
consists in the realization of "emptiness," the Buddhist truth that all
things lack a substantial self, that all things are impermanent and depend

in the most fundamental sense on other things. Applying this wise realization in each case leads to apparent contradiction, and irony. The bodhisattva seeks to lead all beings through the perfection of morality and into the ultimate state of enlightenment, understanding all along how none of these components—beings, morality, enlightenment, the one leading—exist on their own as independent self-sufficient entities.[8] Morality is "empty" and so is the practitioner, as is the end toward which it is practiced—"enlightenment."

This does not mean, of course, that there is nothing to which the bodhisattva must attend. Instead, "emptying" morality deepens the practice of attention by altering the understanding in terms of which each element in the equation is conceived. Here, for example, is how the *Large Sutra on Perfect Wisdom* "empties" the overarching concept of karma, the fundamental principle in terms of which all morality in Buddhism proceeds. After invoking the principle of "emptiness," the sutra says: "in ultimate reality there is no karma or karma result, no production or stopping, no defilement or purification."[9] For a system of morality premised on karma and the gradual purification of human "defilement," this is a radical and paradoxical statement. The teaching of "emptiness" is introduced into moral consideration in order to undermine grounds for dogmatism and "grasping" in the practice of morality. Grasping the idea of karma dogmatically, the bodhisattva will practice morality in a mental framework that will ultimately fail to liberate, even if there are in the meantime many quite valuable benefits.

The same sutra explains how the bodhisattva is to teach the perfection of morality in view of the teaching of "emptiness": "And so he admonishes them in morality—May you beings guard morality, but do not put your minds to that morality, for within it there is no core."[10] Having "no core," no substantial, independent self, is the basic meaning of "emptiness." Practicing morality in view of one's own independent standing, on behalf of one's own betterment, and in pursuit of one's own enlightenment, the bodhisattva will inevitably fall short, no matter how many moral accomplishments might have accrued along the way. Exactly how the bodhisattva is to fulfill this paradoxical demand is difficult to grasp and will be deferred over and over until we arrive at the sixth perfection, the perfection of wisdom. But that deferral is precisely what bodhisattvas face—they begin their Buddhist practice within the parameters of their original understanding of the world. How could they begin otherwise?

This understanding, however, is invariably grounded in the unenlightened assumption that all things, especially oneself, are best understood independently, that is, on their own without reference to anything else. Like most of us, bodhisattvas at earlier levels of practice assume that things stand on their own and can therefore be grasped in isolation from other things. They take the language of things to validate a certain understanding of things and cannot at the outset think otherwise. But the practice of the perfections is meant to disrupt that understanding and to show how the depth of things is more truthfully disclosed through the "emptiness" of linguistic signs and their referents. So the same sutra goes on to say: "It is thus that the bodhisattva fulfils the perfection of morality with a mind free from signs."[11]

The realization that all moral rules are "empty" works toward freeing the bodhisattva from an inappropriate attachment to them. Holding the rules in one's mind without "clinging" to them, without "grasping" them dogmatically, yields a certain degree of latitude in their practice. The moral rules are understood as means, not ends, and when these means come into conflict with important ends, the bodhisattva learns to practice the rules flexibly. Therefore, Śāntideva writes what earlier Buddhists could not have written: "One should always be striving for others' well-being. Even what is proscribed is permitted for a compassionate person who sees it will be of benefit."[12] If moved to do so by wisdom and compassion, the bodhisattva is considered justified in breaking the Buddhist rules whenever the situation warrants it. Although few texts make this point explicitly, given the dangerous antinomian rationalizations that might follow from it, the few that do explicate the idea do so on the basis of a rigorous application of Mahayana principles. Rules are conventions that generalize what is best to do in situations of a certain kind. Situations and people do not always fit these generalizations, however, and when they do not, creative flexibility is essential.

"Emptiness," the connectedness of all things, deepens everything by disclosing the complex foundations upon which all things arise. Seeing these complexities more clearly, bodhisattvas recognize that the best intentions behind the rules will not always be fulfilled by inflexible application. Occasionally some other course of action is more effective in pursuing the highest good, and wisdom is the ability to see when and where that is so. Nevertheless, clear restraints are imposed on this flexibility: The bodhisattva, "coursing in the perfection of morality, beginning with the first thought of enlightenment, guards morality. But he does not aspire for any fruit from his morality, which he could enjoy in samsara, and it is only for the purpose of protecting and maturing beings that he courses in the perfection of morality."[13]

CRITICAL ASSESSMENT:
A CONTEMPORARY PERFECTION
OF MORALITY

Karma as a Moral Principle

Nothing is more fundamental to the conception of morality in Buddhism than the principle of karma. It would be natural to assume from this fact that karma would be a frequently discussed topic in Buddhist moral philosophy. Ironically, it is not. Few Buddhist texts really discuss the idea, and rarely is its meaning debated. Instead, karma appears in Buddhism as a basic point of departure inherited as a presupposition of moral discourse from earlier traditions. In its simplest form, the concept of karma stipulates that actions reap rewards and punishments in proportion to their moral quality, and that these just effects inevitably transpire, whether in this life or a future one, simply as the internal structure of the cosmos itself without the assistance of divine intervention. The idea works brilliantly. It supplies Buddhists with justification for moral effort by showing how good and bad acts always entail appropriate consequences. It gives people good reason to believe that what they do and how they do it matter a great deal.

Much of what most of us already do believe about moral matters accords with the Buddhist idea of karma. Most of us believe that what we do affects who we become, and that this matters. It matters who we are and that we actively engage our freedom in making choices that cultivate better lives. Whether we are intentionally engaged in the cultivation of character or not, we are nonetheless forming and reforming ourselves by virtue of what we do. Karma sets the stage for decisions and actions, and structures their effect. Having made a particular decision, I will always be the one who embraced that choice—at that time, in that way—to particular effect. Having chosen or acted, that choice or act is now deposited and embedded into my character. In effect, the act *is* me, along with all of the other acts I have chosen.

The choices we make, therefore, are never lost and are always right now shaping us. We can feel the past pressing upon us in this way; it is never something that, being past, is truly gone. The fact that our actions are not retractable does not mean, however, that the future is determined. Karma shapes the context and contours of all decisions, but it does not make them. Although particular acts cannot be undone, others yet to come can be differently construed, so that we make some degree of alteration in the course of our lives. This naturalized basis for the concept of karma makes persuasive sense in contemporary moral settings.

Every choice we face provides us with an opportunity either to embrace or to break the hold that the past has had on us. No matter how often we have chosen a certain way in the past, so long as we are human, we retain the freedom (to always varying degrees) to disown earlier patterns and to break out onto a new path. But all of our previous decisions are weighing heavily in the direction of the character we have formed for ourselves through previous actions, thus making decisive change difficult. Decisions made do weigh on us, and their presence is lasting. This is why human freedom is so profound in its significance, awesome in its magnitude. All of us, to the extent that we are human and free, remember with terror and regret bad decisions that we have made in the past. These memories sensitize us to the responsibilities that accompany our freedom and help us to grasp just what is at stake each time we choose.

If the solitary ethical decisions we have been considering so far have the power to move us in the direction of greater forms of human excellence, or away from them, then how much more do the unconscious "nonchoices" that we make every day through habits and customs that deepen over time, engraving their mark into our character. Some explications of karma are exceptionally insightful, in that their understanding of character development takes full account of the enormous importance of ordinary daily practice, the customs of behavior that we habitually do during the day, often without reflection or choice. These include the ways we do our work and spend our time, the customary ways we engage with others, the ways we daydream, or cultivate resentment, or lose ourselves in distractions, down to the very way we eat and breathe.

This is clearly a strong point in Buddhist ethics. On this understanding of karma, which was closely related to the development of meditation, ethics is largely a matter of daily practice understood as the self-conscious cultivation of ordinary mentality in an effort to approximate an ideal defined by images of human excellence, the awakened arhats and bodhisattvas.

Karma is one of the most ingenious cultural achievements to emerge from ancient India. It has enormous promise for future world culture—a

way to understand the relationship between moral acts and the kinds of
life that they help shape. Not all of the traditional teachings on karma will
be so easily adaptable to contemporary global culture, however. What
follows are critical discussions of four dimensions of the concept of karma
that may require further adjustment before this ideal could fulfill its
promise as a contemporary moral principle in and beyond the circle of
traditional Buddhist cultures.

KARMA AS COSMIC JUSTICE

The first dimension of the Buddhist doctrine of karma that warrants reflective scrutiny is its assertion of ultimate cosmic justice. All of the world's
major religions have long-standing traditions of promise that at some point
good and evil lives will be rewarded with good and evil consequences and
that everyone will receive exactly what they deserve. But all of these
religions are also forced to admit that this doctrine contradicts what we
sometimes experience in our own lives. Good people may just as readily be
severely injured or die from an accident, or die early of disease, as anyone
else, and people who have lived unjustly and unfairly will not necessarily
experience any deprivation in their lives. Some people seem to receive
rewards in proportion to the merit of their lives, while others do not.
Among those who do not appear to get what they deserve, some seem to
receive more than merit would dictate, and others less.

That all of these outcomes are common and unsurprising to us should
lead us to question the kind of relationship that obtains between merit and
reward. One way to face these realizations is to conclude that the cosmos is
largely indifferent to questions of justice and human merit. If our experience is that rewards are not always meted out in proportion to merit, so that,
for example, a morally sound person is no more or no less likely to die early
of a disease than anyone else, then maturity and honesty of vision on this
matter may require that we question traditional assertions that cosmic
justice will always balance merit and reward. Although we certainly care
about matters of justice, it may be that the larger cosmos does not.

The religious claim that there is a supernatural connection between
moral merit and ultimate destiny may derive from our intuitive sense that
there ought to be such a connection. We all sense that there ought to be
justice, even or especially in settings where it seems to be lacking. Our
sense that the corporate criminal ought to be punished and that the
innocent child ought not to suffer from a devastating disease are clear

manifestations of our deep-seated sense of justice. Virtue and reward, vice and punishment, ought to be systematically related and where they are not we all feel a sense of impropriety. But whether that now intuitive sense is sufficient reason for us to postulate a supernatural scheme of cosmic justice is an open question that has remained as closed in Buddhism as it has in other religions. The form that this closure takes in Buddhism is the doctrine of rebirth, which plays roughly the same role as ultimate guarantor of justice that heaven and hell do in theistic religions. As it is traditionally conceived in Asia, karma needs to be supplemented by the metaphysical doctrine of rebirth to support its often counterexperiential claims about the ultimate triumph of cosmic justice for the individual.

KARMA AND SOCIAL JUSTICE

A second question about karma follows from the first, and is in fact the primary critique that has been leveled against the idea of karma since it was introduced to the West. This is that the idea of karma may be socially and politically disempowering in its cultural effect, that without intending to do this, karma may in fact support social passivity or acquiescence in the face of oppression of various kinds. This possible negative effect derives from the link made between karma and rebirth in order to give assurance that apparent injustice in the short run of a single lifetime will be rectified in the long run of multiple lives. If you assume that cosmic justice prevails over numerous lifetimes, and that therefore the situations of inequality and injustice that people find themselves in are essentially of their own making through moral effort or lack of it in previous lives, then it may not seem either necessary or even fair to attempt to equalize opportunities or struggle for justice. If you believe that the child being severely abused by his family is now receiving just reward for his past sins, you may find insufficient reason to intervene, even when that abuse appears to be destructive to the individual child and to the society.

It is an open question, of course, a historical and social-psychological question, whether or to what extent the doctrines of karma and rebirth have ever really had this effect. We know very well that Buddhist concepts of compassion have prominent places in the various traditions, and we can all point to Buddhist examples of compassionate social effort on behalf of the poor and the needy. Nevertheless, we can see where the logic of this belief might lead, in the minds of some people at least, and we suspect that it may have unjustifiably diminished or undermined concern for the poor and the disadvantaged in all Buddhist cultures. The link between karma and rebirth can reasonably be taken to justify nonaction in the socioeconomic and political spheres and may help provide rational support for acquiescence to oppression. If and when this does occur, then the Buddhist teaching of nonviolence can be distorted into a teaching of nonaction and passivity, and be subject to criticism as a failure of courage and justice.

If the truth is that the cosmos is simply indifferent to questions of human merit and justice, that makes it all the more important that human beings attend to these matters themselves. If justice is a human ideal, invented and evolving in human minds and culture and nowhere else, then it is up to us alone to follow through on it. If justice is not structured into the universe itself, then it will have been a substantial mistake to leave it up to the universe to see that justice is done. Although, given our finitude, human justice will always be imperfect, it may be all the justice we have. Moreover, the fact that religious traditions including Buddhism have claimed otherwise may be insufficient reason to accept the assertion of a cosmic justice beyond the human as the basis for our actions in the world.

KARMA AND THE FRUITS OF ACTION

A third area of inquiry in which to engage the concept of karma concerns the nature of the reward or consequence that might be expected to follow from morally relevant actions. In pursuing this line of questioning, it is helpful to distinguish, as Aristotle did, between goods that are externally or contingently related to a given practice and goods that are internal to a practice and that cannot be acquired in any other way.[14] When we focus on any morally relevant action, this distinction helps us sort out the difference between goods or rewards that may or may not accompany that moral act because these are only contingently and externally related to it, and rewards that are directly linked to the practice, available through no other means, and therefore internal to that specific practice.

If we look at a single act—for example, an act of extraordinary kindness, as when someone goes far out of the way to help someone else through a problem—we can see many possibilities for rewards that might accrue through some contingency entailed in that relation. The person receiving assistance may in fact be wealthy and offer a large sum of money in grateful reciprocity. Members of his family may honor the practitioner of kindness, and his or her reputation in the community for compassion and character might grow. Such a person may become known as a citizen of extraordinary integrity, leading to all kinds of indirect rewards. These are all good consequences and all deserved. But they are all contingent outcomes, all goods that are external to the moral act itself. They may or may not be forthcoming. Indeed, on occasion contingent misunderstanding may give rise to exactly the opposite outcome. The practitioner of kindness may not even be thanked—no external rewards whatsoever. The same act of generosity may be misunderstood, resented, reviled, or lead to a denigrated reputation that the person never over-comes.

On the other hand, the rewards or goods internal to that act of kindness are directly related to the act and are not contingent on anything but the act. When we act with kindness, we do something incremental to our character—we shape ourselves slightly further into a person who understands how to act with kindness, is inclined to do so, and does so with increasing ease. We etch that way of behaving just a little more firmly into our character, into who we are. That is true no matter whether the act is positive or negative in character. Acts of kindness may or may not give rise to external goods such as rewards of money or prestige, but they do give rise to a transformation in character that makes us kind and concerned about the well-being of others. Internal goods derive naturally from the practice as their cause.

Our question, then, is what kinds of reward does the doctrine of karma correlate to virtuous or nonvirtuous acts, and how should we assess that dimension of the doctrine? Familiarity with the Buddhist tradition prevents us from giving a univocal answer to this question: Different texts and different teachers promise many different kinds of reward for karmically significant acts, depending on who they are and who they happen to be addressing. Both internal and external goods are commonly brought into play. From acts of generosity we get everything from the virtue of generosity as an internal good to great wealth, an external good, with a variety of specific alternatives in between. Teachers often lean heavily one way or the other, from emphasis on external goods such as health and wealth to a strict focus on the internal goods of character, the development of virtues like wisdom and compassion.

Consider this example from the Dalai Lama, where he is primarily interested in external goods. "As a result of stealing," he writes, "one will lack material wealth."[15] Since we all know that successful thieves and corporate criminals may or may not live their lives lacking in material wealth, we can only agree with this claim insofar as we assume that the author is referring to an afterlife, some life beyond the end of this one. That is to say that only the metaphysics of rebirth can make this statement plausible. Otherwise, the doctrine of karma cannot truthfully guarantee such an outcome of external rewards.

Had he been focused on internal goods instead of external, he might have said: As a result of stealing, one will have deeply troubled relations to other people, as well as a distorted relation to material goods. As a result of stealing, one will find compassion and intimacy more difficult, be further estranged from the society in which one lives, feel isolated and unable to trust others—making one even more likely to commit other unhealthy acts, and leading ultimately to an unfulfilled and diminished existence. These results of the act of stealing have a direct relation to the act; every act pushes us further in some direction of character formation or another and further instantiates us in some particular relationship to the world. External goods, while certainly important, cannot be so easily guaranteed except insofar as one offers that guarantee metaphysically by referring to lives beyond the current one.

Although, promises of personal rebirth aside, there would appear to be no necessary connection between moral achievement and external rewards, there is a sense in which moral achievement does often make external rewards more likely, even if this is never a relation of necessity. This is true because the more human beings enter the equation, the more likely it is that a human sense of justice will intervene, drawing some connection between acts and rewards. People who characteristically treat others with kindness are often treated kindly themselves, although not always. Those who are frequently mean-spirited and selfish are often treated with disdain. Honesty in business often pays off in the form of trusting, faithful customers, while the habit of cheating customers will often come back to haunt the merchant. These dimensions of karma and of moral relations are clear to us, and we are thankful that they exist. But it would seem that their existence is a human and social existence rather than one structured into the cosmos.

All we can say, therefore, is that things often work this way, not that they always do or that they must. Sometimes unscrupulous businessmen thrive; on occasion, kindness and honesty go completely unrewarded. These occurrences make it impossible for us to claim a necessary relation between moral merit and external forms of reward. Although it is clearly true that to some extent virtue is its own reward, what we cannot claim is that other kinds of reward are meted out in the same way. Evidence shows us that they are not, even if the human exercise of justice often directs external rewards toward those who are deserving.

We can summarize this by saying: How you comport yourself morally has at least three ramifications: (1) it shapes your character and helps determine who or what you become; (2) it helps shape others and the society in which you live, now and into the future; and (3) it encourages others to treat you in ways that correspond to your character—they will often do onto you as you have done onto them, although not always. The first and second outcomes can be counted as goods internal to ethical action; our actions do shape us and they do have an effect on the world. The third is external, that is, contingent, in that it may or may not follow from the ethical act. The more human justice there is, the more the distribution of external goods is likely to match the extent of our merit.

Thus, insofar as we can think this matter through, some dissociation between merit and external rewards is important to maintain. Although good acts do lead to the development of good character, being good does not always or necessarily lead to a life of good fortune. Therefore, if there is a contingent relation between merit and reward, it would be wise to articulate a system of ethics and a doctrine of karma that do not rely heavily on this relation, in spite of the long-standing Buddhist tradition of doing so for purposes of moral motivation.

KARMA AND COMMUNITY

Fourth, let us consider the extent to which karma can be adequately conceived as an individual consequence or destiny as opposed to one that is social or collective. Although there are a few interesting places in Buddhist philosophy where a collective dimension to karma is broached, it is true that this concept has been overwhelmingly understood in individual terms. For the most part, Buddhists have focused on ways in which the karma produced by my acts is mine individually rather than ours collectively. Although most references to karma in contemporary Buddhism are also conceived individually, there are serious philosophical difficulties with this way of understanding the impact of our moral actions. Perhaps most striking is the view that my acts and their repercussions remain enclosed in a personal continuum that never flows out into the larger society and continues to be "mine" forever; this view reinforces a conception of the

world as composed of a large number of discreet and isolated souls, a view
that a great deal of Buddhist thought sought to undermine.

Although the primary direction of Buddhist thinking may have been
to undercut the entire question of ultimate individual destiny through the
alternative possibility of "no-self," the question continued to surface and
to demand an answer. It may very well be, however, that Buddhist
attempts to satisfy the desire behind the question by offering the concept
of rebirth to allay fears about the after-death continuation of individual
existence has the additional and unwanted effect of blocking further
development along the alternative paths clearly laid out in the early
teachings. It stands in the way of the achievement of a broader vision of
the meanings of "no-self" and a more effective and mature understanding of the ways each of us continue to affect the future beyond our
personal lives. Personal anxieties about death are a powerful force in
the mind, so strong that they can prevent other impersonal and transin-
dividual conceptions from rising to the cultural surface.

The line of thinking that began to develop most explicitly in early
Mahayana texts that imagined complex interrelations among individuals
recognized that the consequences of any act in the world could not
be easily localized and isolated, and that effects radiate out from causes
in an ultimately uncontainable fashion, rendering lines of partition between selves and between all entities in the world significantly more
porous and malleable than we tend to assume. Expanding the image of
the bodhisattva, Buddhists began to see how lines of influence and
outcome commingle, among family members, friends, coworkers, and
co-citizens, such that the future for others "arises dependent" in part
upon my acts, and I become who I am dependent in part upon the
shaping powers of the accumulating culture around me. This type of
thinking, based heavily on the expanding meaning of "dependent arising," was forcefully present in several dimensions of Buddhist ethics. It
may be, however, that we have yet to see the development of this aspect of
Buddhism to the extent of its potential, and that it was regularly curtailed
by what must have seemed more pressing questions about the after-life
destiny of individuals.

There is a variety of ways in which an individualized concept of karma
continues to perpetuate itself in spite of a wealth of ideas in the Buddhist
tradition that would open it up to larger, less self-centered perspectives.
The basic ideas of "impermanence," "dependent origination," "no-self,"
and later extensions of these ideas such as "emptiness" are prominent

among them. But all of these ideas run aground on the concept of rebirth, and it is there that the Buddhist teachings on karma become questionable. All four critical questions raised here about karma derive their impact from the association that karma has with rebirth.

In several respects, rebirth stands in the way of an effort to understand karma in purely ethical terms. Rebirth encourages us (1) to assume a concept of cosmic justice for which we have insufficient evidence, (2) to ignore issues of justice in this life on the grounds that justice will be done in future lives, (3) to focus our hopes on external rewards for our actions, like wealth and status in a future life rather than on the construction of character in this one, and (4) to conceive of our lives in strictly individual terms, as a personal continuum through many lives, rather than collectively where individuals share in a communal destiny contributing their own lives and efforts toward enlightenment for all.

Moreover, the Buddhist doctrine of "no-self" is one of the best among several places in the teachings where we can begin to see beyond the individual interpretation of karma that has dominated the tradition so far. If the idea of karma is to be a truly comprehensive teaching about human actions and their effects, then the concept will need to be enlarged to encompass all of the ways in which the effects of our acts radiate out into other selves and into the social structures that support our lives. This extension of the doctrine has already begun, however, and will not be difficult to pursue, since it can be grounded on the extraordinary Mahayana teaching of "emptiness," the Buddhist vision of the interpenetration of all beings. Following this vision, we can imagine a collective understanding of karma that overcomes limitations deriving from the concept's original foundation in the individualized spirituality of early Buddhist monasticism.

A naturalized philosophical account of the Buddhist idea of karma can insightfully reflect these and other dimensions of our human situation. Separated from elements of supernatural thinking that have been associated with karma since its inception, its basic tenets of freedom, decision, and accountability are impressive, showing us something important about the project of self-construction, both individually and collectively conceived.

Morality and Meditation

There is a very important intersection in Buddhist practice between morality and meditation. Meditation plays several roles in the cultivation of morality. We can summarize these by presenting them in four categories.

First is mindfulness. Attending to the moral dimension of the situations in which we find ourselves requires that we be able to pay attention, that we not pass by morally relevant situations without even noticing them, as when we are distracted or enveloped in daydreams. The practice of mindfulness as a form of meditation generates the mental conditions under which it is possible to see the moral dimension of everyday situations. Even more significant, the practice of mindfulness cultivates awareness of and sensitivity to the situations of others. When we are in moods of self-enclosure, when we have shaped ourselves by long periods of self-absorption, we lose the capacity to see and feel what is happening right next to us in the interior space of family, friends, and others. In so doing, sometimes urgent and obvious situations of need are ignored. The perfection of morality calls for heightened sensitivity; it requires that we be awake and attentive to the numerous overt and subtle ways in which our actions are right now having an effect on those around us, and ways in which they could or should be having an effect. Insensitive to others, we may be unaware of the subtle forms of harm we are doing and we may be oblivious to all of the ways we might be of assistance to others.

The meditative cultivation of mindfulness opens us to see situations in a way that is attentive to the sensitivities and needs of everyone involved. It instills a perceptual capacity that most people lack, the ability to perceive nuances in everyday life that signify something important but that typically elude our attention. In this sense, meditation opens a space of receptivity within that attunes our minds to what is going on right now all around us. Occasionally, and painfully, it shows us the harm that we have been causing but could not see. As meditation proceeds, it awakens us to opportunities for sensitive and just treatment of others that were previously closed to our attention. In the meditative space of "no-self," we become capable of "disinterested" action, that is, action that is not predicated primarily on what is good for us. This is a condition of moral freedom from our own tendencies to become bound up within ourselves, inattentive to the world of others around us.

Second, a contemporary perfection of morality might also suggest another role for meditation to play, one that extends the domain of morality to encompass unintentional acts that the classical teachings on karma did not include. Although most Buddhist teachings on the

principle of karma restrict its sphere to acts that are performed intentionally, we assume today that intention does not cover the entire range of our
moral responsibility. When we are negligent, we are held legally accountable for the injuries that we cause even though we did not intend to harm
anyone. This would imply that we have a responsibility to be aware of
the unintended but potential consequences of our actions. Through
meditative awareness, we can learn to be more mindful of the possible
outcomes of our actions, regardless of what we intended those consequences to be. Similarly, we have a responsibility, both individual and
collective, to strive to understand and be sensitive to the unintended
consequences of the social institutions that we set in place to govern our
societies. Institutions are established with certain intentions and outcomes
in mind, intentions that purport to be socially beneficial. But these
intentions are often accompanied by additional unintended consequences
that may lead to prejudice and injustice.

These negative effects can be hidden in our unexamined institutions
and social customs. It is very easy not to perceive injustices that we
ourselves have unknowingly helped to institute. It is even more difficult
to see these injustices when they are embedded in routine practices that
have come to be assumed in our social world. The "normal" way things
are done can hide insensitivities in which we are all complicit. Racism was
not intended by many of us who lived in twentieth-century America, but
that lack of intention did not prevent extensive racial injustice. Ecological
disaster is not intended by those of us in developed nations with typical
habits of consumption, but that lack of intention does not remove the
responsibility that we will share for having brought that outcome to pass.
Meditation names the activity that strives to engender mindfulness
through a variety of reflective and unreflective means. It can be structured
to yield forms of awareness that put us in touch not just with the overt
and obvious ramifications of our acts but also with a much richer and
more comprehensive account of how we effect the world around us.

A third function of meditative mindfulness in the perfection of morality is the capacity to keep a desired ideal in view. Consistently mindful of
the enlightened "good" we seek, we are much more likely to move in the
direction of that ideal. Unable to keep that ideal in mental view, we are
unlikely to undergo the kinds of change that we claim to pursue. When
we lack this meditative focus, images and thoughts of possible ideal ends
are weak and undeveloped, vaguely coming and going through our
minds without depositing much significant effect. Mindfulness cultivates

a well-honed "thought of enlightenment" in the form of a set of images and conceptions of what our selves and societies ought ideally to be. This dimension of mindfulness in the perfection of morality significantly expands the scope of our responsibility. In the realm of ideals, we are responsible not just for particular acts of good and evil but also for the quality of the overall conception in terms of which we make judgments about which acts fulfill the moral ideal.

Fourth and finally, meditative mindfulness shows us our regret and employs this awareness to enable freely chosen change. In regret, we sense what we ought or ought not to have done or said, who we have become through our acts, and who we might have become instead through some preferable course of action. This is important because, without the ability to raise our regrets into conscious attention, we are unable to learn from the past. Failing to use the past intentionally, we tend to repeat it, and begin to think of its weaknesses as inevitable rather than alterable. But regret poses a series of difficult questions, and it is to them that we now turn.

Regret: Meditating on Moral Failure

Regretting past decisions that we now regard as personal failures is a dimension of moral experience that we all share. We all have regrets. But we may not have considered carefully what to think and do when we fail to live in accordance with our moral convictions or our guiding "thought of enlightenment." In most traditions, the cultivation of a sense of regret and shame is considered essential to the possibility that we will learn from our mistakes and, over time, enlighten ourselves morally. Buddhists, like other religious people and societies, have constructed ritual occasions to cultivate feelings of regret and shame for moral wrongdoing in order to foster conditions conducive to moral transformation. There are repentance ceremonies and confessional occasions intended to highlight moral transgressions and to generate feelings of shame strong enough that guilty parties will be motivated to avoid further moral failure. Feelings of shame are profoundly unpleasant, and few of us will not be compelled by strong motivation to avoid these feelings of failure by doing what we ought to do and avoiding moral mistakes.

Nevertheless, it may be important to ask: Are these profound feelings of disappointment and self-admonition essential to moral change, or should the role of shame ideally be more limited? And is it possible that, for some of us at least, the experience of moral shame can become destructive and not at all beneficial? A good place to begin in responding to this question is to acknowledge that the capacity to regret and to be ashamed of what we have done is essential, virtually synonymous with the ability to live morally. To be "shameless"—that is, incapable of being ashamed of one's actions or character—is to lack moral sensibility altogether. But to acknowledge that the capacity to feel shame is essential is not the same as conceding that shame is the best way to cultivate moral depth and sensitivity.

We can take our lead on this question from Śāntideva, one Buddhist philosopher who we will be consulting throughout our study of the six perfections. Śāntideva claims that although feelings of shame and regret over moral failures are quite natural, they should not be cultivated because they do more to upset the stability of mind required for moral correction than they do to help instill it.[16] Indeed, he says, the thing to focus on in meditation when you have experienced moral failure is your "thought of enlightenment." More important than dwelling on your failure, he claims, is meditating on the very ideals that your actions have transgressed, because it is the strength and viability of these ideals that will be your best ally in preventing moral failure.

Although neither Śāntideva nor other Buddhist philosophers provide an explanation for why or how this is so, here are some considerations that seem important in our setting. We cannot help but feel badly when we fail to live up to the ideals that we have adopted for our lives. We regret mistakes and condemn ourselves for having made them. If the ideal that we have violated is profoundly important to us, we will feel deeply ashamed of ourselves. If we have moral principles at all, the feeling of shame is inevitable. But the question is whether to cultivate that sense of being ashamed of oneself, whether to follow our natural inclinations to dwell on the mistake, reliving it frequently in the imagination in the process of chastising ourselves. Although it is perfectly natural to do just that, it is not at all clear that this is the best way to motivate yourself to achieve the moral ideals that you want to maintain. One reason for thinking that it is not beneficial is that shame is a deeply disturbing emotion. It entails self-condemnation and, at least for a while, self-loathing. While engaged in feeling of shame, we despise our weakness and to some degree ourselves. We lose our self-respect and question our moral capacity. For whatever time we engage in it, we wonder whether we really can live in accord with these ideals. The stronger our feeling of shame becomes, the more we denigrate ourselves and undermine our self-respect.

Wherever it develops in that way, the experience of shame has the power to weaken us. Rather than helping us find the strength needed to stand up and start over by asking ourselves which ideals are worthy of our renewed attention, we attack ourselves when we are most vulnerable. In doing so, we undermine the self-respect needed to get ourselves back on our feet. Shame takes an already bad feeling of failure and deepens its wound; it exacerbates the sense of failure by turning us against ourselves. In this sense, there is an important difference between self-acceptance, which shame disallows, and accepting that on this occasion, for whatever reasons, we have failed to live in accord with our values, which would be the necessary condition of any effort to undertake moral change. Shame is so profound a feeling that it can disable our capacity to refocus on our ideals by forcing us to dwell on the mistake rather than on what is now needed. When we ought to be gathering the energy and sense of confidence needed to commit to change, shame worsens the problem by consuming that energy and confidence in a trial of self-doubt.

Even if all this is true, however, most of us would wonder whether we really have any choice in the matter. When we are ashamed of ourselves we are under the sway of a powerful emotion, and it is not at all clear how we might get out from under its all-consuming impact. The Buddhist remedy for that problem is meditation, and practitioners make the claim that meditative practice can be sufficiently powerful to overcome the damage caused by the feeling of shame. By "meditation," here, we need only mean the intentional redirection of mental energies from the destructive self-loathing demanded in the experience of shame to the constructive task of moving beyond the moral failure toward resources necessary for avoiding that failure. Meditating on the situation at hand, we deflect our mind from the pain of past failure to the ideals that we have been so far unable to actualize.

Having already acknowledged what went wrong, rather than meditate further on it, we place in mind that aspect of our ideals that we have failed to practice. Rather than relive the wrong, over and over, thereby making it a constant and debilitating fact of our mental makeup, we redirect those energies toward the positive ideal that we would hope to embody. While the feeling of shame entails focus on our failure, meditation encourages focus on the values to which we aspire. This turns a disabling state of mind into one that empowers. It allows us to move our minds from the shame of our disease to our aspiration for health, from the regret of failure to the hope for a new start.

Feelings of regret and shame are so powerful that it takes a skillful meditation to overcome them. Many of us have not developed this skill and are therefore at the mercy of our most powerful feelings. But the possibility of developing this skill—essentially, a skill of freedom—is an exciting prospect within the perfection of morality. It enables greater focus on the "thought of enlightenment" and confers greater freedom on the practitioner. Rather than finding ourselves enslaved to feelings of self-loathing that will further weaken our state of mind, we entertain the possibility of a mental freedom that has the power to engage in constructive interior work even in devastating circumstances. The self-respect needed for life is not a given; it must be cultivated and learned, and only then can it be included among the resources available for the development of moral capacity.

Moral Rules and the Function of Prohibition

The realm of morality is most widely known in all cultures as a realm of rules and prohibitions. The Buddhist rules, like those in other cultures, take the form of negative commandments about what "thou shalt not" do. What makes rules universally necessary is that human beings come into conflict with each other, not just occasionally but regularly, and our natural inclinations not only fail to inhibit this tendency but they also fuel it. It is not that we intend harm to each other so much as that harm is a natural outcome of our each pursuing our own ends. Without the restrictive effect of moral prohibition, we would continue to cause harm to each other to such an extent that most of us would fail to achieve our aims.

The Buddhist rules start with the "five precepts" that prohibit harmful conduct; they demand that we abstain from killing, stealing, sexual misconduct, lying, and taking intoxicants. This list bears more similarities to lists from other cultures than differences, because the purpose of moral codes is to define the social conditions under which it is possible for people to live successful and satisfying lives, and these do not differ substantially between human communities.

As we have seen, the Buddhist moral code includes two types of rules, a primary list of infractions against others that are universally recognized (within certain differences of nuance), and a secondary or conventional list of injunctions that are wrong only in the sense that a community has agreed to consider them wrong for specific reasons of religious practice. The conventional rules are interesting in that, rather than mark necessary requirements of communal life, they seek to establish an intentional way of living that could have been structured in some other way. They are based on a communal agreement that these particular procedures structure a way of living that conforms to the chosen ideal. In this case, the agreement was that the Buddhist rules are the best way to enact a life of Buddhist enlightenment.

For those who join the Buddhist community and commit themselves to this way of life, the rules constitute an objective standard for measuring conduct for all members of the community. The standard is not objective in the sense that anyone in any society would agree that these rules correspond to the correct way to behave. They would not, since there are many other reasonable codes of conduct in other societies. But it is objective in the sense that it stands out in front of all Buddhist practitioners as something clearly defined against which conduct can be measured in very straightforward, factual ways.

The objectivity of the code is strengthened by its having withstood the test of time. The ideals posited in the moral code have evolved out of the cumulative experiences of earlier generations and are given the status that they have based on good reasons and practical outcomes. Because of their meditative focus on the idea of the "self," Buddhists were extremely perceptive in recognizing the extent to which our self-absorption and rationalizing will take us in pursuing our own ends. The moral code stands against human egotism and forces us to confront it. Although in some cases newcomers to Buddhist communities obey the rules primarily out of fear of punishment, it is hoped that over time their motivations mature so that they obey the rules primarily because they are "our" rules, the rules that "we" have adopted to help implement the ideals that the community has chosen to pursue.

The fact that the moral rules tend to list prohibited acts—what you should "not" do rather than what you ought to do in a positive sense—demonstrates that the community takes these negative acts of harm as the greatest danger it faces. And this is no doubt true of any community. The negative form of the commandments, however, may make it seem that morality consists in refraining from doing harm, that the good is simply an absence of evil. That would be a serious misconception—enlightenment does not consist in simply avoiding wrong. Awakened bodhisattvas are not those who most carefully "toe the line" of monastic regulation. Otherwise, enlightenment would amount to no more than cautious timidity, the placid state of refraining from negative encounter with others.

Instead, the enlightened being is best imagined as the one who faces up to his or her tendency to do harm to others by pushing through it to a transformed mode of relation to others. The domain of morality is much larger than prohibition, although prohibition and injunction are always where it must begin. That is simply a beginning, however. Based on the law of karma, individuals are accountable not just for what they do but also for what they fail to do.

This way of putting the matter implies that the moral rules of Buddhism are preliminary, something that is undertaken at an initial level but that lose central significance as progress is made in practice. That is how many Buddhists have articulated the place of prohibition. This is not to say that morality is preliminary, but rather that prohibition is the preliminary dimension of morality. Why and how that is so can be seen in the relationship between three different levels of moral practice, which we might call custom, morality, and compassion. To some extent these correspond to the three stages of morality defined in classic Buddhist texts such as the *Mahāyāna Samgraha* and outlined earlier in this chapter.

The prevailing customs of proper human relationship, what we sometimes call etiquette, is what we first learn as children. It is also what novices initiated into the monastic community would learn in the form of the particular ways of acting appropriate to the monastery. Etiquette is simply a socially proven means of choreographing ourselves in relation to one another so that we can live effectively with each other. These polite customs resemble morality in this way, but fall short of morality by taking the form of means. The practice of etiquette is the initial means of approaching morality. Acting politely is acting as though out of moral concern; it is proper behavior that approaches the moral virtue that it intends to instill through habitual performance. The practice of etiquette is a form of education into the deeper resources of morality.

In the same way that etiquette resembles morality while not yet embodying it, morality imitates compassion while still falling short of it. Although from an earlier perspective it appeared that morality was an end and etiquette the means, from this higher perspective morality is also a means, albeit an exalted one, with compassion as its end. The effort to treat others morally resembles in effect having compassion for them, although it does not yet arise from that more exalted source of motivation. Morality imitates compassion and points us toward it, but if compassion were already present there would be no need for morality. It is only because we lack compassionate concern for others that we must constrain and shape our actions by adhering both to proper etiquette and to the restrictions of the moral code. Nevertheless, as Buddhists imagine the perfection of morality, compassion is engendered and brought into being through the habitual practice and internalization of morality.

In the same way that morality leads us beyond and sets us free of etiquette, the ideal is that compassion eventually enables awakened bodhisattvas to do freely and with love what at first they had learned to do dutifully through the prescriptions of the moral code. Appropriate action first takes the form of prohibition and commandment; then it matures into what we know we ought to do; finally, if the perfection of morality has been approximated, it becomes what we desire to do and therefore do naturally without effort or hesitation. The earlier stages of controlling one's behavior in practice, which from some points of view can seem unduly punitive, simply open the space enabling one to see what will eventually seem obvious—that the self is not defined by the immature conceptions and feelings that give it orientation in earlier stages of moral practice. As this earlier orientation loosens its grip on our minds, we move into forms of self-understanding whose previous boundaries have been substantially enlarged.

Morality and Community

Although, as we have seen, the idea of karma has been largely conceived in individual terms, there are certainly suggestions found in Buddhist literature for use in developing the collective and social side of the perfection of morality. It is clear to us now that the moral character in each one of us is deeply affected by the upbringing we receive in our families, by the contacts we have with our friends and neighbors, by the education we receive in schools, and by the larger culture in which we are enveloped. Equally important is the effect that each of us has on the social world around us. The quality of our engagement in this world, the extent to which various forms of human excellence are actualized, matters fundamentally to the culture as a whole and to each individual in it.

Classical Mahayana Buddhist texts picture this communal engagement of the bodhisattva brilliantly. Morally cultivated individuals have a transformative effect on those around them. They exude a sense of possibility that others absorb, whether they are aware of it or not. The "noble" character that the sutras describe is catching; it radiates out into the minds of others and from them, in greater and lesser degrees, passes on to others the sense of nobility that is possible in human beings. Those with integrity of character serve to integrate others, often in ways unknown even to them.

Equally true, of course, is the opposite, that negativity of character extends to others as an influence of corruption, undermining the sense of shared enterprise that a community needs to sustain itself. At least as common as excellence of moral character, corruption of character has profound affects on the community as a whole. Like a contagion, negative character affects everyone in its proximity. It pushes others toward self-protective modes of behavior and makes more plausible the alienated idea that morality is an imposition on individual priorities and desires. It is easy to see the social corruption that occurs through those who have become immoral. Less obvious, but just as important, is to see what it means to be amoral.

To become amoral is to reduce morality to a strictly prudential concern; one attends to it and restricts one's activities, but only to the extent that it is instrumental in fulfilling one's desires. Indifferent to the well-being of others and unaware of one's own role in their welfare, amoral people resent the restrictions on personal pursuit that morality inevitably requires. That resentment commonly leads to some degree of disdain for morality, a disdain that is frequently given rationalization through an ideology of stark individualism. But the distance and isolation that is taken for granted in such a conception of private life is an illusion. We exist interdependently, and the quality of our lives is shaped by how we fit ourselves into this interdependent whole. We are not separate from others in this way, and whatever we do it will have a moral impact on others around us. The outcome of an amoral posture is severe personal limitation, and its effects undermine community. Unpracticed in moral accountability, the amoral person fails to cultivate a dimension of character that is essential and suffers along with the society in proportion to the damage that has been inflicted on everyone.

It is common to assume that morality is a very limited sphere of our lives, active just on those occasions when a difficult decision presents itself. These are moral dilemmas, situations of uncertainty where we must make a complex decision. Although it is true that we occasionally do confront such situations and that these pivotal events define our character in important ways, much more important is an understanding of morality as everyday practice. This is the type of moral thought most frequently enjoined in Mahayana sutras under the category of the perfection of morality. In these sutras it is rare to find a focus on moral quandaries, exceptional and occasional puzzles that tax our moral understanding. The reason for this is that much more basic, and thus more important, is mindful focus on the moral opportunities that present themselves every day as a forum for practice.

Conceived in this way, the practices arranged under the category of the perfection of morality are more like a regular fitness program than the occasional act of confronting an exceptional dilemma. Morality is constructed out of practical concerns, and without regular practice we will be untrained and thus unfit to confront the most important moments of moral life. Moral practice is a lifelong pursuit, one that must be situated within the overall quest for excellence represented in the six perfections as a whole. Like the other five perfections, the perfection of morality entails a reach for excellence that pushes us beyond our current state of moral conditioning. Exercising our moral capacity, we stretch it out beyond what it was. Morality is perhaps the most practical of all the perfections, and practice is precisely what it takes to attain excellence. When we succeed or fail in our encounter with a difficult moral choice, what is indicated about us has much less to do with that particular act than with the lifelong regime of discipline that has led up to it. Unpracticed in moral matters, we can no more expect to excel when put to the test than can the long-distance runner who has yet to do any serious running.

Mahayana Buddhist texts describe the bodhisattva as being involved in the moral education of others. The bodhisattva serves as a teacher and as a model of what is being taught, and seeks a transformative influence on others. When this influence is simply that of being admired and imitated, no critical questions come to mind. But when someone actively seeks to shape the lives of others, suspicions are raised and moral questions emerge. In what ways and to what extent should anyone intervene in the life of another? When someone you know is involved in what appears to be destructive or immoral activity, is it appropriate to intervene in order to stop them? At what point, under what circumstances, and to what extent should you intervene in the life of others to prevent them from harming themselves or others?

On the one hand, the bodhisattva vows to oppose destructive forces in the world and to prevent their appearance wherever possible. There are often good reasons for intervention on behalf of others, especially those in close relation or proximity to us. On the other hand, the sovereignty and integrity of others is important, because without this freedom no moral life is possible. Respecting the dignity of others, we allow them to choose as they do and to live with the karmic implications of their actions as best they can. Yet practicing compassion for others, we do what we can to prevent self-destructive acts that will disable their chances of leading a morally worthy life. Should we practice noninvolvement in the self-destructive acts of others, allowing them to fall into a situation that might become irretrievable, or do we violate their freedom and integrity by preventing them from making a disastrous decision? We can imagine situations in which this would seem an impossible choice, where neither intrusion nor nonintrusion would be satisfying options: the situation of a friend and drug addiction, or one's own adult children involved in a foolishly destructive policy in raising their own children.

The examples of these complicated dilemmas show us that moral choices are not always between actions that are right and actions that are wrong, not always between clearly good and evil options. On occasion they are, and when that is the case moral decision poses little dilemma, even when carrying out that right action is not easy. More commonly, however, morality is a sphere of considerable ambiguity. Choices need to be made not between good and bad but between competing goods, or between two options that appear to be equally destructive. Occasionally, there is a conflict between morality and compassion, where following the rules of appropriate behavior prevents a person from acting out of the deeper concern of love. As Buddhist morality evolved, repeatedly facing complicated choices that could not be satisfactorily resolved through simple recourse to the rules, greater nuance and flexibility were added to the image of what people would need to become if they were to be capable of an authentic moral life. In Mahayana Buddhism, this evolution reinforced the importance of the ethical framework within which morality would be practiced. Thus, character and wise judgment came to be the most highly prized ideals, while conformity to the specific details of the moral code receded in significance.

Recognizing the complexity of social circumstances and the dangers of moral rigidity, Mahayana Buddhist philosophers sometimes advocated what we might call a "relaxed attachment" to the traditions of Buddhist morality. While attending to moral rules with considerable scrutiny, they stressed a deeper responsibility to wisdom and compassion, which on occasion would "overrule" the rules. Although morality is a standard against which the actions of any individual can be judged, the variety and uniqueness of moral situations demands that moral excellence include as one of its crucial elements a strong sense of perception and judgment to enable practitioners to sense when and how the rules are applicable to any particular set of circumstances. Every situation is in some way unique, requiring that responsiveness and attunement to that uniqueness be a fundamental part of moral judgment. The most appropriate actions are shaped to each unique situation so that the action fits the situation with wisdom and compassion.

A morality sophisticated enough for contemporary circumstances will require several elements that can be learned in part from Mahayana Buddhism: that the moral rules are conditioned by the particular history of their development, even when they aspire to universality; that moral life therefore entails much more than getting in line with the rules; that sensitivity to the concrete details of the moral situation is vital in any application of the rules; and that holding the ethical ideal in mind as a criterion governing the applicability of the rules is one way to prevent immoral applications of moral precepts. All of this entails the realization that although the bodhisattva is to strive toward the perfection of morality, what "perfection" entails in any context is always open. In a world of change and interdependence, moral certainty is not possible, and moral choice always includes risk. Refusing to shy away from these risks, we commit ourselves to the creation of a world in which compassion and moral sensitivity increasingly become the human norm.

Morality and the Self

We have seen that morality is one of six perfections and that the perfections are each a domain of ethical self-cultivation. By means of the six perfections, the bodhisattva develops his or her character and does this in pursuit of enlightenment. This way of putting the matter, however, may give rise to an important objection. The objection is that priority appears to be given to one's own pursuit of excellence, while "morality" is most importantly a concern for the well-being of others. If my own quest for the perfection of morality focuses this narrowly on the issue of who I become as a result of moral practice, is it not likely that I will fail in the primary point of moral consideration—that I turn away from self-concern in order to attend to the well-being of others? And if I concentrate so forcefully on the perfection of my own moral conscience, does this not ironically rob me of the compassionate attentiveness to the welfare of others that moral practice is meant to cultivate, thus rendering both my own moral self-transformation and openness to others impossible?

This objection is important and gives us the opportunity to take a closer look at how the "self" is positioned at various stages in the practice of the six perfections. Let us begin by considering a distinction between morality and ethics. Ethics is defined for our purposes here as the overall quest for human excellence—enlightenment in Buddhist terms—while morality is one dimension of that quest, the practice of attention to the needs and happiness of others so that our own quest does not unjustly interfere with their pursuits. In the simplest terms, ethics concerns the overall discipline of self-cultivation—what I ought to do in every dimension of my life—and morality concerns one central dimension of that quest—the way I ought to treat others. Moral questions ask how to give others their due, ethical questions concern what kind of human being I ought to become.

It is true that all of the perfections begin as a means of cultivating one's own character. The perfection of morality, for example, is meant to show us how to become a certain kind of person in relation to others. That is only the beginning, however. Once engaged in the cultivation of morality, practices of selflessness begin to direct concern outward beyond the self toward others and the society as a whole. This process is gradual, however, and it begins exactly where we are, that is, in a posture dominated by self-concern. Initially, therefore, even our concern to be moral is a form of self-concern. But it is precisely this concern that initiates the process of moral self-cultivation within which we enlarge the domain of the "self" to encompass those who were previously understood to be outside of its sphere.

Concern for our own moral standing is a prerequisite without which we never even begin to turn toward others in moral concern. Lacking the fundamental transformation in one's own relationship to the world that moral self-cultivation activates, we are incapable of care and concern for others. The objection that concern for one's own moral worth will always undermine a true morality of concern for others fails to take into account all the complex phases of development required in authentic moral achievement. The objection is based on the naïve hope that morality is already fully present within us, and that nothing significant needs to change in order to activate authentic moral relations with other people. But this is not the case. Only by transforming self-understanding through stages of development is it possible to acquire the kind of compassionate outreach to others that is the ideal aim of morality. But this is not where the process begins.

The transition featured here moves us from morality as self-concern to morality as open concern for others. Distinguishing these two, we imagine the qualitative difference between morality that is maintained through a sense of duty or self-discipline and an increasingly effortless morality that arises out of a transformation in self-identity. In the first instance, where morality is maintained through discipline and duty, we imagine ourselves resisting our natural inclinations in order to be fair to others or to do what is right. Our motivation is that we want to be a different kind of person—a moral person. Resisting contrary inclinations that derive from our own self-absorption, duty and discipline make possible the unnatural results of helpful outreach to others. As we realize that selfish lack of concern for others is an immature and unattractive state, we learn moral mindfulness. Although by this means we increasingly maintain moral conduct, the motivation for acting morally on behalf of others is that it serves our own ends—it makes possible our own self-transformation into an admirable person whose selfish inclinations have been drawn under the wraps of a formidable self-discipline. We see the benefits that morality can bring to our own lives.

In the second instance, imagining an effortless morality, something basic to the self has changed—its very identity—to such an extent that concern for the welfare of others has come to be included within it. Through a gradual change in identity, "self-" concern enlarges to encompass concern for others, thus enabling a relation to others that no longer requires the same discipline of self-curtailment. At the highest level, this is an "effortless" morality in which the self/other dichotomy has been transformed in a fundamental way. Moral outreach of this "higher" form is not a matter of duty and does not work against natural inclination. No "internal" impediments need to be resisted, since the boundaries of the "self" have been enlarged to encompass the other so that we care for others as we care for ourselves.

The difference between these two moral identities is that while in the first instance, acting on your behalf, I intend my own moral self-transformation, in the second instance I act for you without self-directed intentions. Although in some situations the actions may be the same, the mental processes that have given rise to them differ enormously. One instantiates a highly refined discipline and intention for self-sculpting, and the other shows the ultimate effects of that intentional discipline in the form of an enlarged personal identity. In truth, however, because the motivations behind the actions vary significantly, the actions themselves will probably differ as well. The first action, which works against natural inclination, requires a disciplined concentration, while the second can appear to have the joy and ease of effortless movement. Indeed, in the second, the very distinction between self and others has been complicated to the point that one realizes instinctually that one's own well-being is inseparable from the well-being of others. Through the processes of moral self-cultivation, the difference between living for oneself and "living large" on behalf of everyone is functionally diminished.

This process is a matter of gradual change, of course, a change from seeking goodness in the particular form of advantage for oneself to seeking goodness as such, or in Buddhist vocabulary, a transformation from seeking enlightenment for oneself to the broader quest for enlightenment itself. The dichotomy that has been drawn here for contemplative purposes is an abstraction from complex and varied processes that cannot be easily reduced to types. It is a polarity that finds virtually all of us in the middle somewhere. Nevertheless, in the contrast between the two poles of moral discipline and moral expansion, we get a clear sense of both the process of change and the ideal at which it aims. What it highlights, among other things, is that morality is both a debt that we owe to others and a debt that we owe to ourselves. It brings us into profound relation to others and into equally profound relation to our own "thought of enlightenment," that is, to the kinds of self-enlargement that we hold as our personal ideal.

In order to get this centrally important Buddhist point into perspective, recall that the bodhisattva's "awakening" entails an expansion of awareness out beyond the typically tight grasp of the "self." Both through steady, disciplined enlargement of perspective and in occasional moments of insightful or affective breakthrough, a taste of nonself-centered expansion breaks the pattern of egocentric self-enclosure. In the experience of compassion, we let go of ourselves and open up to others. When opening out in this way, the very boundaries that give identity to the self are expanded. The discipline of the perfection of morality is precisely this process of self-enlargement, the gradual opening to others in more and more inclusive ways.

To understand this process of self-expansion, consider how our sense of moral "duty" shows us something about the moral boundaries that define us. When do we feel a "duty," a sense of moral obligation to help others? When a mother realizes that her child has been severely injured, does she respond to this crisis out of a sense of duty? Not at all. Her immediate act of loving care derives from a much deeper impulse. In caring for the child, she is not sacrificing herself but fulfilling herself. Her identity includes the child—the child's pain is her pain. Her desire to ease the child's suffering is as spontaneous and natural as the desire to ease her own. Who we are is defined by the radius of close relationships, and typically the pull of obligation is not required for us to act on their behalf. But as the circle widens beyond those with whom we share family or other close identity, we do encounter at some point the realm of "moral obligation," and correspondingly the boundaries of the self's identity. Is it morally unbearable for us that our neighbors lack sufficient food while we are well fed? One hopes so. Members of another ethnic group slightly further away in our own community? Perhaps. Elders in a far-away society about whom we know almost nothing? The further we move out from the closest circle of identity, the more our relations to others will fall under the discipline we typically call "moral obligation." Where we are not spontaneously compelled to act, but still feel we ought, at that juncture we are guided by moral obligation because there a strong sense of identity has not developed.

Those who are most profoundly cultivated in the disciplines of morality will feel some degree of obligation to reach out to hungry beings wherever they are found on the planet. Beyond this sense of obligation, however, stands the personification of an ideal—the bodhisattvas—who respond to the needs of strangers not out of a sense of moral obligation but out of a far deeper sense of identity with all living beings. These bodhisattvas—people like Mother Teresa—no doubt begin their path with a sense of moral obligation but conclude it having shaped their own identity to include the welfare of others as an integral part of themselves. Although it may be true initially that I respond, if at all, to the hunger of unknown people in other cultures out of a sense of moral obligation and not out of a deeper sense of identity, it could occur through the practices of morality that my identity is so enlarged that I actually experience the links between their well-being and my own. When this occurs to the extent that my feelings for them are engaged, my actions will begin to be motivated by compassion rather than duty.

This is the image of the bodhisattva's perfection of morality, an expansion of the self that includes others in the innermost domain of self-concern. Buddhists sometimes refer to this expansion as an experience of "no-self," but it could just as well be conceived as a magnificent transformation or expansion of the self. Although moral practices begin by cultivating the sense of duty or obligation that we owe to others, it comes to ideal fruition in the irrelevance of this same sense of duty made possible by an enlargement of the self toward the ultimate goal of profound reverence for life.

Moral progress, both for us as individuals and for us collectively as a society, will consist in the ability to respond to the needs of ever larger and more inclusive circles of human beings and then beyond that sphere to all living beings. From these basic structures of Buddhist thought it is possible to realize that the long-standing moral problem—the question: why should I be moral?—depends in a very direct way on who or what this "I" is, that is, on the depth of self-understanding implied in the one asking the question. Wherever this question assumes the substantiality of the self, the isolation of the self, and that the self's identity is fundamentally nonrelational, it is very difficult to answer. Remove these assumptions, however, and place someone fulfilling the bodhisattva image in the position of the inquirer, and the question loses its relevance. Indeed, it begins to look like a truly unenlightened question.

When we understand all things, especially ourselves, as constituted through relations to others, the larger issue of identity begins to take on a new look, and along with it, the kinds of moral questions that will be posed. Seen from an ideal of the bodhisattva image, those who are hungry will be fed not because it is the bodhisattva's duty to feed them or that they have a right to be fed, but rather because of a sense of common belonging and shared identity so fundamental that a compassionate response becomes "natural." Whenever we think of moral life as a duty imposed upon us by the moral law, we hold the motivation for moral action outside of ourselves and continue to alienate ourselves from deeper sources of motivation.

The complexity and importance of moral self-cultivation are such that it is incumbent upon us to end these reflections on the perfection of morality with three qualifications:

First, although our hopes for ourselves and the images of compassionate, awakened bodhisattvas provided by the Buddhist tradition encourage contemplating the possibility of living in the world in a state of risk-free moral perfection, this is not a helpful goal. No matter how far we extend the cultivation of selfless, compassionate concern for others, and no matter how far our innate sense of conscience and responsibility take us, as long as we are human we face the limitations of human understanding and the reality of moral risk. This is simply to say that in our deepest reality we are finite and that in human life good and evil always coexist. Although moral conflict may take place in the cultivated individual at higher and higher levels of development, the difficulty of moral choice and the necessity of conflict remain as persistent realities within us. Indeed, one of the paradoxes of moral life is that we initially become attuned to the moral demand upon us often as the result of some failure that now stands before us as a judgment of guilt—one now requiring our attention.

Second, moral self-cultivation is not simply the prerogative of individuals; whole cultures and societies also engage in it, and this social background constitutes the basis on which individuals will undertake their own personal regime of moral development. Larger, social morality is the presupposition for individual morality, even when on occasion individuals appear to reject the moral code of their society in order to establish a "higher" level of morality. "Appear" is the relevant word in this sentence, because in the act of advancing beyond the moral customs of a culture or criticizing a society's failure to live in accordance with their professed morality, the individual serves as an instrument of the society for developing and deepening its morality. This development, however, is only possible upon the condition of certain institutions—moral institutions—and these are by definition social in character. The importance of moral institutions is that they create and sustain the most basic conditions in which human beings can live together successfully. Without moral conditions, the personal pursuit of excellence in any form becomes impossible, even inconceivable. For this very important reason, individuals always live under an obligation to serve these conditions—the institution of morality—even when that service requires that they take a moral stand within and in opposition to their society.

Third, and finally, it is important to understand that morality is not the final or only dimension in the cultivation of enlightened character. Morality is just one of the six perfections, one vital dimension of a comprehensive ethics for Buddhism or for any culture. Sometimes moral concerns are so powerfully present and so urgent that they may seem to be the only issues that matter. When this urgency is deeply felt, moral concerns may overwhelm everything else. Other aspects of life may be suppressed or sacrificed to the domination of the moral demand. In this situation, moral sensibilities can become a form of bondage that undermines the overall quest for an enlightened world. For such a bodhisattva, it is not the pleasures of desire or the self-absorption of ambition that bind; it is an overwrought sense of moral duty that distorts life, conceivably rendering someone incapable of nourishing either themselves or others.

But, in spite of the power of moral concern, morality is not the end or goal of human life, and the location of the perfection of morality at the second level of self-cultivation out of six shows clearly the Buddhist understanding of that point. In truth, a life that is only moral would strike us as barren, perhaps joyless, as well as underdeveloped in the broader scope of possibilities. On the other hand, let us reaffirm, before moving on, that a life of self-cultivation lacking in the moral dimension will invariably be inadequate, immature, and unworthy of our full admiration. These two realizations—that morality is essential but insufficient to a mature practice of enlightenment—show us the importance of understanding how all dimensions of human life fit together in a comprehensive "thought of enlightenment."

THE PERFECTION OF
TOLERANCE

TRADITIONAL BUDDHIST IMAGES OF
THE PERFECTION OF TOLERANCE
(*KSĀNTIPĀRAMITĀ*)

Ksānti, translated here as tolerance and elsewhere frequently as patience or forbearance, has been a central virtue throughout the long history of Buddhism. It was one of the ten perfections of the Buddha praised in the early Pali sutras and continued to develop in range and significance in the unfolding of Mahayana Buddhism. Śāntideva goes so far as to claim that "there is no spiritual practice equal to tolerance."[1] Then, having given more cursory treatment to the first two perfections—generosity and morality—he backs his claim by devoting a full chapter to the perfection of tolerance. There and elsewhere we begin to see the qualities of human character encompassed by the perfection of tolerance.

Ksānti means "unaffected by," "able to bear," "able to withstand," and in that dimension indicates a strength of character, a composure, and a constancy of purpose that allow a bodhisattva to continue pursuing universal enlightenment in spite of enormous difficulty.[2] Emphasizing that basic dimension, this third perfection could also be translated as the "perfection of endurance" or the "perfection of composure."[3] Bodhisattvas who have trained in this virtue are imperturbable and well-composed, calm and focused in the midst of adversity. Through deliberate self-cultivation, they build the capacity to withstand danger, suffering, and injustice, to resist the onslaught of negative emotions, and to think clearly under the stress of turmoil. They attain an "admirable constancy" that, even in face of enormous opposition, equips them to move effectively when others have been overwhelmed.[4]

Buddhist texts counterpose this strength of character to a range of character weaknesses—the tendency to lose focus, to become fearful, to react in anger to abuses or slights that injure the ego or the body, as well as to yield to the temptations of surrender and despair. Mentally unaffected by abuse or danger, the ideal bodhisattva conserves his or her energy for positive steps toward awakening and is not overwhelmed by the self-destructive temptations of fearfulness and surrender, anger and retaliation. Self-controlled and powerful in composure, the bodhisattva maintains the stability and presence of mind to make the best possible move in a wide range of situations. Whereas "tolerance" and "patience" are often interpreted as forms of passivity or weaknesses, the perfection of tolerance is thought to generate a remarkable power. Impressed with the vitality and significance of this third perfection, a sutra says: "In consequence, the bodhisattva perfects himself in tolerance, and enjoins tolerance on others; he speaks in praise of tolerance, and also of those others who develop tolerance."[5]

Sensing that *ksānti* covers a broad range of virtues applicable to a variety of human situations, early Mahayana texts began to divide the perfection of tolerance into several subcategories. The *Perfection of Wisdom Sutras* recommend that the bodhisattva "develop two kinds of tolerance," the ability to withstand physical and mental abuse and the capacity to engage in the pursuit of truth without fear.[6] Later Mahayana texts prefer a threefold division, broadening the perfection of tolerance to encompass (1) the capacity to tolerate all forms of personal suffering; (2) the capacity to tolerate injuries of body and ego caused by other people; and (3) the capacity to tolerate more comprehensive visions of reality that undermine long-standing habits of mental insecurity.[7] In this section we seek to understand what the classic texts of Mahayana say about the perfection of tolerance by tracing these three dimensions.

Endurance: Tolerance for Discomfort, Hardship, Poverty, and Pain

Perhaps the most widely recognized Buddhist phrase is the first noble truth, the Buddha's initial assertion that "life is suffering." This claim has prompted a great deal of critical questioning, even rejection of Buddhism, on the grounds that its negative assessment of human life fails to emphasize human happiness and the joy of life. But this response is based on a misunderstanding, a misreading of the way suffering is positioned in

Buddhist thinking. The mistake is understandable, though, given the stark form that this pronouncement takes: "Life is suffering." Without working through the meanings of the Sanskrit *dukkha,* suffering—the reasonable tack taken in introductory books on Buddhism—let us simply rephrase the first noble truth in order to get on with the point behind this first meaning of the perfection of tolerance. Suffering in human life is unavoidable; life always entails periods of suffering. All human beings, no matter how privileged their circumstances, will encounter hardship—we will all get sick, we will all injure ourselves, we will all encounter disappointment, we will all face obstacles, we will all feel the pain of depression, and at some point, we will all confront our own death.

Although every one of us knows that, we nevertheless hide from its truth; we wish otherwise, hope otherwise, and invariably become disillusioned when we encounter pain in spite of our best efforts at avoidance. The Buddhist first noble truth is a frank, startling call to awaken from this avoidance and to face the truth of suffering directly and wisely. As the Buddhist teachings unfold around the first truth, we recognize that, far from a passive rejection of happiness in preference for despair, the teachings demonstrate enormous insight into the human situation by outlining paths of action for overcoming the destructive impact of human suffering. Buddhist teachings begin with a stark warning: Life does entail suffering and, unless you face that fact thoughtfully and courageously, your own habits of response to it may deepen the impact or negative effects of suffering, pushing you toward diminished forms of life.

This is where the perfection of tolerance begins. In this first sense, tolerance requires adjusting our attitude toward suffering and its opposite so that, gradually, we gain the capacity to see the inevitable alternation between these two poles of human life with insight and understanding. The classic texts present images of awakened Buddhists facing difficulties of all kinds with strength and resolution, without wasting the energy of life in destructive habits of dejection and despair that just add suffering upon suffering.

Śāntideva's *Bodhicaryāvatāra* mocks the readers' destructive habit of despair in the face of hardship. The text asks, rhetorically: "If there is a solution [to your problem], then what is the point of dejection? What is the point of dejection if there is no solution?"[8] The text goes on: "There is nothing desirable in the state of dejection."[9] In other words, if you respond to difficulties primarily with lamentation, with feelings of dejection or claims of unfair victimization, you will simply be wasting your time and deepening the wound. For, if something can now be done about the problem, get busy, do something constructive. And if this happens to be an unavoidable situation, one completely beyond your control, there is still no point in wallowing in dejection—find some path of human well-being that you *can* control and get back into the movement of life. Overindulgence in the emotions of loss brings about further loss. Our instincts in this respect are frequently self-destructive. From a Buddhist point of view, living wisely would entail transforming the way we respond to difficulty.

If all of the six perfections are based on the expectation that human beings develop the freedom to sculpt themselves and their circumstances in liberating ways, then the perfection of toleration is essential to this effort. Without the developed capacity to face difficulties that arise in constructive ways, there is little hope of enlightened movement or progress. Building calm endurance through insightful understanding of our circumstances, we avoid stagnation and the deepening of suffering that goes with it.

So early Buddhist texts maintain that the first step toward overcoming self-destructive habits in response to suffering is developing the ability to accept suffering as part of life. This is why the "truths" of Buddhism begin here—they require at the outset a psychologically difficult admission: that suffering will inevitably be part of life and that everything depends on how we face up to that fact and how we cultivate our capacity to see it through constructively. As the Dalai Lama explains, the acceptance of suffering opens up two beneficial possibilities: first, that we will be able to think clearly about what can be done about it, and second, that we will "prevent negative thoughts and emotions from taking hold of us," that is, we will prevent ourselves from making matters worse by wallowing in pointless feelings of regret and injustice.[10]

Śāntideva puts this point succinctly: "Only through suffering is there escape."[11] Only *through* suffering is there escape—not around it, not bypassing it, but directly through acknowledging it, facing up to it, and pressing through it deliberately will we have found an adequate means of dealing with suffering. Such tolerance or patience with regard to suffering is far from passive acquiescence or the cowardice of denial. Indeed, it takes up the issues of life with a directness and resolution that both call for and develop deep sources of strength.

Perhaps the most prominent reason we hold for not accepting suffering is that we believe it to be unjust. That we, and not someone else, have contacted a devastating disease; that our home, and not someone else's, has burned to the ground, inspires the cry "why me?" When the justice of fair distribution of pain and joy seems to be lacking—and it will often seem lacking to the one who is suffering right now—then it becomes especially difficult to accept the pain that has been allotted us in order to move on. All religious systems have ways to address this issue of injustice in the distribution of suffering, and the Buddhist way is through the teachings of karma and rebirth. Many traditional and modern texts ask practitioners to regard all suffering as just repayment for one's own acts of injustice either earlier in this life or in previous lives. Employing that technique of mind, it becomes easier to accept the illness or the disaster that has befallen us rather than someone else.

One traditional text on the perfection of tolerance makes this clear: "The tortures that one currently endures have their causes in one's past conduct. Even if one does not commit in this life anything that deserves a reprisal, one atones for the wrong doings done in one's previous lives. One is in the process of repayment, and one should endure one's pain with grace. There is no reason to rebel."[12] Taking the blame oneself for one's own suffering forestalls the profound sense of injustice that often prevents us from moving on when suffering befalls us. We may, however, "have reason to rebel." In the constructive section of this chapter, we will want to assess this strategy of avoiding self-deceptive dangers in our sense of injustice and ask about its applicability for us today.

Much of the chapter on tolerance in the *Bodhicaryāvatāra* is addressed to particular difficulties in life that bring suffering, some having to do with fear of the truth (our third dimension of tolerance), some dealing with suffering in human relations (our second dimension), and some taking up unavoidable misfortune in life: discomfort, poverty, sickness, old age, and death. To make this last category of hardship vivid, the author names particular annoyances that are common in life and directs us as readers to an appropriate attitude in relation to them: "The irritation of bugs, gnats, and mosquitoes, of hunger and thirst, and discomfort such as an enormous itch: why do you not see them as insignificant? Cold, heat, rain and wind, journeying and sickness, imprisonment and beatings: one should not be too squeamish about them. Otherwise distress becomes worse.... Therefore one should become invincible to suffering, and overpower discomfort."[13]

From the Buddhist perspective outlined in many sutras and treatises, seeing discomfort as "insignificant" and losing one's squeamishness about more severe forms of suffering requires practice, in this case the practice of meditation. Meditation is effective in this arena because it allows us to "practice" tolerance in a neutral set of circumstances prior to the actual situations of suffering or discomfort that we will face in life. So the Dalai Lama says: "This is why we need to put the practice of patience [tolerance] at the heart of our daily lives. It is a question of familiarizing ourselves with it, at the deepest level, so that when we do find ourselves in a difficult situation, although we may have to make an effort, we know what is involved."[14]

In fact, like many traditional Buddhist monastics, Geshe Sonam Rinchen asks us to "regard suffering as happiness," that is, to see in every moment of life, especially the most vivid, an opportunity to awaken from our own patterns of self-deception and avoidance.[15] As he puts it: "Seeing hardships as an adornment is to see them as an opportunity and an asset. If you begin by willingly accepting minor hardships, your capacity will gradually increase....It is possible to regard suffering as happiness. If we willingly accept difficulties, each hardship we face will simply increase our courage."[16]

From Buddhist points of view, meditation is the key to developing this kind of tolerance, the intentional shaping of mind both in formal settings and in the midst of everyday life. By deliberately "practicing" our relation to difficulties of all kinds, Buddhists claim, we can gradually reduce their negative consequences and cultivate a state of mind that cannot be undermined by the difficulties that now overwhelm us. As Śāntideva claims: "There is nothing which remains difficult if it is practiced."[17] For Buddhists, this is as true for the practice of positive states of mind as it is for avoiding destructive mental states—if we work it through enough times, deliberately and wisely, we will master it.

We understand today that virtually all of the Buddhist sutras and most of the subsequent literature advocating the perfection of tolerance were composed in the setting of Buddhist monasticism. The authors were monks who had devoted their lives to the pursuit of disciplined states of mind and wrote perceptively from those states. But it is also true that for the most part they wrote for a monastic audience, and it is on this point that we will need to inquire about the applicability of ideas drawn from monastic circumstances to nonmonastic lives—our own. Monks and nuns were by definition those committed to a life of simplicity, poverty, and contentment in very sparse circumstances. They cultivated contentment by reducing desires, developing a focus on dimensions of life that would render unimportant many of the pursuits of comfort and pleasure that preoccupy those who have not chosen that life. Reducing distractions to a minimum, they disregarded possessions, pleasures, and sexual instincts, and sought to control their minds and attitudes in relation to everything beside the point of their quest. That, as least, was the ideal.

Models for their style of life came directly through sutra accounts of the life of the Buddha. With tolerance, patience, and endurance, the Buddha lived a middle path between the sensual indulgence that guides ordinary lives and an ascetic rejection of the world. Earlier in his life, the ancient narratives tell us, the Buddha practiced asceticism; he sought control over his body and mind through disciplines that are for the most part unimaginable to us today. In ancient India, ascetics pursued powers, called *tapas,* that enabled extraordinary human capacities. But in the life of the Buddha and in the early Buddhist texts, we see a rejection of these extreme physical practices of asceticism in preference for practices of mental development. As one historian puts it: "The physicality of the extreme ascetic act was replaced by the controlled and restrained mental attitude of the possessor of *kṣānti*, the perfection of tolerance."[18]

The practices of the perfection of tolerance bring about a "serene confidence of mind" that allow pursuit of one's goals in life regardless of external circumstances. Thus, as one sutra claims: "While the bodhisattva courses thus, he is not afraid. He is impregnated with the strength that he has gained, and that enables him to persist in his endeavors and to think: 'It is not the case that I shall not be fully enlightened.'"[19]

Patience: Tolerance in Human Relations

From early Buddhist sutras up through the writings of contemporary Buddhist masters, a great deal of attention has been given to the ability to tolerate differences between human beings. Overcoming a variety of immature postures toward others—everything from impatience to anger and hatred—was thought to be essential to the practice of the bodhisattva. Attaining composure, "an admirable constancy" in dealing with others, was regarded as an invaluable achievement, one worthy of the title "perfection." The variety of topics that fall under this category is staggering, but when Buddhist teachers home in on the most important of them, it is almost always the difficulty of anger. Developing the capacity to tolerate insults, injustices, and other potentially harmful actions by others with a composed and serene comportment was thought to be essential to bodhisattva practice. Ārya Śūra puts it this way: "The admirable constancy of those of strong character which ever ignores the offences of others is called tolerance—the lovely name results from its virtues: knowing compassion, it acts for the aim of the world. They say that patience is the principal religious observance of those whose minds are devoted to the aim of others, for the fault of wrath obstructs what is beneficial to the world, as a dam obstructs the waters."[20]

Śāntideva, too, writes his chapter on the perfection of tolerance to focus on hatred and anger. This chapter begins with the strong claim that the "generosity and morality performed throughout thousands of eons— hatred destroys it all. There is no evil equal to hatred, and no spiritual practice equal to tolerance. Therefore one should develop tolerance by various means, with great effort."[21] He continues to describe how readily we become "disfigured by hatred" until the beauty of human life has disappeared. "In short," he claims, "there is no sense in which someone prone to anger is well off."[22] Hatred was one of the "three poisons" named in early Buddhism, three states of mind that destroy lives, and hatred was universally chosen as the most deadly of all. For these reasons, the perfection of tolerance, the capacity to react with equanimity when others harm us, has been singled out in Mahayana texts as a necessary condition for the spiritual life of the bodhisattva. "Bodhisattvas do not get angry in situations in which harm comes from all directions. . . . They do not engage in blaming, reviling, striking, threatening, or harming others for the sake of retaliation. They do not cling to resentment."[23]

A variety of techniques is offered in the sutras and other texts for getting past anger and hatred. Calming meditation is considered the most effective because its focus is on state of mind, especially on bringing passions such as anger to a still point. But there is also a variety of techniques related to insight meditation, techniques that encourage the practitioner to transform his or her understanding of the situation in a way that dissipates passionate antipathy. The three most common are (1) meditative reflection on the thought that every negative thing that is done to us is a direct karmic result of our own past actions; (2) contemplative reflection on the idea that those who treat us unjustly and with malice are, unbeknownst to them, serving us as our teachers in the perfection of tolerance; and (3) reflection on the basic Buddhist concepts of "dependent arising" and "no-self" in order to depersonalize interpersonal relations. We will consider these three one at a time.

First, conjoining the ideas of karma and rebirth, Buddhists have frequently attempted to understand everything that happens to them as a result of their own actions both in this life and in past lives. If the harm that is being done to us by another is really the response of justice to our previous act of malice, whether we remember that act or not, then we have little reason for anger or a sense of injustice. A contemporary Tibetan teacher, Geshe Sonam Rinchen, explains it this way:

> A negative action we performed in the past resulted in a bad rebirth. The harm we experience now is the remaining negative momentum of that action. Why do we resent the person who helps us to end the effects of previous wrong-doing? In fact they are doing us a favor. We willingly undergo unpleasant medical treatment, even an operation, to avoid more intense suffering. If we try to retaliate when harmed, we simply perpetuate the whole cycle.[24]

Shifting our understanding of the matter to redirect the cause of the harmful act done to us back on our own past acts, we relinquish all rationale for anger and hatred. Thus, one text says: "When the bodhisattva meets with slander or insult, when he is struck with a sword or a stick, he knows on reflection that the cause of such a treatment lies in his past actions."[25]

The second technique commonly employed by Buddhists to alter one's attitude toward those who have done us harm is to regard them as the only ones who could possibly teach us the perfection of tolerance. They become, in effect, our teachers, even though they are completely unaware of the role they are playing or its value. That shift in perspective alters the way we conceive of the event; it focuses all attention on what we might learn from the situation in which we now find ourselves. The *Bodhicaryāvatāra* offers this shift of perspective by asking practitioners to think of their opponents as honorable in the same way as the Buddha because, like the Buddha, they present us with an opportunity to develop this essential Buddhist virtue.[26] Here is how the Dalai Lama explains it:

> It is also very helpful to think of adversity not so much as a threat to our peace of mind but rather as the very means by which patience is attained. From this perspective, we see that those who would harm

us are, in a sense, teachers of patience. Such people teach us what
we could never learn merely from hearing someone speak. . . . From
adversity we can, however, learn the value of patient forbearance. And,
in particular, those who would harm us give us unparalleled opportunities to practice disciplined behavior.[27]

A third technique for overcoming anger through a transformation in
understanding focuses on self-understanding. From a Buddhist point of
view, at the basis of all human anger is a misconception of the "self."
Misunderstanding who and what we are, we act as though our own
personal well-being is the only thing that really matters. So when anyone
does harm to us, we treat that occurrence as a major affront to justice,
something for which recompense must immediately be made. Overcoming this false and immature sense of self is, of course, central to the entire
history of Buddhist thought and practice. Emphasis here is firmly on
the basic concept of "no-self." Buddhists claim that when you have
awakened to the truth about yourself, you will be able to tolerate much
of what now drives you into fits of anger and depression. Here is how
Ārya Śūra places the "no-self" concept in relation to the perfection of
tolerance:

> Worldlings are stupefied by adherence to false belief in a self, contemp-
> tuously imagining that all the rest are "others." Therefore, their minds
> overpowered by abuses, they become weary because they lack toler-
> ance. The minds of illustrious persons, being guided by compassion,
> perform auspicious acts through tolerance; having abandoned the view
> of self, such minds are not agitated by another's offence, because of
> their passion for virtue. Wrong discursive thought is the cause of
> anger—that fever in the heart—on the part of those who are weak in
> resolution; but right discursive thought establishes mental tranquility,
> which is the abode of tolerance."[28]

Taking the view of selflessness that had been so thoroughly cultivated
at the heart of Buddhism, Śāntideva brilliantly exposes the selfish mis-
understandings that are at the root of our behaviors. He writes:

> 62. If you argue that your dislike of one who speaks ill of you is
> because he is harming living beings, why then do you feel no anger
> when he defames others in the same way?

63. You tolerate those showing disfavor when others are the subject of
it, but you show no tolerance towards someone speaking ill of you
when he is subject to the arising of defilements.

64. And my hatred towards those who damage sacred images and
stupas or who abuse the true teaching is inappropriate, since the
Buddhas and bodhisattvas are not distressed.[29]

Shredding the convoluted rationalizations that we all go through in
placing ourselves above others, Śāntideva goes on:

79. When your own virtues are being praised, you want others to be
pleased as well. When the virtues of others are being praised, you
do not even want to be pleased yourself.

80. After arousing the Awakening Mind out of the desire for the
happiness of every being, why are you angry at them now that they
have found happiness for themselves?

81. You desire Buddhahood, which is worthy of worship throughout
the three worlds, expressly for living beings. Why do you burn
inside on seeing them have some slight honor?[30]

Many classical Buddhist texts employ the concept of "dependent arising" to undermine passionate feelings of anger and frustration by attempting to understand how the person treating us badly might have come to
behave that way. Through an analytical form of meditation, practitioners
attempt to understand what causes and conditions have rendered this
person insensitive to the well-being of others. Since all people are shaped
by factors that lie outside of their control, contemplating the factors that
have led others to treat me so badly softens my anger. If I can see the way
you have been treated in life, the way your parents raised you in an
atmosphere of violence and misunderstanding, I will be more able to
loosen my judgment and consider not just how I have been injured but
how you have been injured as well. Here is how Śāntideva approaches
the issue: "A person does not get angry at will, having decided 'I shall get
angry. . . .' Whatever transgressions and evil deeds of various kinds there
are, all arise through the power of conditioning factors, while there is
nothing that arises independently."[31]

Anger toward someone who has been conditioned by negative causes
to act this way would be, Śāntideva concludes, "as inappropriate as it
would be toward fire for its nature to burn. . . . So anger towards them is

as inappropriate as it would be towards the sky if full of arid smoke."[32] Nothing is entirely self-generated, we learn, and since anger and ill-will are thoroughly unpleasant, clearly no one would decide to be that way if they could help it. The Dalai Lama adds that tolerance is advanced by the "ability to discriminate between action and agent."[33] This means that it is important not to condemn the person even though it may be important to make a statement in condemnation of what someone has done. There are some acts that we have no right to forgive, but there is no one who does not deserve our forgiveness. Considering the person "ill with hatred," the texts advise turning one's attention to whatever healing might be possible. This is the way the *Treatise on the Great Perfection of Wisdom* describes the bodhisattva: "When he is tormented and insulted by someone, he knows that that person is ill with hatred and driven by rage. The bodhisattva heals him through one of his salvific expedients without feeling any aversion towards him."[34]

It is very difficult to determine just how passive and receptive the bodhisattva ideal in classical Buddhism would require one to be. Some texts stress the strength and rigor of the bodhisattva, the ways in which his task is to "upset accepted attitudes."[35] Elsewhere, thoroughgoing passivity is idealized. For example: "If those beings take away from me everything that is necessary to life, then let that be my gift to them. If someone should rob me of my life, I should feel no ill will, anger or fury on account of that. Even against them I should take no offensive action, either by body, voice, or mind."[36]

In the diverse history and geography of Buddhism, there has been a variety of different positions on the extent to which an ideal bodhisattva should go in accepting the harmful actions of others. Some contemporary teachers are deliberate in maintaining tolerance as a form of wisdom and strength. They make clear that not everything is to be tolerated. Geshe Sonam Rinchen writes: "Practicing patience means not getting upset and remaining calm, but does not demand that you allow yourself to be manipulated or exploited by others and their disturbing emotions."[37] Furthermore, the Dalai Lama suggests that tolerance

> should not be confused with mere passivity. On the contrary, adopting even vigorous countermeasures may be compatible with tolerance. There are times in everyone's life when harsh words—or even physical intervention—may be called for. But since it safeguards our inner composure, tolerance means we are in a stronger position to judge an

appropriately non-violent response than if we are overwhelmed by negative thoughts and emotions. From this, we see that it is the very opposite of cowardice.[38]

The same mental posture of tolerance under the onslaught of abuse is recommended when we are being praised or admired. The bodhisattva is not to get mired in these emotions either, but to maintain the same equanimity we found in response to another's rage. Composure is maintained through profound understanding and a well-grounded meditative mind. The image of the perfection of tolerance in this second dimension, therefore, is of a self-composed, patient bodhisattva who cultivates a spirit of gentleness and compassion in the face of both bodily and mental abuse from others. Such a person, the sutras claim, is fit to be a teacher.

Tolerating the Truth about Oneself and the World

In "A Song on the Six Perfections," the great Tibetan yogi Milarepa claims that "beyond being without fear of what is ultimately true, there is no other tolerance."[39] Although we have followed some of the great treatises on the six perfections in dividing the perfection of tolerance into three types, we also follow virtually all Buddhist philosophical writing in realizing that no matter how many types are differentiated, they all come down to this final version: the capacity to tolerate or face what is ultimately true about oneself and the world. This, the classic texts maintain, is extremely difficult. We all live by means of a variety of rationalizations, explanations that we provide for ourselves or that our society provides for us that blunt the sharp edge of reality and soften the impact of the truth.

As we have seen in each perfection—generosity, morality, and now tolerance—the final steps in each case require the appropriation of wisdom into the perfection. What that means is that at some crucial stage, practitioners must come to understand the "emptiness" of all things, and then in view of that understanding they must transform the very meaning of the perfection that they have learned. What is difficult about this final maneuver is that it is frightening. The comfortable truths already learned appear to be undermined and all solid ground seems to slip away. At that juncture, many turn back, because it may easily seem more palatable simply to live in the partial truths one has already learned than to endure the more pointed truth of their "emptiness." Describing that point on the bodhisattva path, the *Large Sutra on Perfect Wisdom* says: "A doer of what is hard is the bodhisattva who, while coursing in perfect wisdom, does not lose heart when the perfection of wisdom is being preached, and does not mentally turn away from it, who persists in making endeavors about the perfection of wisdom and who does not turn back on the supreme enlightenment."[40]

It is hard enough, these teachings seem to say, just to live unselfishly. But to look deeply into the possibility that there simply is no self requires a courage that comes with the perfection of tolerance. One of the primary points of the entire Buddhist tradition, however, is that although there are many ways to approach selfless living, the most direct and most profound is the realization of "no-self." At the outset, however, and at many points along the way, this far-reaching truth is not comprehensible. It can be believed, it can be taken on faith, and in occasional insights, it can be partially understood. But it cannot be comprehensively grasped. For that reason, in the initial and some subsequent stages along the way, trust in the *dharma*, or "faith" is considered useful. It is useful in that it keeps the practitioner going, it allows you to continue working—meditating, practicing, thinking—even though you cannot articulate even to yourself how things really are or why these practices are worthwhile. Realizing this, Nāgārjuna claims: "When one's mind is grounded in faith, one escapes doubt and regret. When the power of faith is strong, one can seize and espouse the dharma; and this is called *dharmakṣānti*."[41] *Dharmakṣānti* means tolerance of the dharma, patient acceptance of the teachings about the nature of reality even though they are not yet within your grasp.

One of the best places in Mahayana Buddhist literature to get a sense of the kind of realization at stake here is the chapter in the *Vimalakīrti Sūtra* called the "Dharma Door of Nonduality." After the opening question is posed by Vimalakīrti to the other great bodhisattvas—how to talk about nonduality—in the first stanza a bodhisattva claims: "The attainment of the tolerance of the emptiness of things is the entrance into nonduality."[42] Paraphrasing, we could say that only when you have worked your way into the perfection of tolerance, only when you can face the "emptiness" of all things—yourself included—without being frightened to the point of turning back, will you be standing at the entrance into nonduality, the essential feature of enlightenment.

What is nonduality? In this Mahayana Buddhist setting, it is a vision of reality that derives from the "emptiness" of all things, the truth that nothing exists in and of itself, that things are always in process of change, and that this change occurs through their fundamental dependence on other impermanent things. Nothing is completely separate from other things, and nothing remains the same over time; hence the duality or division between things is ultimately an illusion. From this point of view, reality as it is bequeathed to us through our culture's common sense is an illusion, a dream from which we must awaken if we are to see the truth. This new truth, however, is not simply a new set of beliefs. On the contrary, it transcends the very conceptual form that the old truths once assumed. It is not graspable, not something that can or must be believed. It is not an assertion about how things really are because "all assertions can be refuted and confounded."[43]

The sutras advise that, given the unnerving quality of this insight, it is necessary initially to be patient with it, to allow it to seep into the mind through gradual meditation and reflection. The full force of the insight requires tolerance at the highest and most important level—the ability to look directly into the truth and not become frightened, not turn back to the comfort of the already well-known world. One Buddhist text puts it this way: "the acquisition of the wisdom of impermanence, suffering, emptiness, and non-self, then the rejection of such wisdom, and finally the ability to endure such a doctrine constitute *dharmakṣānti*," tolerance for the truth.[44]

There is a sense in which the teachings ought to evoke fear and bewilderment because the common sense that they dislodge serves as our current connection to "reality." Unsettling that connection, although liberating, is also frightening. The perfection of tolerance is, finally, the ability to see what emerges as it is without turning back in fear and trembling.

The classic Mahayana texts are clear that in the final analysis the perfection of tolerance is "intended for the benefit of others."[45] Ārya Śūra calls it "the method of action for world-benefit of that one who is at all times well-composed."[46] Being "well-composed" in the perfection of tolerance, the bodhisattva becomes "a servant to the world."[47] Serving the world entails a good deal of suffering, in that there is much that one must be able to tolerate. "But this suffering" he continues, "will produce great benefit. Delight is the only appropriate response to suffering which takes away the suffering of the universe."[48] And ability to endure suffering voluntarily on behalf of others is attained through wisdom, insight into the ultimate selflessness of reality. Therefore the *Large Sutra on Perfect*

Wisdom proclaims: "A bodhisattva, who courses in the perfection of tolerance, exerts himself through wisdom . . . to mature all beings; this is the perfection of wisdom of a bodhisattva who courses in the perfection of tolerance."[49]

CRITICAL ASSESSMENT: A CONTEMPORARY PERFECTION OF TOLERANCE

Ksānti, the primary Sanskrit word employed to name the third of the six perfections, covers a range of meanings in English. In our efforts to understand it and to see how it might stand as a contemporary ideal of self-cultivation, we will work back and forth between the English words "tolerance" and "patience" in order to reflect the full depth of this Buddhist ideal. Buddhist monks and nuns are renown for their calm patience, their ability to tolerate and endure what would drive the rest of us to extreme reaction. This has been true throughout the long and impressive history of Buddhism. Images of serene kindness and resolute pacifism abound in the tradition.

Our task now is to pose critical, evaluative questions for this tolerant ideal. For example: Are we to tolerate anything and everything? Be patient and willing to wait forever, no matter what? And if not, how do we draw that line, using what criteria? We want to think clearly about the extent to which we today can concur with the Buddhist tradition that the perfection of tolerance is indeed fundamental to a form of enlightened character that would resonate with the contemporary world. And to whatever extent we can agree on the importance of a tolerant patience of character, we will want to shape the contours of that virtue, to sort out which dimensions of it might prove admirable for us today and which might not so easily stand up to contemporary ethical scrutiny.

The Intolerable: Are There Limits to Tolerance?

In Western societies since the period of the Enlightenment, toleration has been considered essential to the practice of democracy. Because human beings differ from each other in a broad range of ways, living together peacefully requires our willingness to put up with ways of living that we might prefer to condemn. This thoroughly modern conception of toleration is included in the Buddhist use of the term—the aggressive curtailment of others' thoughts and actions is to be avoided whenever possible. But serious questions have arisen in liberal democratic societies: Is it always possible, or always preferable, to be tolerant? Can a culture or a person afford to tolerate everything? As soon as we reflect on this question, we realize that the answer must be "No." Some actions and some ways of living should not be tolerated. We should not tolerate acts of senseless cruelty, we should not tolerate murder, rape, and violence in many forms. We should not tolerate racism, sexism, and homophobia.

If tolerance is to be integral to our contemporary "thought of enlightenment," it cannot be grounded in a simple lack of convictions, a state of passive indifference. It must not require of us that "nothing matters," because the values to which our ideals would commit us would necessitate a passionate striving for the alleviation of destructive suffering and for global enlightenment. Tolerance cannot, therefore, be a neutral state, a state of blank dispassion, since compassion is an essential part of it. An exalted ideal—the further awakening of humanity—will establish parameters for the practice of tolerance. With this goal in mind, tolerance cannot mean the uncritical acceptance of everything based upon indifference to ends; instead, it must mean that we come to tolerate some things, mindfully, for the sake of a larger, more important goal. In this sense, tolerance will not be able to stand alone as a perfection; it will need to be combined with others capable of providing the guidance it needs for perfection. In the same way that generosity can be abused or be potentially destructive unless combined with wisdom, in order to be a perfection or an ideal, tolerance must be reinforced by other traits of character that would serve to bring it to perfection.

If the perfection of tolerance is not a condition of ethical neutrality, a state of nonjudgment or a lack of conviction, then we might begin to give it substance with a formula like this: The perfection of tolerance is the art of understanding what, when, and how to tolerate. Shaped this way, tolerance would necessarily be guided by a "thought of enlightenment" and by a profound conviction that all human beings deserve to live under conditions that will allow them the pursuit of happiness. The goal of tolerance would be to generate and preserve those conditions; it would not include passively allowing these conditions to be violated. Therefore, nothing should be tolerated that would undermine the conditions human beings need to lead free and worthwhile lives.

Tolerating injustice to others, or tolerating pointless suffering that could be prevented—these are not tolerance at all; in fact, they may be forms of immoral neglect and cruelty. Those who tolerated Hitler, those who tolerated American slavery, participated in their evils. To tolerate such acts is to collaborate in them, which cannot be the appropriate image for perfect toleration. In the case of genocide or slavery, it would be better to react to these evils in anger or rage than to allow them to continue. Sometimes there are very good reasons to be intolerant. The act in question may be destructive of its victim, it may also destroy the actor himself, and it may dangerously undermine the society in which it is being carried out. Any of these reasons may justify the refusal to tolerate some activity or development going on in the society around us. Meekness and complicity in the face of some acts of evil imply anything but enlightenment. These may be better described as cowardice or indifference, a failure of moral nerve. Therefore, indiscriminate tolerance not only falls short of perfection, it may collude in the perpetuation of some form of evil.

Realizing this, our conception of tolerance requires greater complexity and nuance than the traditional Buddhist narratives suggest. To practice the perfection of tolerance, we must understand how to tolerate others without undermining the commitment that we have made to values implied in our "thought of enlightenment." Authentic tolerance must arise from a source of power and confidence rather than from weakness. Rather than a form of surrender in life, tolerance must be underwritten by exuberant compassion and a commitment to noble values. How can we gather these ideals together into a unified conception of tolerance?

Anger, Patience, and Self-Control

As we have seen in our description of Buddhist accounts of the perfection of tolerance, anger is singled out as the most deadly barrier that any striving for enlightenment might face. Anger is the most deadly of the "three poisons," and among the illnesses of the mind, the most difficult to cure. As we all know from personal experience, anger is the feeling that is most difficult to control and the one most likely to lead us into actions that in retrospect we understand to have violated our own ethical convictions. For these reasons, anger is one of the most frequently discussed Buddhist topics. The Dalai Lama, Thich Nhat Hanh, Robert Thurman, and virtually every other Buddhist leader in our time has written extensively and impressively on this theme because it is so clearly linked to the ability to practice a worthwhile "thought of enlightenment." Let us attempt to think carefully about it.

In order to avoid the "poison" of anger, Buddhist monks and nuns have gone to great lengths in their practice. To begin our reflection, here are two examples from Buddhist texts that display the mental effort to displace anger. From the *Perfection of Wisdom* literature, we find:

> Moreover, a bodhisattva should not be afraid if he finds himself in a wilderness infested by robbers. For bodhisattvas take pleasure in the wholesome practice of renouncing all their belongings. A bodhisattva must cast away even his body, and he must renounce all that is necessary to life. He should react to the danger with the thought: "If those beings take away from me everything that is necessary for life, then let that be my gift to them. If someone should rob me of my life, I should feel no ill will, anger or fury on account of that. Even against them, I should take no offensive action, either by body, voice, or mind."[50]

In another story, a monk asks permission of the Buddha to go to a barbarous region to teach Buddhism to cruel and abusive people. Interrogating him, the Buddha asks:

> "If they abuse, revile, and annoy you with evil, harsh and false words, what would you think?"
>
> Monk: "In that case, I would think that the people are really good and gentle folk, as they do not strike me with their hands or with stones."
>
> Buddha: "But if they strike you with their hands or with stones, what would you think?"
>
> Monk: "In that case, I would think that they are good and gentle folk, as they do not strike me with a cudgel or a weapon."
>
> Buddha: "But if they strike you with a cudgel or a weapon, what would you think?"
>
> Monk: "In that case, I would think that they are good and gentle folk, as they do not take my life."
>
> Buddha: "But if they kill you, what would you think?"
>
> Monk: "In that case, I would still think that they are good and gentle folk, as they release me from this rotten carcass of the body without much difficulty. . . . "

> Buddha: "Monk, you are endowed with the greatest gentleness and
> tolerance.... Go and teach them how to be free, as you
> yourself are free."[51]

These stories present for our reflection the image of selfless, nonretaliatory saints who under no circumstances respond to severe abuse with
anger. Their extreme tolerance, however, pushes us to raise questions
about the limits of tolerance and about whether there may be occasions
when anger is appropriate. In order to get a slightly different perspective
on these same situations of injustice, imagine either one of the monks in
these stories a second-party observer to someone else who is being treated
in this cruel and unjust way—observing injustice not to the monk himself
but to someone else there in front of him. If the monk passively tolerates
this situation of cruelty to another person, can we regard that as an image
of the perfection of tolerance? Clearly not; our reaction to it will not be
one of admiration.

What is the difference? Obviously, the stories differ only in who is being
treated with injustice. Why would that difference make the enormous
difference that it does? Why would toleration in one version be praised
and in the other condemned? Perhaps the difference is only this: that in one
story—the situation of indignant self-defense—there is the possibility that
the monk may be acting selfishly, while in the other that is highly unlikely.
In both versions, injustice is being allowed, to oneself in one story and to
another in our second revised account. We might ask ourselves: under what
circumstances would our ideal dictate ignoring the demands of justice,
allowing someone to act in such a way that justice is undermined?

It would be helpful if, in the extensive canon of Buddhist stories, there
were stories like the one we just imagined, stories in which monks were
praised for standing firm against injustice to others. In that case, we
might find that while justice was to be upheld for others, suspicions
remained about the ways in which we perceived and responded to
injustice to ourselves. But, in fact, stories concerned with protecting
others against violence and injustice are not featured in classical Buddhist
literature. Noticing that, we realize that the task of supporting and
upholding justice is not among the central virtues of classical Buddhism.
What we find in the classic texts are stories that valorize selfless tolerance
of harm to oneself alone, rather then narratives that instruct Buddhists
about how to act in face of injustice to others.

Perhaps the most influential Western views on anger are Aristotle's. Unlike his Buddhist counterparts, who were at the same time treating anger as the worst of the human "poisons," Aristotle came to regard anger as a virtue. Paraphrased, his account goes like this: The ideal person ought to get angry when the sense of justice that holds a community together has been broken—the greater the injustice, the more anger and retaliation are required to reestablish an optimal balance of justice between people. Anger, on this account, is the middle path. The two extremes that ought to be shunned by the "enlightened" person, says Aristotle, are the irascible person, who is always getting angry, and the nonirascible person, who is incapable of anger.

The irascible person lives in a self-protective state of mind that skews his judgment. He always feels that what has been done is an affront to his dignity, even when nothing of the sort was intended. Although he does not notice injustice to others, he is always ready to fight injustice against himself. Mired in the illusions of self-absorption, his judgment is always out of accord with the reality of the situation. He is incensed whenever his interests are at stake and insensitive whenever the interests of others are under assault. He gets angry at the wrong times or for the wrong reasons, and his anger is far out of proportion to what it is about. This person's anger is out of control, as is his self-concept and his overall relation to others.

The opposite—the nonirascible person—is incapable of adequate response to injustice, whether to himself or to others. He is indifferent, or cowardly, or riddled with such self-contempt that he cannot rise to the occasion when someone treats him cruelly or unjustly. He simply lets go of any claim to justice on his own behalf. In doing so, he takes no responsibility for the maintenance of justice in society. Aristotle, like others in the Western tradition of thought, finds this nonirascible person "slavish." Such a person has no backbone, no will of his own, no self-respect. He goes along with whatever anybody else insists upon, no matter how unfair or cruel. He cannot make a stand for what is fair and right in the world because he is too fearful, or indifferent, or lacking in self-respect.

Tolerating injury, patiently ignoring injustice, is for Aristotle far from the ideal. In his view, anger is the more admirable response to injustice, a balanced anger that is justified by the evil that has happened and always meted out in just proportion. On Aristotle's account of the matter, anger is not always to be avoided, not always a "poison" to your character.

Sometimes, he claims, circumstances will justify an angry response. With this challenge as an experiment, we can test the Buddhist point of view on anger, asking ourselves whether or to what extend we ought to adopt it as our own ideal.

At the outset we should recognize that each of these positions—the Aristotelian and the Buddhist—implies a specific sense of the self. Aristotle's society prized the honor of the individual and praised the individual for defending this honor against unjust violations by others. The self takes responsibility for defending its own sphere against encroachment and is diminished to the extent that it fails to rise up in protective self-defense. When individuals are responding to injustice in appropriate forms of anger, they are defending not just their own "self" but their society as a whole, as well as the very possibility of justice. Failure to retaliate against unjust violation of one's own sphere implies a withdrawal from honorable participation in that social world. Aristotle concludes, therefore, that anger is an essential emotion for any society or self interested in justice.

In contrast, Buddhists claimed that the highest realization is that there is no such "self" and that the most admirable forms of social interaction are based upon the deep unselfishness that derives from this realization. In this mindset, protecting oneself against the encroachments of others would not so clearly be a virtue. In fact, acts of self-protection of this kind were considered counterproductive, even destructive, because all self-protection just hardens a narrow sense of self and makes a larger vision of nonself-centered justice and compassion impossible. The more you think of your "self" as needing to protect itself against others, they concluded, the less capacity for unbiased judgment you will have, a capacity grounded in selfless wisdom.

Thus, the challenge that Buddhism poses to us is: Can we imagine a human being beyond the protective sense of self implied in Aristotle's ideal of correct anger, and a society in which that nonretaliatory sense of self constitutes the normative ideal? We can get a glimpse of this ideal even without Buddhist assistance. Although the position is not entirely clear, Westerners will recognize an alternative to Aristotle's ideal in Jesus' claim that we ought to "love our enemies" and that, when slapped, we ought to "turn the other cheek." In this view, love trumps justice as the highest image of human perfection, and the admirable self is at its best when not preoccupied with self-protection.

Aristotle argues that a coherent society needs justice and that justice requires the protection provided by indignation and the passionate retaliation against injustice. Furthermore, he claims, these states of mind are available only through the condition of anger. If injustice does not make us angry, how could we possibly rise to the occasion of struggling against it, especially when that fight endangers our very lives? The challenge of Buddhism for us is not just to imagine a human being beyond that sense of self, but to work out a conception of it that accords with contemporary reality. That would require our answering the following question in the affirmative: Can we make a mental distinction between the nonirascible person who, lacking anger, does not insist on justice (Aristotle's image of slavelike character) and the nonirascible person who does so insist? Can we imagine someone who does not respond to cruelty and injustice with anger and retaliation, but who nevertheless, through some other resource of character, takes an equally energetic and effective stand against it?

I think we can. Major steps in this direction are provided by several historical events in the twentieth century. One is the story of Jackie Robinson's effort break the racist barrier in American baseball that had kept him and others out of the major leagues. Robinson endured what it seemed no one could endure—constant insults from angry players and spectators, racist taunts, violent attempts to injure him, and threats to his life. Throughout, he refused to explode in angry retaliation but kept his cool in such a way that his oppressors would eventually be humiliated, not him. It is not that he did not experience anger. We are told in fact that behind the scenes Robinson fumed, blazing in the "correct anger" envisioned by Aristotle. But, unlike Aristotle's ideal, Robinson would forgo acting on this anger out of the vision of a higher ideal, the prospect that from his success might come a change in the mind and character of racist America.

A further step in this direction can be seen in the lives of Mahatma Gandhi, Martin Luther King Jr., and Thich Nhat Hanh. These three twentieth-century heroes fought injustice, not only forgoing retaliation but also reacting without anger, each standing firm in the realization that truly to overcome the evil in one's enemies one must face them in a posture of love rather than contempt or hatred. Each realized that the means you employ will always help shape the end you receive—violence will always beget some form of violence. Each realized that the mindset of retaliation—an eye for an eye—eventually blinds everyone, as Gandhi was able to say so clearly.

Martin Luther King's nonviolent resistance to racism was inspired by Gandhi's example, and by Thich Nhat Hanh, whose opposition to the

Vietnam war was based in part on the Buddhist "perfection of tolerance." The killing practiced by all sides in Vietnam brought Thich Nhat Hanh to his feet in opposition. With astonishing energy, he worked to put an end to the violence that war would only intensify. But what drove him toward this goal was not anger. Instead it was a profound sadness about the unnecessary suffering and ignorance of humanity and a hopeful vision for what might come to be instead. These emotions fueled a passionate resolve to act. The motivating passion was compassion rather than hatred or anger. In Thich Nhat Hanh, this overriding sadness and love gave rise to the powerful conviction to do whatever he could to elevate human understanding and to overcome our addiction to violence as a means of settling human disputes. In this response to injustice, we see a form of passion very different from anger giving rise to courageous, thoughtful, and energetic action.

It may be that the elucidation provided by Thich Nhat Hanh's writings and seminars on anger will over time do more to change the human world than any possible political act. Anger, he says, is not only not essential to the insistence on justice but it also cannot possibly bring that justice about. Thich Nhat Hanh's kind of angerless insistence on justice is certainly not indifference, and it is not in any way lacking in courage or passion. On the contrary, it is a state of profound compassion that engenders both conviction and the courage to insist on peace and justice.

The kind of selfhood implied in this way of thinking about anger has undergone a fundamental reorientation. Rather than insisting that "injustice not be done to me," it insists with equal passion that "injustice not be done to anyone or anything." Its reorientation dislodges the "self" from center stage. Anger as a response to injustice presupposes a kind of selfhood that will at some point stand in the way of justice. Even if the anger in question is not anger about what was done to oneself, but rather anger in response to injustice to others, the very posture of anger sets up so potent a dichotomy between the good that I (or we) represent and the evil that I (or we) oppose that my retaliatory acts will only evoke further antipathy and retaliation from the other.

A posture of compassion and understanding, on the other hand, that includes or encompasses those propagating evil works effectively to undermine that evil by drawing the unjust into the circle of *us*, those about whom we also care. Such a posture entails a larger vision of shared community that includes even the one whose violence and injustice violates that same community. By contrast, the kind of vehement exclusion of the other implied in anger tends to replicate the crime in an effort to accomplish justice. But justice can only be accomplished by a form of understanding in alignment with it, and neither anger nor revenge can bring this level of understanding into being.

From this Buddhist point of view, anger always implies shallowness of vision. Arising spontaneously in moments of passion, anger is thoughtless, as we all know from experience; it is not grounded in a deep understanding of our shared humanity. Anger is always shortsighted, even if in defense of something as important as justice. It is invariably egocentric and exclusionary. But the gap between anger and the selfless state embodied in Gandhi, King, and Thich Nhat Hanh is enormous, and needs to be bridged by intermediary steps. These steps can be considered stages of cultivation. Anger, like other emotions, can be cultivated and educated, gradually, over time. You can train yourself through practices, meditative and otherwise, so that you are not blinded by anger when it arises, and in such a way that angry responses are not out of control, so that, over time, they are more and more thoughtful and more proportional to the wrong that has evoked it. Anger can be either more or less ensnared by delusions of the self; it can be either more or less selfless, even if at a very high level anger is replaced by love.

As with generosity, in the arena of tolerance, selflessness is not enough. "Perfection" requires that, in addition to unselfishness in orientation, wisdom guide the decision of what to allow and what to oppose. Most important, it is the perspective provided by wisdom that shows us how to act for the long-term betterment of everyone involved. By acting "nondualistically," wisdom shows us how to end the cycles of retaliation by treating even the perpetuator of evil as one of our own. Wise tolerance will neither allow his evil acts to be repeated nor position the doer of evil beyond the scope of our care and compassion. That is the social meaning of "nondualism."

As the Dalai Lama understands it, this level of tolerance is far from "mere passivity." As he explains: "None of the foregoing is meant to imply that there are not times when it is appropriate to respond to others with strong measures. Nor does practicing patience in the sense I have described it mean that we must accept whatever people would do to us and simply give in. Nor does it mean that we should never act at all when we meet with harm. *Sö pa* (patience) should not be confused with mere passivity."[52]

Few of us, however, can claim to approximate this ideal. We are not Jesus, nor Thich Nhat Hanh. When we are treated unfairly, our initial response will be anger. So the more practical question for us is how to deal with anger when it does arise. Assuming that we have not already perfected our capacity for tolerance and wisdom in its use, what mechanisms for controlling and shaping anger will be useful? As in other cases, the Buddhist claim here is that practice is the key, and in this they are surely correct.

The most important kind of practice for Buddhists, in this case and others, is meditation. Meditative practice allows us to work situations over in our minds before they occur; it allows us to go back over circumstances in which we were inflamed by anger in order to get a feel for alternatives. Doing this, we encounter a potentially explosive situation in premeditation, so that when a situation like the one we imagine comes up we engage it in a premeditated or thoughtful way. Premeditation, we know from legal contexts, is defined by sufficient time and opportunity to consider something thoroughly in advance. The practice of some forms of meditation offers just this advantage. Where our initial inclination is to strike back in a violent state of mind, having worked it through the mind in advance, having considered the ethical ramifications of such a response as well as alternatives to it, we stand a much better chance of acting in accord with our overarching "thought of enlightenment" than we would if our meditation had not contemplated that situation ahead of time.

Thich Nhat Hanh's teachings on anger do not take the simplistic tact of advising people not to get angry. Anger is a sudden and natural reaction, and when the conditions are right anger will arise. Thich Nhat Hanh focuses instead on the more practical question of what to do with your anger once it has taken over your body and mind. Perhaps the first step is to recognize that anger is not an optimal response to any situation. That recognition, then, would guide us to cultivate a desire not to be overtaken by anger. When anger overwhelms us, we are controlled and dominated by it and therefore lack freedom of choice.

To initiate the effort to regain freedom over it, we meditate on past occasions of anger, especially on those that have done damage to ourselves and others. The desire to avoid anger develops to the extent that we have reflected on the past and on the potential damage that this state of mind brings into being. Second, we need to learn to notice our anger when it arises and identify it for what it is. Enveloped in our anger, typically we do not see ourselves at all. We can see only the person or the deed that right now enflames us. We are so focused outwardly that we are not sufficiently self-aware to see the anger that has possessed us or what it is right now doing to our minds. Desiring to avoid anger, we learn to identify its symptoms and signs.

From the moment of noticing an angry state of mind, the best tactics are diversionary. We can divert attention from the situation or person that has inflamed us to something else. One, already mentioned, is the anger itself and its detrimental effects. Another is to juxtapose the state of anger and its likely consequences to our stated goals, to our ethical ambitions—seeing how one will block the other, and asking which we would like to pursue. Another, assuming that we have developed this skill, is to engage in conscious, deliberate breathing. Aware that respiration and mental state are interdependent, we deepen our inhalations, bringing more oxygen into the blood and brain, and calm ourselves down to the point that clear thinking can begin to help us. Diversionary techniques like these coax our minds away from what has impassioned it. Typically, the power of our passions, especially anger, is so overwhelming that we have no direct control over them. Often the best we can do is to redirect the energies of anger in another direction, divert them into more constructive channels.

Analysis of the situation before us provides another effective technique to prevent being overtaken by anger. Anger arises dependent upon certain beliefs. Identifying those beliefs, we can often undermine the severity of the anger itself. Extreme anger is usually based on the assumption that the person who has offended us intended the offense; we assume malicious, deliberate harm. But we all know that this often turns out not to be true. When we see that the infraction was really an accident, or based on yet another misunderstanding, that it was careless but not maliciously intended, we quickly calm down into another, less provoked state. Anger will also be diminished if we come to think differently about the importance of the wrong done to us—if it now seems to have only slight overall consequence or effect on our lives, or if, on reflection, its damage seems easily reparable.

More important in Buddhist terms, we can also trace the wrong, whether intentional, malicious, or not, back to its causes and conditions. "Dependent arising" shows us the important question: Why would this person have acted so cruelly? Upon what would such an act depend? Following this line of thought, we can often see how it depends on many prior conditions—the way this person was treated, either recently or over time, by everyone—his parents, family, friends, at work, and on the street. If we can see that others, including ourselves, operating under similar circumstances, would have probably reacted similarly, then the weight of blame we attribute to this person is diminished. Understanding is always the solvent that cools our anger and directs us to more constructive relations. Meditation is the womb in which understanding is nurtured.

Practicing the Perfection of Tolerance

The mental attitudes of intolerance and impatience take an enormous toll on all of us. Residing in these closed and rigid postures, we resent the situation in which we stand, and that resentment undermines flexible points of view from which we might engage the world effectively. When impatient or intolerant, we diminish ourselves and others by inhabiting a rigid smallness of mind. The perfection of tolerance includes a patient willingness to accept present reality as the point of departure for transformative work in the world. The patient person is content to be wherever he or she is right now, no matter what this situation happens to be. Contentment in this case is not letting go of effort and striving; what it releases is the struggle, the unnecessary conflict that stands in the way of lucid assessment and sustained conviction.

Accepting the reality in which we stand, tolerant people do not indulge in moods of resentment; they do not waste energy resenting that things are as they are. In the grip of resentment, we falsify the world, refusing to face the reality that has come to be. Wise patience does not struggle in this way; it does not exhaust resources of mind and body wishing that things were other than they are. Resentment of the real undermines our best efforts to see what we face and to deal with it constructively. Ideally, the practices of tolerance and patience would release us from the grip of these agitations, freeing the mind to deal with the situation calmly and directly. Letting go of unhelpful distractions, we are in a much better position to participate thoughtfully and effectively in the world.

Painfully, I recall my own past moods of impatience. I am annoyed that my son cannot move or do something with the quickness and agility that I can. The slow pace of action upsets my rhythm and state of mind in spite of the fact that I understand his disability very well. Although I hasten to disguise it, I know that my impatience is displayed for him to see, in my attitude, my rigidity, and my shortness of temper. I know very well that anyone's degree of clumsiness or agility is just a genetic given, a gift or an obstacle that nobody "deserves" in any sense, but my impatience overwhelms this knowledge.

Impatience jangles my nerves; it severely diminishes my mind and character. More important, it is upsetting to the one I love because in my impatience he can sense a voiceless accusation, an unnecessary and unhelpful insinuation of inferiority. Unconsciously internalizing my impatience, he becomes even less able to perform the task; he gets frustrated and loses confidence. The effects of my impatience will make it even more difficult for him to make a wholehearted effort in the future. It hardly matters that the harm done is not intended, because it is done and I am its cause. Lacking thoughtfulness, not attending to the destructiveness of this impatient state of mind, I continue to diminish myself and others without taking the time to find the freedom to get out of this state.

Impatience and intolerance imply presumptuous and arrogant states of mind. We are presumptuous when we fail to think about what others need, about the differences between people that must be taken into account. We are arrogant when we assume a posture of superiority and look down on the differences that define everyone. Arrogance reflects a mind out of accord with the world around it, one that misunderstands the situation at hand and unknowingly acts with profoundly destructive consequences. These destructive consequences are widely shared. Both the one being demeaned and the one who shows disdain are diminished by this smallness of character.

Practicing the perfection of patience or tolerance requires a humble stance in the world, an honest, uninflated sense of oneself. But humility is not one of the perfections; in fact, it is not a virtue that we can work on like any other. This is so because we come to be humble not through a series of accomplishments to our character but rather through humbling realizations about who and what we are. We become humble when we are willing and able to look directly at our own weaknesses and failures. These shortcomings are substantial in all of us, but only the humble person has the honesty to own up to them and face who they are, all fronts aside. Such honesty often comes through times of humiliation, hardly the kind of experience we willingly seek. From this point of view, humility is not lack of awareness of who we are, as is often assumed. Instead, it is a profoundly felt sensitivity to the extent of our own limitations.

Discernment of this kind entails a lucidity that few of us possess, both with respect to our own smallness and to the depth and power of the reality that lies beyond us. Patient, tolerant acceptance arises out of such a clarity of mind. It is not that, when humble, we lack awareness of who we are, but rather that, in humility, we step into a profound sense of our true place in an immense universe.

For the perfection of tolerance, wisdom is the art of understanding when to be tolerant and how. This is why tolerance or patience is a skill of character that is so difficult—it depends on the insight and subtlety of mind to know when it ought to be practiced and when not, and in each case how to practice it to good effect. The appropriateness and effectiveness of patience, like generosity, is context dependent, and the capacity to see these subtle nuances of context takes wisdom. In this way, patience is a matter of balance, wisdom to sense the whole of the situation in which we find ourselves and to act in accordance with just proportion and sound timing.

Both balance and timing indicate to us that it will not always be appropriate to be patient or tolerant. Wisdom guides us to ask—tolerant or patient of what? For what reasons and on behalf of what larger goal? Knowing when to be patient entails knowing how to place this present situation in the context of overriding goals, especially one's "thought of enlightenment." Limited practices of patience must fit into a larger scheme of practices aimed at more and more encompassing ends, both personal and communal. There are times, clearly, when it is unwise and unenlightening to wait patiently, times when, for the good of everyone, only direct action will do.

As the art of putting things into perspective, wisdom also teaches us how to contextualize problems, how to understand what worries us in a light that is liberating rather than debilitating. Recall that Buddhist wisdom is associated with the realizations that all things are impermanent and contingent. Cultivating the ability to tolerate the problems and difficulties that are almost always on our minds, awareness of their impermanence and contingency is essential. Keeping impermanence in mind, we realize that this problem, like all others, is transient. Although it weighs heavily on my mind right now, I can attain a perspective that predicts its transformation and eventual disappearance. That slight distance from the problem enables us to avoid being crushed by the perceived weight of problems.

In addition to seeing the transience of the problem, wisdom points to its contingency. All things just depend. They come into our lives due to particular conditions, and when those conditions change so will the problems. This formula—the Buddhist teaching of "dependent arising"—assists in understanding the status of difficulties. They are contingent and can be altered by changing the conditions upon which they currently depend. Understanding this empowers action and helps reduce the extent to which we waste time and energy bemoaning what has happened as though that state is permanent and unavoidable. Getting wise perspective encourages us to see the reality before us for what it is without lamentation or resentment. Accepting the problem as a problem does not undermine effective work to solve it. Indeed, it is exactly what makes skillful response possible by bringing pointless struggle to an end.

Throughout Buddhist history, the perfection of tolerance has been among the most valorized practices and mental attitudes. Buddhists recognized that the kind of self or ego displayed in acts of impatience, intolerance, and anger was the antithesis of their spiritual ideal. Practices of the perfection of tolerance were aimed at overcoming the states of mind entailed in intolerant rejection and angry retaliation. This potent emphasis in traditional Buddhism, however, tended to obscure the fact that there are also dangers of character inherent in this same character strength. Wherever tolerance or patience is unduly valorized or distorted, we are vulnerable to the harm that excessive passivity may cause to ourselves and to our society. Recall that the perfection of tolerance is the cultivation of the wisdom to discern when and how to be tolerant. It cannot be a universal obligation that we always tolerate, or that we tolerate everything. Drawing those lines of separation, however, is extremely difficult, which is precisely why wisdom is needed in addition to the selflessness upon which tolerance is based.

The distortion to the perfection of tolerance that is most important to understand is one in which acts of toleration mask or suppress suffering. In this situation, patience with abuse is a sign of weakness and self-condemnation. We allow harm to be done to us because we lack a strong enough sense of ideals and the courage to admit the damage that is being done to ourselves and others. This kind of tolerance is not rooted in respect and compassion for all beings, but in its lack. That is the danger in the traditional virtue of patience that women have come to recognize in the last half century—that when we lack a healthy self-respect, we may condone abuses to ourselves and disguise their destructiveness with unwise claims about the virtue of "patience" or "tolerance." Wherever tolerance is simply passivity under all circumstances, we are far from its perfection.

True tolerance is not paralysis, and it is not a form of weakness. Thus, tolerance is distorted when it becomes an unreflective habit, when it is what we always do. Patiently accepting cruelty or unjust demands of self-sacrifice, we distort tolerance. Although monks and nuns have been particularly vulnerable to this distortion of tolerance, so is everyone in a hierarchical society. Acquiescing to degrading circumstances, what was once humility turns into humiliation. "Perfect" tolerance finds the appropriate middle ground between self-obsessive intolerance and self-inflicted humiliation. Locating that space requires wisdom, and practice.

Bodhisattvas vow to enlighten all beings, to extend wisdom and compassion to everyone. That includes themselves. We owe it to everyone, including ourselves, to see to it that respect is maintained. One of the most famous maxims in Immanuel Kant's ethics asserts that we should always treat others and our own self as ends and never simply as means. In the same way that the aggressive, self-obsessed person denies respect for others, the excessively tolerant, servile person denies respect for him or herself. The perfection of tolerance wisely avoids both extremes.

Tolerating Misfortune and the Contingency of Life

For some traditional Buddhists there is no such thing as misfortune. All fortune—good, bad, and indifferent—is justifiably earned, they claim. We deserve whatever we get in life. Grounded in the view of cosmic justice inherent in the Buddhist teachings of karma and rebirth, this idea is not always easy to practice. But for those who are adept at practicing it, it does have powerful ramifications. Whoever accepts these teachings to the extent of being able to live in accord with them has no reason to resent what has happened. When misfortune befalls such people, their understanding of karma and rebirth ameliorates its sting. Whatever has happened to them—no matter how terrible or how wonderful—it was their own actions in life that have produced this new state of affairs. Adopting this view, you would have every reason to tolerate everything that happens to you and no reason to resent or bemoan the consequences that your own actions have earned.

In this way, the doctrines of karma and rebirth make the practice of tolerance much easier. Although on the surface it may appear that others have done an injustice to you, a profound understanding of the teachings deflects that blame away from others and onto your own past choices. What a Buddhist believer in karma and rebirth must learn to tolerate is not others but his or her own past. This past is self-created, justifying the harm or benefit that is now being suffered. Although we can certainly bemoan our own acts and blame ourselves for our miserable state, what we cannot do under the dominion of these teachings is to claim injustice. Although we will soon want to assess possible negative consequences that these doctrines have on the practice of the perfection of tolerance, first we acknowledge ways in which the teachings of karma and rebirth have made a strong and positive contribution to moral life.

Resentment and egocentric claims of injustice have ruined many lives. When we are injured, the force of the experience is so powerful that we are in no position to judge where fault and blame ought to be placed. But we do it anyway, and our judgments are so potent that we cannot help but relive the experience of injustice over and over in our minds. Resentment fades very slowly, if at all, sometimes mounting over time to destroy the quality of lives that cannot move on. To whatever extent the Buddhist idea that "what we suffer is self-caused" has helped to overcome the destructive force of resentment and bitterness on human lives, it must be appreciated and praised. In addition, it gives the strength of purpose to think that our efforts to be just, kind, and thoughtful will be amply rewarded in the long run, even if not now in this life. Karma and rebirth give us reasons not to be discouraged and to remain firm in our resolve to live well, no matter how little it seems to avail us at the time. These are some of the ways in which these teachings have had enormously positive effects.

Whatever positive effects the ideas of karma and rebirth have had or currently have on practitioners, however, we cannot escape the possible negative repercussions of these ideas, or the larger question of what in fact we ought to believe about cosmic justice. Although it is perfectly possible to live in a traditional Buddhist society and accept the truth of these ideas in unquestioning faith, it is unlikely that this will be possible for us—the likely readers of this book. In a worldview at least partially shaped by modern science and not so much by traditional South Asian cosmologies, there is little chance that we will be able to convince ourselves that the universe has been structured in such a way as to include systematic cosmic justice. It seems to us that some things just happen. It is not that these events do not have causes; they do. It is rather that these causes are oblivious to the question of whether or not we deserve the particular outcomes that we receive. For most of us, although we are indeed causal agents affecting our own lives, not everything that happens to us can be explained this way. Some things just happen—both wonderful and tragic things, whether we deserve them or not. Wayward meteorites, rare diseases, wandering into the life of the perfect lover, and lottery wins are all examples of fateful consequences that few of us will be able to regard as having been self-determined or deserved, even though any one of those could be the event that most significantly shapes the relative success of our lives.

If that is true, then perfecting our powers of tolerance will be all that much more important. On this scenario, what we must learn to tolerate is not just the impact that our own actions have had on our lives but also the much more difficult fact that our lives are also shaped by outside forces and contingency, or luck. Doing that would entail accepting that, in addition to the causal role that we play in our own lives, there are other determining factors, and that some turns of fortune are contingent upon factors that are both beyond our control and indifferent to our moral stature. Our sense of justice, now highly evolved, is offended by that prospect. We would prefer that things be arranged otherwise and that all people get what they deserve. We notice that sometimes dishonest and cruel people live long and prosperous lives and that on occasion humble, hard-working people are crushed by violence and injustice. We notice these injustices and feel strongly that this is wrong, that it ought not to be so. But the sense that things ought to be structured so that people get what they deserve will not necessarily convince us that they are in fact structured that way.

For those, like me, who are not convinced and who look out into a cosmos that appears to acknowledge nothing of our human concept of justice, it is inevitable that we ask: If the idea of cosmic justice promulgated in all the major world religions is in truth a comforting illusion, a way of consoling ourselves in the face of an indifferent universe, then what is the most fruitful way to live in the absence of that consolation? If honesty in belief disallows our adherence to the ideas of rebirth or heaven as a consolation for undeserved suffering and reward, then how can we proceed in spiritual life in the most thoughtful and effective way possible? What resources in the Buddhist tradition are still available to generate strength for life when we are threatened by what appear to be unjust consequences such as accidents and disease?

One place to begin responding to that line of questioning is with the realization that life is a gift—an unasked for, unearned "given." None of us asked to be here or expected to be here. But here we are. Realizing that, it is hard to find a good reason not to accept the gift, whatever it happens to be. When both Hindus and Buddhists claim that in the larger scheme of things becoming a human being is the most precious opportunity, they are on to something important. Although the framework for that Hindu and Buddhist claim is the doctrine of reincarnation, and for us it is not, the moral is the same: Do something extraordinary with your freedom. Not striving for the richest source of freedom available to you, and instead living in fear, resentment, or despair, simply makes no sense as a response to life understood as a gift. A perfection of tolerance suited to contemporary culture should help us respond thoughtfully when we are threatened by injustice, helping us to engage what remains of our lives as imaginatively and energetically as our resources allow.

Being impermanent, dependent, and contingent is not just the fate of human beings. Everything we can name depends on a variety of causes and conditions, and everything is always subject to change. In this sense, we are no different from anything else; like all things, we too are "empty" of permanent, unconditional status. Therefore, like the lives of flowers, insects, stones, and ideas, we are contingent upon factors beyond our control. Our existence is vulnerable for good or ill to larger forces, forces that may serve to make us rich and happy or may crush us undeservingly before our time. This is to say that risk is a fundamental feature of existence, human and nonhuman.

We all live in a state of risk. Learning to live effectively in the midst of vulnerability without being frightened into loss of nerve and incapacity is essential to the perfection of tolerance. Although we can never eliminate threats external to us, we can work internally to transform the ways we face these threats and the ways we react when things go badly. Whether a quest proceeds under mostly hospitable conditions or whether it struggles through seemingly unending adversity, the quality of the quest remains to some extent under our control.

The realization that all of us are at risk is widespread; most people fear that fact and understand it through their fear. A few, however, transform the knowledge of their vulnerability into life-affirming wisdom. Without resorting to consoling beliefs, they are able to face risk and contingency in a way that prepares them to tolerate misfortune when it strikes and to absorb turns of great fortune in ways that do not undermine their character. Most of us do not respond to the vulnerability of our lives so skillfully. The contingency and risk of human life evoke a variety of unhelpful responses, and avoiding these should be a major component of the perfection of tolerance. These inappropriate responses are evasive and self-deceptive, and in those ways contribute to the dangers of misfortune.

When things go badly, responding badly will just make it worse. Reacting insightfully and with resolve, we may be able to move adeptly beyond crises and take something of them up into our larger quest. When things go badly, for whatever reason, we are tempted in several self-destructive directions of response. We may become resentful, dwelling on the expectations of entitlement that we had previously cultivated. We may become cynical, convincing ourselves that nothing will go well or that nothing matters. We may find ourselves falling into despair, accompanied by self-destructive withdrawal and resignation. In each of these ways, we adopt a mindset suited only for surrender, for giving up, and that reaction exacerbates the misfortune we already had.

The perfection of tolerance is the meditative discipline of working with everything that assaults us, discomforts us, and forces suffering on us. Holding the mind steady, we learn to examine the pain, seeking to locate dimensions of our character that are not so severely affected by the apparent crisis and from which we can respond with resolve. Contemplating these, we begin to open a spiritual power not otherwise accessible. Patiently sitting still with our suffering entails neither wallowing in it nor celebrating it, but instead promises a freedom from its tyranny. Patience of this sort is far more than passive endurance. It is the energy to pass through suffering without allowing it to get us wholly in its grasp.

As we have seen, in traditional Buddhism, the recommended mental strategy for controlling one's reaction to misfortune is to consider everything that has happened to you to be the result of your own actions—your own karma—either in this life or those before. When we assume this, we have only ourselves to blame and no reason to be angry with others or the cosmos. Although blaming ourselves for our misfortunes will in some cases make us resolute not to repeat the mistakes that give rise to suffering, there are other cases in which directing our anger and feelings of displeasure inward upon ourselves may be harmful, even debilitating. Sometimes an excessive self-blame may do far more harm than good. In some cases, self-contempt is crippling, because addiction to self-indictment undermines the basis on which commitment to anything worthwhile in life can be made. If, as it seems to me, not all misfortune is self-caused, and if self-cause is only one possible factor among several that bring suffering into being, then blaming yourself for all misfortune will turn out to be intellectually dishonest. When you are really not to blame, taking the blame upon yourself may be just more delusion. Enlightenment always entails a willingness to recognize and tolerate the truth.

Tolerance of Uncertainty

The most difficult challenge associated with the perfection of tolerance is tolerating the truth of uncertainty that derives from human finitude. Having learned to accept the uncertainty of life and its very real risks, we are now asked to tolerate the uncertainty of all the wisdom we have acquired. Mahayana Buddhist texts unflinchingly proclaim that the highest realization, the truth that is most difficult to encounter, is that all the teachings of Buddhism and all the other "truths" you have acquired are "empty." Recall that "emptiness" was the term used to coordinate the realizations of "impermanence," "dependent origination," and "no-self." To say that all things without exception are "empty" is to say that all things change over time because what they are is dependent on other equally impermanent things. Change and dependence imply that there is "no-self" to anything in the sense of a permanent identity that is what it is, independent of other things. Being "empty" and having "no-self" are thus the same realization.

But what, then, does it mean to say that in addition to everything else to which it applies, "emptiness" is applicable to itself; "emptiness" is itself "empty"? Insight deriving from long-term reflection on this one thought in Buddhist history is extensive. One outcome of this meditation is the realization that no doctrine is final, permanent, and beyond doubt. "Emptiness" was in many ways a teaching about how to live well in view of the prospects of human finitude. Through reflection on this teaching, Buddhists contemplated the uncertainty of human thinking and sought ways not around this insight but through it to greater and greater realization. They sought to learn through experience how to live well in the absence of certain knowledge, yet without being rendered immobile by the fear of being wrong or getting stuck in sheer hesitation.

Buddhist sutras warn against the fear that will arise when you truly encounter what it means that human understanding is always open, never final. One reaction to this reflexive realization is to think that inquiry is pointless, that if we cannot know the truth definitively there is no point to the quest for truth. But that overreaction is based more on fear than on clear reflection. Being uncertain is not being wrong, and in no way does it render pointless the quest for understanding. Indeed, Buddhists maintained that understanding this one point with clarity—the "emptiness" of all things including knowledge—would eventually establish grounds upon which fearless, lucid thinking could take place. "Eventually" is the correct qualifier, however, since the texts spend most of their time worrying about the initial reaction that may drive people back from the effort of the search itself. Encounters with the threat of meaninglessness were analogous to an initiation rite for Mahayana Buddhist monks and nuns. Passing through it was a sign that the "thought of enlightenment" had taken hold in their minds and that a glimpse into the depth of human finitude would not frighten them into turning back for the safe grounds of conventional knowing.

It is natural to be impatient in the conceptual domain of life. We feel secure and protected when we know the truth, and insecure when we do not. Those feelings frequently drive us to firm conclusions, to the security of indubitable knowledge, as quickly as we can get there. We are impatient with inconclusiveness in the quest for understanding, and that very impatience drives us to anxiety-riddled misunderstanding. We seek definitive, nondebatable answers, and in such a search tend to close down more than open up. Closure is our word for the end of a search, but it is also the description of a state of mind that prevents imaginative, fearless reflection. The desire for closure is the impetus to dogmatism. In a dogmatic state of mind, we insist on one version of the truth—ours. We want the discussion terminated and thinking to cease, both ours and others'. But this posture of dogmatic insistence is amenable only to authoritarian modes of social interaction. It does not fit well with a plurality of others who are equally interested in the issue and in the truth. Perfecting our tolerance of uncertainty, we also perfect our ability to be at ease with others who see things in different ways, whose views do not concur with ours.

Although the dogmatic posture of certainty is "normal" in any society—openness always being the exception—the extension of this closed-minded position is the very definition of madness and insanity. The madman always knows the truth and proclaims it in a self-aggrandizing manner. His rigid closure of mind is dogmatic in the extreme, and the threat of differences of opinion are too much for him to bear. The madman's mental posture is not the opposite of ordinary sanity; it is simply an excessive version of it—more of the same. Awakening from this temptation to close one's mind, the person of profound tolerance differs not just from the insane but from the ordinary mode of knowing as well.

Afraid of the openness of reality and frightened by the finitude of human life, we all grasp for closure. Our ideal becomes the "grasp," a posture of holding on that has the final truth in its clutches. This temptation is everywhere in our lives and among the most difficult to resist. Only through meditative extension of patience in the pursuit of truth and tolerance of the posture of not knowing do we begin to overcome this form of "normal" mental illness. Modern Western thought has produced something closely related to the realization of "emptiness"—"historical consciousness," the consciousness or awareness that everything is immersed in history, that everything becomes what it is through the shaping powers of historical conditioning and change whenever constitutive conditions change. The ability and willingness to understand ourselves historically is similar to the ability to see the "empty" character of all things—that is, its relational and always changing character.

In this insight, we realize that everything is a product of history, of dependence and time, including ourselves. Through it, we understand that all human thinking is subject to future doubt and revision, no matter how certain we may be about our knowledge. The upshot of historical awareness is not that we cannot know the truth, but that doubt and openness are essential ingredients to any quest for understanding. Similarly, realizing that all human knowledge is "empty" or "historical" does not in any way amount to saying that knowledge is not valid, or that it is pointless. It is rather a profound look into both the dependent character of everything and the reality of ongoing change that pervades the entire cosmos.

One way to restate this insight is to say, as Socrates did, that the highest wisdom is to know that we do not know, where "knowing" implies finality and the end of the quest. Every time we overcome an old way of understanding something by discovering a new way to look at it, we are tempted by this same certainty, the arrogant conclusion that this time the end of the quest has really arrived. Every new sense of clarity provides grounds for a new form of blindness. A serene patience or wise tolerance expresses the determination to acknowledge this insight into the openness of all human inquiry. Patience provides us with the ability to keep our minds open, always alive to the possibility that a greater, more comprehensive truth stands nearby in the waiting. The perfection of tolerance takes this skill as one of its most profound, and those who strive for perfection in this dimension of life possesses a tool of great transformative power.

Cultivating a Community of Tolerance

As we know from modern history, tolerance is also a virtue that communities and governments must cultivate. Collective tolerance is the community's desire to make it possible for different people with different conceptions of what a good life is to live together in some degree of harmony and good will. In the Asian societies in which Buddhism was born and developed, there were long-standing traditions of religious tolerance. Numerous religious groups somehow managed to live together without becoming aggressively fearful of the differences between themselves. This has been largely true in India and in China and in many of the cultures that have existed on the periphery of these two cultural giants, exceptions notwithstanding.

In modern contexts, where democratic ideals of decision making prevail, tolerance becomes much more than leaving one's neighbor alone, much more than mutual indifference. It entails an aspiration to work together toward the common good, especially in discussions and debates that lead up to decisions about how to shape the institutions that serve all of us. For the most part, Buddhists in traditional Asian societies have been content to practice a political neutrality, leaving the political dimension to others. Political necessity prompted that approach. Buddhist monastic institutions existed and thrived on the goodwill of the monarchical governments that ruled these lands. They received support and sustenance from their societies in exchange for their contributions of education and guidance in religious matters. A largely unspoken agreement guaranteed their verbal support of the government and prohibited their interference and disagreement in matters of policy.

For the most part, Buddhists were quite willing to accept these limitations on their participation in politics in exchange for freedom to practice their way of life. Although there were certainly exceptions to this general rule in the long history and geography of Buddhism, they were clearly exceptions to a very dominant pattern. Moreover, the pattern of a hierarchical ordering of political power was duplicated in most Buddhist monastic institutions. In a community predicated upon the cultivation of enlightened character, democratic dispersals of power seemed to make no sense.

In modern settings, however, Buddhists have adapted skillfully to democratic political institutions, as though these were very much in keeping with Buddhist principles. Buddhists have, in a variety of contexts, argued for tolerance of differences between groups, protecting both peace and the rights of everyone to pursue their own ideas of the good. Although very clear about the limitations of politics, Buddhists have come to see their own responsibility to work for the improvement of the social conditions in which the pursuit of enlightenment takes place. It would appear that this historical pattern will only gather strength and that cultural conditions will increasingly open a place for Buddhist participation in debates about social policy. If democratic societies are constituted around ongoing debates about how to arrange institutional structures within which individuals and smaller groups can pursue their own visions of the purpose of life, then it is hard to imagine that Buddhists will not become active participants.

This has been one of the primary difficulties with some traditional governments, and certainly with modern totalitarian regimes. They often reserve the right to impose their own conceptions of the good—their own "thought of enlightenment"—upon everyone, cutting short the discussions and debates that serve to extend these visions further through comparison with other ideas. A perfection of tolerance worthy of a developed global Buddhism will clearly seek to practice openness to as many points of view as possible. A perfected form of collective tolerance would not require that Buddhists regard other forms of understanding as true. It would only require that they offer others an opportunity to persuade them, a chance to present their ideas in the setting of open-minded reflection on the common good.

Such a posture of tolerance may still seem a contradiction—that Buddhists would regard another point of view as false or misleading and at the same time commit themselves to protecting the right of the other to propagate that view. But what Buddhists would be protecting in taking this position is not so much the other person's view as their freedom to think and decide on their own how they ought to live. The value at stake is autonomy, and Buddhists have a strong incentive to protect this overriding value. This would not entail that Buddhists be indifferent to the effects that the opposing view might have on their society. Indeed, Buddhists may find that they must oppose some particular position, arguing that it not become a part of public policy. There is no need for anyone to forgo their right to resist the influence that ideas or behaviors may have on the culture as a whole. But there is an implied requirement that they engage in opposition peacefully, that debate and persuasion be the means through which political action proceed.

We have seen in this chapter that tolerance takes its ideal form when it is placed in conjunction to a wise sense of justice. Although it is greatly beneficial to be patient and tolerant for the sake of justice overall, it is neither good nor wise to accept acts of injustice with patience and tolerance. For this reason, cultivating a community of tolerance would also require cultivating the place of justice among Buddhist ideals. For a variety of historical reasons, the concept of justice is not very well developed in Buddhism. Justice is not one of the many ideals that Buddhists have debated and extended over the long history of this tradition. We have given two reasons for this lack of emphasis: (1) that in order to maintain their position in Asian societies, Buddhists were expected to maintain neutrality whenever politically difficult issues of justice were at stake, and (2) that the doctrines of karma and rebirth functioned to assure everyone that an overarching cosmic justice was always in effect, thus alleviating the pressing demand in Buddhism for a political concept of justice that would help maintain justice here and now.

Both of these reasons for the weakness of a concept of justice in Buddhism are in the process of evaporating. For one, the spread of democratic political regimes will gradually come to mean that Buddhists need not and should not abandon the political domain. Politics is the social practice within which what the sutras called the "necessary conditions" for enlightenment are distributed. And two, as Buddhism becomes both global and contemporary in its orientation, confidence in cosmic justice through the idea of rebirth is likely to become questionable. Buddhists might recognize that justice is our responsibility as citizens of the world rather than something that will naturally be done for us. For both these reasons, Buddhists are likely to take an interest in systems of justice that would help make possible a true community of tolerance. This development would confirm, not contradict, the most impressive elements in the Buddhist tradition. Indeed, what is now called "socially engaged Buddhism" is already well underway, and the ideal of justice is quickly becoming a well-honed dimension of the Buddhist tradition.

Justice, like any ideal, is always vulnerable to distortion, however. An individual's and a community's sense of justice can be dangerously skewed by the demands of self-interest and self-absorption. Our demands for justice can easily become no more than self-centered demands that our interests be served rather than the interests of others. This is why the perfection of tolerance is so important. Without wise judgment about when and how to tolerate, our claims about what is fair and right are always dubious. This is where the contribution of Buddhism and the perfection of tolerance might become globally significant. Relying only on persuasion and the force of their example, Buddhists who practice the perfection of tolerance in a variety of political arenas will find that the *dharma* is powerfully applicable to dimensions of life not previously incorporated into their practices. In these settings, the perfection of tolerance will be expanded and applied effectively to a wide variety of issues, and this is where we will begin to see how valuable these assets of character perfection are in the contemporary world.

THE PERFECTION OF ENERGY

TRADITIONAL BUDDHIST IMAGES OF THE PERFECTION OF ENERGY (*VĪRYAPĀRAMITĀ*)

In transition from the first three perfections to the final set of three, the classic texts of Mahayana Buddhism announce a significant shift of emphasis. The first three—generosity, morality, tolerance—are appropriate practices for anyone. The final three, however—energy, meditation, wisdom—operate at a higher level of spiritual awareness and therefore tend to be the focus of monks, nuns, and others who give priority in their lives to spiritual practice and insight. At this point in the practice, high levels of energy are required to undertake the practices of concentration and meditation prescribed in the fifth perfection, and in order to sustain the transformation in personal orientation experienced through insight and wisdom in the sixth. Thus, energy marks the transition from one level of practice to another, from preparatory exercises to a loftier level of endeavor.

Ārya-Śūra begins his discussion of the perfection of energy by describing his understanding of this transition. He explains how the first three practices are more commonly undertaken because the motives that might lead one to begin the practices of generosity, morality, or tolerance do not necessarily require a profound sense of selflessness. Indeed, such motives may very well be grounded in ordinary self-regard.[1] Thus, one might happily practice generosity, as many of us do, in hopes of earthly or religious rewards, while unaware of the selflessness that ultimately grounds the first perfection. Similarly, motives for the practice of morality may include various forms of self-concern—fear of karmic consequences, fear of punishment, or fear of damnation and hell—without yet sensing that morality leads to a set of concerns far more comprehensive than personal destiny. Furthermore, many people tolerate what goes on around them simply because they lack the courage to stand up to it or the power to do anything about it. "Patience" in this case is less a sign of depth of character and understanding than it is a symbol of weakness, an indication more of lack of understanding than profundity of it. This is not in any way to demean the first three perfections. It is rather to recognize that the distance between initial motivations and ideal outcome or "perfection" is enormous, and that something beyond the first three practices is required in order to bring these three to a higher level.

The final three perfections, beginning with energy, mandate a movement beyond these initial levels of practice. They are more abstract, less worldly in character, and their rewards are more difficult to visualize. But once they are initiated, the final three perfections begin to provide the basis on which the first three can be more profoundly comprehended and thus more wisely practiced. The transition between the two groups marks a point beyond which focus on enlightenment is more clearly defined. It is in this light that one sutra claims that "where there is energy there is enlightenment."[2]

The word "energy" translates the Sanskrit *vīrya*, a very important and much evolved concept in the history of Indian culture. *Vīrya* derives from early Aryan roots, where its warrior heritage can be clearly seen. In earlier epochs, *vīrya* pointed to the power and virility of the warrior, the one noted for physical strength and courage, the hero of epoch battles. Evolving through the history of brahmanical culture, it came to signify prowess of other kinds, the energy and exertion necessary to make extraordinary accomplishments possible. Early Buddhist texts referred to the Buddha himself as a *vīra*, a great hero, the one who was victorious over the forces of evil—Mara—and whose spiritual achievements would transform the world. For Buddhists, therefore, *vīrya* meant the energy of accomplishment, the effort, courage, and power to see spiritual endeavor through to its completion. *Vīrya-pāramitā* is the perfection of this energy, the power of unyielding commitment to the ultimate goal of universal awakening.[3]

Śāntideva's *Bodhicaryāvatāra* defines energy as "the endeavour to do what is skillful" and juxtaposes against it such vices as "sloth," "despondency," and "self-contempt."[4] "Sloth" is simply laziness, the desire not to exert one's energy in hopes that benefit will somehow arrive without the outlay of effort. "Despondency" is "defeatism," "apathy" and "weariness" of life.[5] "Self-contempt" is the view, put into practice through daily lethargy, that I am incapable of anything significant and cannot expect myself to accomplish much. It defines disappointment into one's own inner identity.

Śāntideva's chapter on the perfection of energy reads like an inspirational lecture. It goads us to look closely at ourselves and to take stock of our current level of effort. "Hey you," it shouts, "expecting results without effort! So sensitive! So long-suffering! You, in the clutches of death, acting like an immortal! Hey, sufferer, you are destroying yourself!"[6] The text points directly to the implicit despair behind our low levels of enthusiasm and meager effort. It chides the easy-going defeatism and lack of pride that emerge when the answer to the rhetorical question "How could I possibly achieve Buddhahood?" is a simple negative assumption.[7] Energy level shapes our understanding of what is possible in life and is therefore critical in determining what kinds of self-transformation we might seek and attain.

Courage was considered an essential component of the quest for self-transformation. As the bodhisattva develops the perfection of energy, he is said to find that "he is not afraid. He is impregnated with the strength that he has gained and that enables him to persist in his endeavors and to think: 'It is not the case that I shall not be fully enlightened.'"[8]

Ārya Śūra defines the perfection of energy as "striving without weariness in the practice of the good," as "striving untouched by the fault of discouragement," and as a movement out of "mental slackness."[9] He attributes great powers to success in the perfection of energy, claiming that "as a general rule the person who is afflicted with depression, though striving is at his disposal, finds even his own tasks arduous; but for the one whose striving is not inferior, the burden of others' tasks . . . can be borne without fatigue."[10] In this and many other Mahayana texts, focus on the "thought of enlightenment" is the most potent technique available to raise the practitioner out of "lassitude" and into a level of energy that can sustain ardent practice and discipline.[11]

But how does one do any of this? How is it possible to develop energy and perfect the capacity for intelligent and disciplined striving? Beyond the motivational force of the "thought of enlightenment," little concrete advice is offered. Here we encounter the weakness of the Buddhist texts that teach this fourth perfection. Very little in the way of technique is offered, even though we might assume that there were such practices circulating in Buddhist monastic contexts. What is given instead is inspirational rhetoric, encouraging discussions, challenges put to the reader in forceful terms. No doubt these texts did inspire. They must have helped to motivate and to enable endeavors that would have not been possible otherwise. Nevertheless, this is one area of traditional weakness that today might be corrected by posing the question in all seriousness—to what extent can one's level of energy be transformed, and through what techniques might that be accomplished?

Two Forms of Human Energy

It is common in Mahayana Buddhist texts to divide the perfection of energy into two kinds, one physical and one mental. Although we might be led to assume that physical or bodily energy has to do with diet, physical exercise such as yoga, and a variety of bodily practices that might have been available in early India, the texts do not specify what exercises would have been included in this list. It is enough, apparently, to know that energy takes a physical form and that developing it to full capacity is one dimension of Buddhist practice. The focus instead is on mental energy, and the implication is clear that mental energy is the most consequential form that energy takes. Although the division between the two forms of energy is frequently made—the bodhisattva "generates physical and mental energy"—nothing further is said about the distinction between them except that "the correct measure of repeated exercise" between the various kinds of energy is important.[12]

Developing the power of mental strength was considered the primary task for the bodhisattva. So Śāntideva writes: "If my mind is weak, even a minor difficulty is oppressive. When one is made passive by defeatism, without doubt difficulties easily take effect."[13] Śāntideva goes on to claim that "affliction in the mind is due to false projections," and that "desire for what is good must be created, meditating carefully on these things."[14] This is simply to say that when we project aspirations and desires onto the world that are unworthy of our highest possibilities, these "false projections" work against the quest for enlightenment by sapping our energies rather than building and developing them.

In his discussion of the perfection of energy, Ārya-Śūra recognizes that most people simply accept their current energy level for what it is and are not aware that self-transformation in this dimension is possible. Developing this thought, he divides all of us into three categories of persons: (1) those who are unable to begin the quest at all, either because they do not recognize the very possibility of transformation or because of their own low self-regard; (2) those who are inspired to undertake the quest but become easily discouraged, distracted by something else, or simply weary of all undertaking; and (3) those who set out and advance boldly and energetically toward their goal.[15] Of course, ancient Indian writers conceived of this quest as spanning many lifetimes rather than one or a fraction of one. But this larger conception of human endeavor underscores the importance of "energy" and "effort" and helps us understand why this perfection is ranked so high on the list of Buddhist virtues when, by contrast, it rarely appears on lists of admirable qualities that we find in other cultures.

Ārya-Śūra proceeds to divide the quest for perfection of energy into three stages, or three "formal undertakings" (*samādāna*).[16] In the first stage, the bodhisattva is focused on a "thought of enlightenment," since it is this thought that will inspire energetic effort all along the path. Taking the bodhisattva's vow, however, requires that this "thought" be broadened to such an extent that, in intention at least, the goal is not one's own awakening but the awakening of human culture altogether. This vow can be a source of frustration, since the goal stands so far beyond what seems plausible in this life. Therefore the bodhisattva is focused on the accumulation of energy in order not to be discouraged or intimidated by the transcendent nature of the final goal.

Ārya-Śūra describes this stage as building a "hardness of armor" that allows one to continue on energetically, even in the midst of one's own suffering, by refusing to dwell on it and, through the teaching of selflessness, coming to see it in impersonal terms. This first level is the stage of dedication, striving to remain in the world of *samsāra* while working diligently toward the liberation of all beings. The second "undertaking" envisions the bodhisattva successful in work on behalf of others, not just strengthening his own resolve but, through the power of that resolution, performing the work of awakening. At this stage, the bodhisattva makes great strides in deepening his practice and builds more extensive reserves of energy as practice matures. The third and final stage coincides with enlightenment and pictures the bodhisattva able to work effortlessly without any thought about his "own" effort or her "own" labor. At this level, exertion is not self-consciously produced. Instead, the text envisions energy made available through sources beyond the open boundaries of the individual self.

If, following the larger vision of the text, there really is "no-self," then the movements of influence between "empty" and interdependent entities enables each to join into power sources shared among them all. The text appears to suggest that energy originating in the individual will is always partial and limited, and that the very effort to live out of that energy alone reinforces the walls of individuality and unnecessarily restricts the extent to which energy can move back and forth between all elements in an interdependent whole.

The Distinction between Ordinary
and Extraordinary Energy

The most important distinction within the practices of energy, emphasized in virtually all classical texts, is that between mundane or ordinary practices of energy on one side and their perfected forms on the other. This is the same internal distinction that we find in all six of the perfections. It separates ordinary practice predicated upon common modes of self-understanding from extraordinary practice taken to the level of "perfection."

As the classic Mahayana texts describe it, the mundane practice of energy is hardly "ordinary"; indeed, it is admirable in virtually every . The bodhisattva at this level meditates on various dimensions of getic practice—on the possible sources of this power, on ways in ch it can be put to use, on how to avoid discouragement, on ways to scend previously generated levels of energy. The bodhisattva adopts ntentional way of living that incorporates a variety of individual tices, and pursues these with a sincerity of purpose and concentration iind as well directed toward the cultivation of energy as possible. In r to generate and maintain this focus, the bodhisattva purposefully vates a desire for enlightenment and uses this desire to motivate ipline.

t first glance, this act of cultivating desire might appear to contradict a basic principle of Buddhism itself, which, as set forth in the Four Noble Truths, seeks to overcome desire as a way out of life's suffering. In spite of that contradiction, however, desire appears at this stage in a bodhisattva's career as an essential element without which no pursuit of perfection is possible. Thus, in describing the path to perfect energy, Śāntideva makes an explicit point of claiming that "one should create desire." Going further, he asserts that "The Sage has sung that desire is the root of all skillful deeds." "Desire for the good" is essential to the quest; you must want awakening in order to have any chance of getting it.[17]

In order to stress and to develop the role that desire must play for the bodhisattva, Śāntideva resorts to an innovative form of rhetoric that had very little role in the Buddhist tradition prior to this historical juncture. He writes: "One should be addicted solely to the task that one is undertaking. One should be intoxicated by that task, insatiable, like someone hankering for the pleasure and the fruit of love-play."[18] How this insatiable desire might play a legitimate role in Buddhism, against the advice of the Noble Truths and much of the early monastic tradition, is a topic we will address later in this chapter. For now it is sufficient to see how pursuit of perfection in any area is based on just such desire. Lacking a desire for enlightenment, there would be no energy for the quest.

Midway along the path, however, something happens that begins to transform the character of this desire. The bodhisattva begins to practice what we have seen in the earlier perfections as "turning over" the merit of his or her practice, dedicating the "roots of good" that would normally be his or hers alone to a larger goal. This larger goal is enlightenment conceived not as an individual possession but as a possible condition of humanity. The transformation implied in this is enormous, an endless movement from restricted boundaries of the self outward toward larger and larger matrices of interconnection. Initially however, it entails a movement from one form of self-understanding to a significantly enlarged self-conception. Instead of pursuing various practices aimed at building and developing the level and intensity of one's own energy, one pursues those practices for another aim altogether, the development of energy as such, not just in oneself but in one's environment as well.

Here the bodhisattva realizes that self-empowerment is too narrow a goal, a goal that, although beneficial at the outset, begins to stand in the way of further progress along the Buddhist path. Whereas that very merit—the good that comes to an individual from dedicated practice— was in the beginning the rationale for practice, it is now seen to have the detrimental effect of reinforcing the habit of self-confinement that Buddhist practice seeks to undermine. It is precisely the surrender of this kind of self-concern that marks the transition from the mundane quest for energy to more highly perfected forms.

But what constitutes the perfection of energy? By what signs can we recognize energetic striving at its most sublime level? Two criteria invariably appear in the *Perfection of Wisdom Sutras*. They are the emergence of selfless compassion and ironic wisdom within the practice of the perfection of energy. The first of these criteria—selfless compassion—is

noticeable in the aim of the practice, the distinction articulated in the
Vimalakīrti Sūtra between "inferior aspirations" and "lofty aspirations."[19]
When a bodhisattva honestly and accurately spells out the goal that
motivates striving, it will be either more or less focused on his or her
own accomplishments or personal spiritual attainment. The extent to
which the motivating goal looks beyond personal success and homes in
on the more exalted goal of awakening for all sentient beings is the first
sign of perfection. The "turning over" or "dedication" of merit accruing
from one's own selfless acts (*parinamāna*) is one important technique
toward this end, one intended to purify the quest for the perfection of
energy. Ārya-Śūra calls it "energy strengthened by compassion."[20]

The second criterion for perfection, and the one featured in the
Perfection of Wisdom Sutras, is ironic wisdom (*prajñā*). Wisdom is the
sixth perfection, the final stage in the hierarchy of practices, and the most
profound achievement for Buddhists. The other five practices can only
reach a level of perfection when wisdom informs them thoroughly,
altering their inner structure and deepest motivation. The difference
between the ordinary practice of energetic striving and that same practice
honed by wisdom is located in the quality of the conception of practice.
Ordinary practice "perceives a basis," that is, it operates as though the
seeker, the act of seeking, and the energy sought are each separate and
self-constituted entities. Ordinary practice "bases" itself on the naïve
thought that all things are permanently identified by their "own-being."
This "common-sense" view fails to see what wisdom enables one to see,
that there is no permanent "self-nature" separating the self from the
energy that it seeks. The *Large Sutra on Perfect Wisdom* puts it this way:

> There does not exist the own-being of all these states.... Endowed
> with this mental energy even at the time of his dying, [the Bodhisattva]
> works the weal of beings, but without apprehending them. He fulfils
> the Buddhadharmas, but does not apprehend them. He purifies the
> Buddha-field, but does not apprehend it. Endowed with this physical
> and mental energy he fulfils all the wholesome dharmas, but does not
> cling to them.... It is thus that the Bodhisattva, who courses in perfect
> wisdom and is endowed with mental energy, fulfils the perfection of
> energy even though dharmas be signless.[21]

The "irony" found at the heart of wisdom is featured in this passage.
The bodhisattva seeks something called "energy" on behalf of all

"beings," knowing all the while that this energy, the beings on behalf of whom it is sought, and the seeker him or herself are all "empty" of "own-being." They do not exist in the way that we assume they do, as independent and settled entities in the world. They exist only in an "empty" manner, that is, by way of thoroughgoing dependence on all of the factors that have brought them into existence, including the projections of the bodhisattva's own mind and the customs of language and perception of the society in which he or she lives. Nevertheless, in spite of their "emptiness"—indeed because of it—the bodhisattva sets out to strive energetically toward the most exalted goal conceivable—the liberation of all beings through wisdom and compassion.

Seeing all things wisely, as "empty" of their "own-being," the bodhisattva begins to live differently in the world. Based on the vision that this perspective enables, this new way of living absorbs energy from the surrounding world and transmits quantities of energy that can be harnessed by others. Wisdom empowers that ability, in part by offering "freedom from the ideas of pleasant and unpleasant" and from all static dichotomies that keep us isolated and closed.[22] Recognizing the contingent and ironic existence of all things, including one's "self," the bodhisattva is not overwhelmed by hardships. Although these hardships do not go away, their presence is "empty" of "own-being" and therefore open to a wide variety of conceptions and attitudes. Not bound to conventional self-understanding and not obligated to experience suffering and hardship as unbearable or insufferable, the bodhisattva attains levels of freedom, flexibility, and energy that are inconceivable in ordinary existence. It is in this light that the classic texts of Mahayana Buddhism envision the perfection of energy, and in this sense that they claim that "where there is energy, there is enlightenment."[23]

CRITICAL ASSESSMENT:
A CONTEMPORARY
PERFECTION OF ENERGY

Energy—*energeia* in its earliest Greek roots—is an ancient concept in Western thought, from Aristotle to Newton and into modern physics. But rarely if ever has it been consciously developed as an ethical term, a metaphor for how human beings ought to be. Indeed, our culture lacks a common term for energy of human spirit, for spiritedness, and this is one place where we might be able to learn from Buddhist cultures.

The role of energy in ethics can be highlighted by reflecting on ways in which we might fall short in life. There are two basic ways in which it is possible for a person to fail ethically. The most obvious of these is to act unjustly, to commit crimes against one's society and oneself, to be a negative, destructive force. But another way is to fail in the positive, failing to live constructively on behalf of oneself and others. This second failure signals a deficiency of energy, a lack of constructive striving toward something worthwhile. Failing in this sense, people may never commit a crime against others or do anything explicitly wrong; their failure consists of not generating the energy of constructive life, thus failing to live a life in keeping with their capacity.

It is easy to see how the capacity for energy of spirit might be important to the conception of the bodhisattva. Imagine a truly good person—thoughtful and compassionate in living—who in spite of that goodness lacks the vitality that significant accomplishments require. This person acts selflessly for the benefit of the community, but lacks energy. Although meaningful contributions are made, they are insubstantial and limited—local in character. By contrast, imagine the same sort of person, thoughtful, compassionate *and* overflowing with energy and the capacity for focused work. The enlightening effect of the second far overshadows the first, even though their compassion and selflessness are equal. The difference between anything done meekly and that same thing done energetically is enormous, and justifies our attention.

So how do we today picture an optimal state of human energy? What image of vitality and effort do we in fact admire in people and maintain as an ideal for our own lives? We might envision a person whose capacity for work and play is simply greater than the rest of us can muster—someone who can retain concentration over extended periods of time and through that disciplined focus accomplish a great deal. No doubt we would assume that this greater capacity is at least in part the result of training and discipline, in the same way that athletic excellence always requires effort in addition to natural gifts. The state of ideal energy should not be conceived, therefore, as an original or natural state, but rather as an achievement, the outcome of discipline and practice.

On the other hand, we might want to resist this image of ideal energy if the one who has achieved it is a joyless disciplinarian, someone who stifles all inclination and preference in order to fulfill the demands of duty. The most energetic people we know often have a sense of ease and freedom about them, sometimes making their outstanding efforts look effortless. They do not strike us as battling against their own instincts. To capture this more highly refined image, therefore, we need to envision the combination of disciplined energy and joyful release, where a well-developed capacity for delight—including delight in the achievements of others—is combined with a strength and confidence that do not arise out of self-centered focus but from some more expansive source.

Just as the *Perfection of Wisdom Sutras* have done, it is natural for us to divide our image of human energy into two kinds—physical, bodily energy and energy of mind and spirit—even as we understand more and more about the interdependence of these two. The ideals of physical energy are embodied for us in the great athletes of our time, from the sprinter to the endurance runner, from the dancer to the mountaineer. In each of these models, pleasure is found in bodily existence, joy in physical movement and exertion. We also see in great athletes a grace and freedom of movement that the rest of us simply do not achieve; these people appear somehow to be more at home in the physical world than we are.

Although we can understand how important mental energy might be, it is more difficult to articulate in a single image. Certainly we would imagine the paradigm of a mentally energetic person as fully awake, attentive, sensitive, and alert. If we were open to the world and interested in it, our mental energy would enable us to be observant and receptive. The receptivity demonstrated by a mind of this kind would not be a condition of passivity, but rather an energized attentiveness, responsive and attuned to the world, capable of both silent receptivity and articulate action. Mental vitality would also require a strong capacity for thinking—thinking that is clear and incisive in getting to the point of the current situation. Reflectively attuned, the energetic mind is propelled by active questioning and is not afraid of critical doubt. The desire to understand would overshadow most forms of reticence. Such a mind would be imaginative in pushing beyond the ordinary, as well as flexible and innovative in pursuing unconventional paths of thought. Thinking of this kind would not enclose itself in abstraction, but would enlarge its exploratory domain through openness to the world.

The successful combination of bodily and mental energy is aesthetically pleasing to observe. Highly energized people are often beautiful, especially so when their enormous energy reserves are focused on something admirable. Typically, however, energy levels come and go; they are rarely stable, and it is easy, when energies are at their peak, to make the mistake of pushing too far and too hard, thus depleting both body and mind, and setting the stage for depression and a low state of spirit. Thus, to complete our initial image of the perfection of energy, we envision a person who understands how to use personal resources to their optimum effect, how to channel energies of various kinds into a single unified effort. Correspondingly, those who most deeply understand this dimension of human life also appreciate rest and relaxation. Although surging with energy, they are not tight, caffeinated beyond the capacity for relaxed presence, but move freely between periods of concentrated absorption and open release. Like cats, they know when to let go, when and how to relax. They also understand how to turn themselves over to the complete release of laughter or meditative receptivity.

In developing this image, it is important to remind ourselves that the potential powers and capacities of human beings are not the same. Each of us is capable of our own specific form of excellence and each to our own degree of potential. The paradigmatic bodhisattvas described in sutras are simply typological images; they make available broad descriptions of overall human possibilities. The particular powers of any one individual—you or me—will be unique and must be individually sculpted. Finally, keep in mind that these qualities are rarely seen in actual embodiments that meet our most exalted expectations. We get glimpses of excellence in people around us, but only rarely do we witness someone whose levels of energy and whose skill in harnessing that energy are truly exemplary. On those occasions when we are privileged to be in the presence of one or more of these excellences, however, we have an opportunity to see human possibility in one of its most impressive forms.

Energy of the Body

The division made in Buddhist texts between physical and mental energy reflects our own assumption that energy exists in a variety of forms between the physical and the nonphysical. Although energy is not a "thing" on which we can place our hands or eyes, it does manifest itself in the most physical of ways as power. Most philosophical and religious efforts to conceptualize the essence of energy focus on the mental—energy of the spirit. We have good reasons today, however, to be attentive to all of the ways in which the physical grounds and supports the mental, and to develop this view in such a way that we question the validity of the distinction itself. This is simply to say that it is incumbent on us to focus considerable attention on the truth that we exist as human bodies, and if we seek some form of transcendence—the image of perfection—then we should consider carefully all the ways in which cultivating physical excellence will provide grounds for the achievement of excellence in other domains. Although we can imagine nonembodied beings—angels or bodhisattvas of a purely spiritual sort—that is not the way human beings have ever existed. Human ideals must therefore continually circle back to questions about our bodily form, provoking us to ask ourselves how we can most admirably take up the challenge of our physical existence.

It seems clear to us today that long-term processes of evolution have gradually given rise to the increasing complexity of our physical being. Our bodies function as they do through a variety of complex systems working in conjunction with one another—respiratory, muscular, digestive, circulatory, and nervous systems, to name just a few. These particular systems permit us to process oxygen, move through space, digest nutrients, and centralize control of our lives through conscious awareness. To live as a human being requires that these systems and others (skeletal, epidermal, glandular, and so on) function effectively and in conjunction with each other. The achievement of excellence in any domain beyond the physical is fully dependent on a high level of function in bodily systems. High levels of physical vitality make optimal mental function possible.

All processes contribute to this vitality, but it might be important to learn from Buddhists to pay particular attention to the respiratory system, the system that makes oxygen available to every part of our bodies, especially the brain, where human awareness is centralized and controlled. Here we notice the conjunction of two different perfections, the perfections of energy and meditation, because it is in the processes of meditation that we come to recognize the enhanced quantity of energy that is made available through practices of conscious breathing that are mastered in Buddhist meditation. Oxygen wakes us up in every sense, and all of us know this intuitively even if not consciously. Bringing this fact to mind and learning ways to take advantage of it is perhaps half of what there is to learn in meditation. Deeper, calmer, and more conscious breathing gives rise to deeper, calmer, more conscious life, from processes of thinking and perception through all dimensions of immediate experience.

Different cultures and different historical periods within any culture conceive of the relation between mind and body in distinct ways. Whether these conceptions are conscious or not, we can see the effects of their differing mind/body relations embedded in linguistic custom and

everyday activities. In the Axial age—the period of emergence of many of
the world's major religions and philosophical systems—a strong tendency
to separate mind and body was felt in most prominent emerging cultures.
The distinction between matter and spirit, body and mind, had far-
reaching historical repercussions. The emergence of religion and philosophy as we know them today were dependent on the ability to conceive of
the superiority of mental function over bodily function and the ability to
imagine the immortality of the individual soul. These were world-chang-
ing, historic ideas without which human culture would not be what it is
today. The emergence of these ideas in India within Buddhism and
Hinduism and in the Mediterranean world in Greek philosophy and
early Christianity provided the conceptual foundations upon which much
of the world's culture of the last two millennia would arise. It is highly
likely that significant influences on these issues flowed back and forth
between India and the Mediterranean world.

Within each culture different positions were taken, some more extreme in separating spirit and matter, and some more moderate. Early
Buddhists took what they thought to be a "middle path" between extremely ascetic separation of mind and body and earlier conceptions that
failed to make a meaningful distinction at all. From our contemporary
point of view, however, the extent to which Buddhists sought to subordi-
nate body to mind was substantial, and this fact links the early Buddhists
to the thinking of their Greek and early Christian contemporaries. All of
them looked down on their bodily existence from the perspective of the
newly emerging spirit. Nevertheless, in our own efforts to imagine an
ideal we will want to think seriously about the limitations of traditional
mind/body dualism and avoid many of the unhealthy consequences that
follow from it. We have good reasons to be aware of all the ways in which
mind and body join together in the spiritual quest, and following this
awareness, construct practices that facilitate their conjunction.

This issue comes into clear view when we consider the character of
"asceticism," religious or philosophical practices of physical discipline
aimed at the subordination of the body to the mind. Strong doctrines of
mind/body dualism tend to give rise to strong traditions of asceticism,
understood as the denial of bodily life and pleasure in order to cultivate
and enrich the spiritual life of the soul. Thus we find early Christian and
Buddhist practices aimed at the repression of all sensuality, all pleasure,
and all positive attention that might be given to the cultivation of bodily
existence. Their practices intentionally cultivated disgust and disdain for

the body. They built an ideal around insensibility, the ability not to sense or feel the world in its physical dimension. Even when we can appreciate its historical importance in the evolution of human culture, it is as difficult for us now to admire this kind of asceticism as it is to conceive of ourselves as embodied spirits seeking escape from the world of matter. These worldviews are unlikely to be persuasive in our effort to construct ideals worthy of our time. They are rapidly being replaced by evolutionary models of body/mind continuity that stress the convergence of the physical and the mental over their division.

Adopting contemporary critiques of mind and body dualism, however, opens other, nonascetic ways of conceiving of disciplines focused on the physical dimension of human existence. Indeed, our admiration of the ascetic discipline of the brilliant dancer or the well-honed athlete begins to show how the coordination of mind and body can yield forms of excellence that could not have been imagined in some previous traditions of thought. Now grounded in the unity of mind and body, ascetic or disciplinary practices focus not at all on the repression of the physical. Instead they are attuned to its mastery—its perfection.

Cultivating both mind and body helps renew our appreciation of pleasure which, because of its association with the body, had been dismissed in ascetic religions that subordinated physical existence to the life of the spirit. Reviving appreciation of pleasure on contemporary grounds makes it possible to see how both mental and physical pleasure provides an experience of freedom, a brief taste of liberation from various forms of enclosure. This possibility, however, only arises in the context of a comprehensive sense of balance and proportion. At this historical juncture, we can understand the rationale for Epicurean and Buddhist teachings of temperance and appreciate how moderation in the pursuit of pleasure is an enlightened practice. The quest for the perfection of energy requires that these teachings of well-tempered enjoyment be understood and practiced at the level of excellence. The point of a well-conceived "temperance" is not to deny bodily pleasure, but rather to enhance it by developing sensibilities that would otherwise be naïve and dull. Thoughtful moderation in every dimension, including physical and sensual pleasure, promotes greater awareness and the sense that through mindful attention to all dimensions of life we are restored and refreshed.

Early Buddhist texts sought to develop a "middle path" between intemperate indulgence and extreme ascetic denial. At neither extreme is freedom to be found because, whether in turning ourselves over to the pursuit of sensual pleasure or in puritanical disgust for it, we are still tied to an understanding of our physical existence that distorts the balanced coordination between mind and body that fluid functioning assumes. The mastery of the physical is not about enjoying less but enjoying more profoundly by means of deeper awareness in view of a wise understanding of how to coordinate different dimensions of our existence, so that each plays a role that enhances the whole.

A brilliant exercise in the cultivation of this possibility is the Buddhist teacher Thich Nhat Hanh's meditation on mindfulness in the conscious act of eating a tangerine.[24] When eating a tangerine, he teaches us, learn to pay attention. Learn to be conscious of the present moment of experience so that mind and body are not always divided. In this exercise of consciousness, Hanh teaches us to do what we mistakenly thought we did already—to actually taste our food. Instead of ignoring the experience of eating, as we almost invariably do, we can develop the capacity to experience it consciously. Tasting, as it turns out, is something we must learn to do by practicing awareness. When we do this, the sense of taste comes out of its dormant, unconscious state and fully into experience. Cultivating mindfulness in meditation is not a matter of transcending the physical but of settling down into it by connecting mental attention to bodily sensation. In a composure of mindfulness, we recognize bodily feelings that are present in spite of our inattention. Cultivating awareness of them, their role in the whole of our lives can be experienced and appreciated.

Understanding as we do how unconscious bodily experience affects and influences our conscious mind, and understanding the variety of ways in which we can improve the quality of our experience by bringing it to conscious attention, we have good reasons to seek the most effective disciplines available to us for enhancing and coordinating mind and body. Eagerness for bodily disciplines that might accompany spiritual disciplines is acutely felt today. There are very few traditional physical practices that have come down to us today as compliments to theological and philosophical disciplines of mind. For the most part, traditional practices of the spirit either exclude the physical from view or take a position that opposes spirit to body.

From India, however, we have an outstanding model for practicing the complementarity of spiritual and bodily discipline in the joining of physical yoga (*hatha*) to intellectual yoga (*jñana*) by way of meditative practices (*rāja yoga*). This coordination of practices is ideal because it gives concrete expression to the realization that all dimensions of life and all dimensions of the human quest are enhanced through the conscious cultivation of the bodily ground from which our mental and spiritual lives have evolved. The cultivation of embodied life as a self-conscious discipline is one of the great legacies that have come down to us from both Indian and Greek culture, and can be developed further through resources from all over the world that are now part of our global human inheritance.

Taking that thought seriously, we can begin to imagine a way to extend the brilliant description of the bodhisattva Vimalakīrti given in the *Vimalakīrti Sūtra*, so that it includes ideals of the body along with the mental and moral perfections. In marvelous passages describing the lay bodhisattva, Vimalakīrti is pictured as generous, moral, tolerant, energetic, meditative, and wise. The description is unusually full because it includes descriptions of his family, his occupations, his worldly activities, and his relations to people in the community. But left out altogether is any reference to his physical presence. We do not know what he looked like or how he moved. We have no image of his posture, his physical strength and stamina, his eyes, his smile. Were the movements of his body easy or forced, smooth or uneven? Was his posture erect or curved, his stamina hardy or frail? Was his voice strong or faint, musical or bland? Were his eyes clear, steady, calm, and penetrating, or timid, restrained, nervous, or self-conscious? Was he emotional, or perceptive, or humorous? How did he laugh? Did he sing, dance, run, play? We don't know how to answer these questions about Vimalakīrti because it would have never occurred to authors of classical texts to tell us. Nor do we know anything about physical existence in the lives of the Buddha, or Jesus, or Socrates, or any other figure in classical antiquity. It occurs to us now, however, that a full picture of the ideals in our minds includes these fundamental dimensions of physical existence. Imagining greatness in the sphere of energy, we need to picture a form of bodily life capable of standing along side of this ideal.

Desire in the Perfection of Energy

One place where the mental and physical dimensions of human life converge is the domain of desire. Our desires cut across the body/mind divide because they always seem to implicate both. Perhaps this is one reason why all classical religions hold desire in suspicion. In the throes of desire, we can hardly tell where matter stops and spirit begins. No traditional religion had given desire a more negative role than Buddhism. Desire was named in the

Four Noble Truths as the singular cause of suffering. Desire was precisely what was to be eliminated in enlightened life.

At this point in the development of Buddhist thought and practice, however, it is not difficult to see the limitation of this perspective. Desires, more than anything else, get us moving in life. They provide the energy for accomplishments of all kinds, including the quest for enlightenment. We can learn to desire the good, we can desire a comportment of peace and compassion, and when they are fully developed, desires can help us work for the enlightenment and health of all beings. The question before us therefore is: What is the relation between human desire and the energy that moves us? How can we conceive of desire so that we can contemplate both the problematic side of desire that early Buddhists saw so clearly and the inevitable role that desire plays in any life of excellence? Addressing this central issue while giving justice to the obvious truth of contrary views, we will come to more clearly understand what the perfection of energy ought to be.

Although reconciliation between these two positions on desire would appear to be very important to a full understanding of the perfection of energy, it is extremely difficult to find a plausible solution in traditional Buddhist texts. We can even find texts that in different sections take both contradictory positions—that desire is the fundamental problem, and that without desire you will not be able to attain enlightened wisdom—but still no systematic reconciliation between the two poles is attempted. For example, in the *Bodhicaryāvatāra*, Śāntideva claims that "when one notices that one's own mind is attracted or repelled, one should neither act nor speak, but remain like a block of wood."[25] The image of a "block of wood" was a traditional metaphor for something fully dispassionate, free of all desire. In contrast to that, however, he says in the perfection of energy chapter that "the Sage has sung that desire is the root of all skillful deeds." "Who would reject righteous desire?"[26] Similarly, the *Vimalakīrti Sūtra* can claim that Vimalakīrti resides in a state of desirelessness, while claiming that the "very nature of desire . . . is itself liberation."[27]

How should we understand this point of tension in Buddhist texts, and how should we understand the role of desire in human experience? First, it is easy to see many of the ways in which desire really does pose a problem for people, not just for those seeking Buddhist enlightenment but for anyone interested in a successful and mature life. Desires frequently cloud our vision and derail our plans. They have a tendency to become so powerful that they distort the understanding we have of ourselves and the world. When we are focused on objects of desire, we see very little else. Greed, envy, anger, and hatred are often the results of uncontrolled desire in their positive and negative forms, and on occasion each of these impedes our ability to see the truth and to alter our actions accordingly. Desires encourage us to emphasize our own needs and perspectives over others and tend to block a wider understanding of the situation in which we find ourselves.

When we understand ourselves primarily in terms of our desires, our self-understanding shrinks. I become "the one who seeks my own satisfaction," "the one who wants this or that," and little more. Unable to see beyond objects of desire, we fail to account for the larger context within which these things stand, often misunderstanding both the value of the things and who we might become in the effort to attain them. The act of grasping shrinks our vision and our character. Narrow, restricted desires can only give rise to narrow, restricted lives. Grasping for them makes it hard to recognize that who we become through our acts and our understanding is much more important than getting what we right now happen to desire. Although these desires do energize us in a certain way, their energies flow only in constricted channels, the narrow world of our habitual wants.

When the pursuit of particular desires becomes a pattern of behavior— a habit—we fall under the spell of addiction. Addictions are desires that distort our judgment, and because of that, restrict our freedom. Even though addictions foster the conditions of pain and diminishment, they demand our attention and obedience. Addictions are inevitably painful. When they are not fulfilled, they become forms of suffering that come to be experienced as desperation. Under the sway of such power, we surrender our judgment as well as concern for the harm that satisfaction of such a desire will inevitably cause. Desperate for the object of addiction, we are indifferent to who we become as a result of getting what we want.

The category of addiction need not be limited to obvious dangers such as narcotics. Even desires for what is generally good can be distorted to become damaging addictions. As we saw in the first three perfections, even the pursuit of something as worthwhile as generosity, justice, or tolerance can become a mental addiction that throws our judgment off balance and ends up having destructive effects on everyone around us. Realizing this, we see that the distinctive power of an addiction is not located in the thing craved but rather in the character of our relationship to it. Wanting something need not be destructive, but allowing it to block judgment, restrict freedom, and derail pursuit of enlightenment is. Captured by craving, energy is diminished and pursuit of the good is short-circuited.

Finally, desires encourage us to rationalize, to make excuses. When there is a conflict between a principle of long-term importance like justice or honor and desire, our desires conspire to hide the truth. When they do, we easily lose awareness of the larger and more important question at stake and end up yielding carelessly and pathetically. Distracted by desires, we are unable to attend to the justice or honor at stake, and without really "deciding," yield to desire by surrendering our purported quest for a noble goal.

Early Buddhists recognized these truths about desire and set out to enact countermeasures in the form of a meditative lifestyle that might lead beyond desire to some form of enlightened character. They practiced the thought that desires lead to suffering and that a noble life requires their eradication. That focus, however, would tend to hide from them another side of desire—the necessary role that desires would nonetheless play in their quest for awakening. What is the positive role played by desire?

Desire is the basis of motivation. It is the source of our energy. Without wanting something enough to motivate our will and energize our action, we are unlikely to pursue or get it. Imagine what it would be to eliminate all desire while still living a human life. Without desires we would be inactive and impotent. Lacking ambition, we would be without purposes and plans. Existing in so dispassionate a way that we desire nothing, we would be indifferent to any outcome; we would not care—about anything. Apathetic, that is, lacking *pathos* and passion, we would be devoid of feelings of any kind as well as the activities and spiritedness that follow from them. Although it is no doubt true that there have been a few aspirants who have understood the Buddha's enlightenment to be a state of complete desirelessness, this is not the image of the compassionate and energized bodhisattva that we are likely to imagine and admire. A richer and more complete conception of Buddhist enlightenment encompasses and elevates desire rather than rejecting it.

In this negative image, all desire is treated as an alien presence within, something that ought to be eradicated. But that idea is hard to reconcile with the traditional Buddhist concept of the components of the self, one of which is the will, intention, or, in other words, desire. What we want or will at any point in our lives—what we desire—plays a significant role in defining who we are. In this Buddhist picture of the self, five interdependent components (*skandha*s)—all in the process of change—define who we are at any moment. Since one of these components is what we will or want in life, this element of the self becomes a significant determinant in constructing our identity. And if the element of will is a fundamental and necessary component of what we are as human beings, then spiritual discipline is best conceived not as the repression of the energy of desire, but rather as its reorientation. The point of ascetic discipline that works against certain desires is gradually to learn the freedom of mastery, the freedom to choose among desires and to shape them, thus avoiding both harmful desires and detrimental relations to desires such as enslavement or addiction. Discipline regulates desire, channels and cultivates it, so that what we choose—life in pursuit of excellence—is actualized over against what would have occurred had we followed the desires that originally motivated our activity.

Those skilled in practices of mindfulness and in the discipline of character know how to assess desires. They consciously evaluate and rank desires, and when some of them are out of accord with chosen purposes—a "thought of enlightenment"—they also know how to extinguish them. Keeping these points in mind, we can still say, in the spirit of traditional forms of Buddhism, that the bodhisattva's wisdom arises from having eliminated desires, as long as what we mean by that is that enlightenment is incompatible with many of our immature, uncultivated desires. Immature desires—based on a narrow self-understanding—are eliminated in the process of enlarging the sense we have of ourselves to encompass aspects of the world or ourselves previously beyond incorporation. Our very best desires, however—those honed by compassionate elevation of vision—need to be cultivated and maintained. Desire of this kind fuels our energy; it propels our most capacious vision.

Developing character, therefore, entails cultivating chosen patterns of desire. The kinds of desires that are worthy of development are those that accord with a well-conceived "thought of enlightenment." But it is not enough simply to have cultivated a "thought of enlightenment." Clarity about goals in life does not necessarily entail that we are living in accord with them, which can only happen when desires and choices actually align with a "thought of enlightenment." The "thought of enlightenment" that you form must be effective in shaping your desires. It must provide grounds for the ongoing evaluation of desires, making it possible to consider and decide which desires among those that come to mind coincide with who you would hope to be. When there is accord between our ideals and our desires, we act with our inclinations rather than against them, and this is the freedom of "effortless action" that is valorized in traditional Buddhist texts.

The Energies of Emotion

Related to the issue of desire in the perfection of energy are the emotions. To what extent and in what ways do the emotions contribute to and detract from a life oriented to enlightened ideals? Early Buddhist answers to this question tended to show a strong distrust of human emotions. Because equanimity was considered an essential characteristic of enlightenment, emotions would generally be seen as either dangerous or detrimental. Strong emotional attachment was considered to be the root of much suffering, and the cure was a form of serene detachment—equanimity—that would regard all outcomes as "equal." Certain practices of meditation were intended to provide freedom from emotional disturbances and to foster conditions for admirable detachment and dispassion. Self-mastery through meditative practice was directed at a serenity that would be free from the ravages of emotional turmoil. Emotional distance of this kind was thought to give rise to a form of wisdom that would be insulated against the damage done by poisonous passions such as hatred, anger, grief, and fear.

These early Buddhist concerns about the emotions are certainly legitimate. We can be consumed by passions like anger or hatred, blinded by resentment, and diminished in a serious way by prolonged grieving. Under the sway of powerful emotions, we are subject to passionate actions that we may deeply regret. But as Buddhist thinking matured, it would become clear that not all emotions are similarly detrimental to enlightened life. Indeed, certain emotional states—for example, love and compassion, awe and wonder, joy and humor—were essential ingredients of the most admirable ideals. Although emotions can indeed blind our judgment and confuse our minds, they can also motivate our striving and stimulate energy in the pursuit of enlightenment.

In order to play this constructive role, emotions need to be shaped and cultivated; they need to be educated. Educated emotions are fundamental to depth of character, and self-conscious development is the primary means to prevent their distortion and excess. Emotional maturity of the kind we would imagine in a contemporary "thought of enlightenment" would be far less vulnerable to the extremes of destructive outbreak.

Although no human being is invulnerable, those who have given mindful attention to the development of their emotional responses will be better positioned to manage the storms of difficult situations. As we all know from our own internal experience, choosing well and acting well have many root conditions, but one of them is feeling well. When we have feelings of compassion, compassionate choices and actions are much more likely to arise than they would be otherwise. Feelings of peace tend to generate peaceful acts. Having an emotional life that is well balanced and suited to an earnest effort to live in accord with a "thought of enlightenment" is crucial.

Although any particular emotional response is involuntary—emotions just happen without our either thinking about them or choosing them—the conditions that give rise to all of our emotions are subject to meditative cultivation. Although we cannot determine how we will respond emotionally to any particular event in life, we can shape the background conditions out of which emotions arise in ways that make enlightened emotional responses much more likely to prevail. The most important of these background conditions is simply the attitude that we take toward our emotional dispositions. A constructive attitude would include honest self-knowledge, a posture open to observe and understand how we do in fact respond emotionally in life, and how these patterns of response both enable and harm us. We must want to understand our emotional life and to educate and shape it, like other dimensions of our character, as skillfully as possible. Instead of thinking of emotions in simple causal terms as beyond our control, we can begin to take responsibility for them in the same way we do other dimensions of our lives.

We know from the history of religions—as well as the history of Buddhism—that varieties of spirituality range from the passionate to the dispassionate. The most common caricature of Buddhism emphasizes the dispassionate side—the image of reclusive monks in meditative, nonviolent serenity. But there are many exceptions to that pattern, from Tantric passion to the emotional ecstasies of devotional of Pure Land Buddhism to Vietnamese, Tibetan, or Burmese monks in political rebellion. There is no good reason to narrow this range of salutary emotions by recommending that a contemporary account of the six perfections would best entail one specific form of emotional life. It is not difficult to imagine enlightened bodhisattvas at both extremes of the range of emotions as well as in the middle. But it is clear enough that, however conceived, emotions are an important part of life and that the attempt to delete them altogether is as mistaken as any effort to get out of the life you have been given. Both insight and active striving are integrally connected to human passion.

Once we realize this point, there is no reason to conceive of enlightening practice as devoid of enjoyment—the experience of joy in the midst of daily activities. There is no point in maintaining a traditionally dour caricature of enlightenment. Can we imagine an enlightened life in which the practitioner does not enjoy the practices in which he or she is engaged? A practice in which he or she forever struggles against the grain of emotional inclinations? Can we imagine an ideal life that is devoid of joy and ecstatic release? It is unlikely that we can or will. Recognizing that desire and emotion are essential components of life, it will become obvious that striving for their perfection rather than their eradication is the wiser and more comprehensive image of enlightenment.

Human Agency and the Unity of Will

Energy of spirit requires that we be moved by a "thought of enlightenment"—that is, by goals, values, and ideals. But this "thought" will have motivational power only if we continually cultivate it and keep it in mind. Attention, concentration, and mindfulness are therefore essential features of the practice of creative ideals. The link between energy and attention is vital. When our mind wanders aimlessly, our energies are scattered and unfocused. As it turns out, having ideals and goals is just as important as attaining them, because it is the activity of movement and striving that keeps us awake and alive.

Thinking and willing a "thought of enlightenment" entails much more than maintaining a general thought. If I seek enlightenment, I must understand what it is that I seek. This understanding will include numerous levels of specificity. It will not be enough to know that I strive to become generous, moral, tolerant, energetic, meditative, and wise because, in each case, I need to understand what that effort would mean. And beyond the many levels of understanding contained within each "perfection," I must have a working knowledge in great detail about the life domains in which I will practice these ideals. Will I cultivate generosity primarily in my family, at work, by volunteering in the public schools, working in the free medical clinic, by direct political involvement, in organizations of international cooperation, or what? I dissipate the quality of any generosity of spirit I can manage and distort its effects if I do not have a sophisticated conception of what I am doing and why. Focus of attention and energy of engagement are required from the most general "thought of enlightenment" right down to the most basic level of specificity in the midst of my life. To be effective, a "thought of enlightenment" must truthfully become many hundreds of thoughts.

There are many risks involved in this enterprise, of course. We can easily be wrong about what it is that we ought to be doing and how we ought to go about it. Finite beings are always vulnerable in this way. We must choose according to our own gifts and inclinations, and having chosen, restrain and limit other alternatives. Giving ourselves wholeheartedly to one set of choices, we turn away from others—occupations, lovers, hobbies, charities, practices, ideals—and it may turn out that our choices were not the best available to us, that they were out of balance or not sufficiently comprehensive. That thought is always unnerving, even when we do not entertain it consciously.

We all have the experience of realizing that we have chosen badly or weakly, or that we failed to choose at all. How we respond to that realization is crucial. Simply ignoring this realization, we risk wasting our time or our lives. Pulling back from it in despair, resentment, or self-pity, we fall into another means of dissipating our lives. Refusing to take the risk of possible failure by opting for resignation or disengagement from life, we make it certain that failure will be our fate. Understanding these modes of failure, tendencies we all recognize in our own experience, we realize that the risk we all face is best addressed by ongoing critical engagement with a "thought of enlightenment." "Critical" here means honest, disciplined assessment of where we are right now in relation to current possibilities. These are always changing, and if we are not honing and evaluating current conditions, we stand in greater risk than we would otherwise.

Energy or spiritedness in life will be dissipated or left uncultivated if the ideals that comprise a "thought of enlightenment" are not cultivated. We can imagine lives that show two different weaknesses. First is that of someone who appears to have no ideals, no "thought of enlightenment" in relation to which energy can be generated. Such a person does have desires, but they are desires that have not been consciously chosen. This person has not identified with particular desires and intentions, and therefore follows desires that are not truly his or her own. In that state of mind, desires arise from whatever conditions happen to prevail, and the one who has them lacks autonomy and control over them. Desires of this sort just happen and, lacking reasons for acting one way rather than another, the person we are describing simply follows their lead. Few human beings live this way in the extreme, but many, if not most of us, fit this description to some extent.

The second weakness is simply weakness of will. In this situation, someone does have ideals and an image of the admirable form of life to which they aspire, but repeated failure to live in accordance with these guiding principles undermines the extent to which this weak "thought of enlightenment" can be effective in generating the energy to live this way. Such a person lacks resolve, and finds it difficult to generate the discipline of mind to stay on course. Although this person does identify with a set of commitments, that identity is so weak that desires lack the guidance and force that would bring them into accord with his or her ideals. Everyone, no matter how strong of character, fails on occasion to act in harmony with higher ideals. But "occasional failures" and "regular lapses" mark the difference between those who experience temporary setbacks and those who regularly default on the integrity of their life. Ārya-Śūra's text on the perfections refers to this state as a consequence of a "weak vow," a commitment that is ambivalent and half-hearted.[28]

To live wholeheartedly, by contrast, is to live a life of integrity, the unity of will through which choices, acts, and energies are integrated around a "thought of enlightenment." When we are unified in this way, we act in accord with ourselves rather than at odds with ourselves. Living wholeheartedly, the feelings and energies that are signified by the "heart" are joined in harmony with the mind and will, such that what we desire aligns with our largest vision of the good. This condition, as we all know from occasional experiences of it, gives rise to an ecstatic form of freedom, a liberation from destructive forces of self-contradiction. Full identification with decisions generates the freedom of maximal energy. When in this state of accord, we are free to be who we have decided to be and not forced to be otherwise. Although this freedom is a result of binding ourselves to a vision of the good, it is *our* vision, the one that we have chosen and continually hone. Only in this freedom do we experience something like the "adroit yet effortless action" that Buddhist texts valorize. Action is "effortless" when it is precisely what we desire.

Intention (*cetana*) or the will was a central concept throughout the history of Buddhist thought and language. Breaking the self down into fundamental components, the seat of intentional action was designated one of five basic elements of personhood—body/physical sensation, feeling, conception, intention or will, and self-consciousness. In the age of modernity, "the will" became central to what we mean by a person. To be a person requires a certain form of self-understanding, an understanding in which we consider ourselves to the primary source of our own decisions and actions. An act that we will is one for which we are the primary agent, one for which we assume responsibility. Gathered together, acts for which we are primarily responsible make up our personal history, the narrative of our lives that demonstrates what kind and degree of coherence holds us in unity. What we call "the will" is thus the basis of agency and the grounds for personal integrity.

Due to this importance in modern culture worldwide, the concept of the will is susceptible to reification, as though "the will" were an identifiable organ like the heart or brain. Buddhist and current intellectual practices of antiessentialism help warn us about objectifying the will in this way. Taking these perspectives seriously, we can nevertheless make use of the concept of the will to help understand the motivational dimension of our characters. Making provisional use of the concept "will" need not mandate the notion of a substantial stage director named "the self." Selves are simply the coordination of motives, feelings, thoughts, bodies, and moments of self-awareness that have come together in this way at this time. Nothing more permanent or independent need be implied. Aligning our thoughts on the will with these limitations, we can begin to see all of the ways that energies rise and fall in relation to the kinds of motivational forces operative in our lives, and then begin to cultivate them.

Courage and the Perfection of Energy

The capacity to face fear and the situations in life that evoke it is courage, and courage is a fundamental component of the Buddhist perfection of energy. In fact, courage has been one translation of *vīrya pāramitā* occasionally chosen for Buddhist texts in English, because courage is among the most prominent manifestations of energy observed in the bodhisattva. Buddhist sutras regularly valorize courage as a potent antidote to spiritual weakness. Courage is a strength of character developed through arduous spiritual exercise; it is the capacity to risk one's current security for the purpose of something greater, the capacity to put oneself on the line even in face of humiliation or danger to oneself.

Although the image of the bodhisattva projected by Mahayana sutras sometimes portrays this courageous person as untouched by fear—someone experiencing no fear whatsoever—it is probably both more accurate and more helpful to real human lives to imagine the bodhisattva facing fear rather than not experiencing it at all. The perfection of energy in the form of courage enables the confrontation with situations in life that evoke fear; it offers the power to stand one's ground and to remain there even in the face of disaster. The absence of fear, by contrast, can only be imagined in a transhuman state. As long as human beings are exposed to risk and uncertainty, with something real to lose, fear will be a part of human experience.

Risk is an essential component to life as we know it. A life that is not open to uncontrollable elements in the world and therefore not subject to fear would be a divine life, the life of a god, not that of a human being. Imagining human life in the form of an ideal—the perfections—we should continue to envision ourselves exposed to the world rather than sealed off from it in divine protection. Only under those circumstances do we face the structural element of finitude that is the basis of human existence. Thus, confrontation of fear rather than its absence is the admirable human ideal that we ought to imagine in the bodhisattva and seek in ourselves, and this is the image that best fits the "perfection of energy." Meditating on and identifying with admirable models of courage, we weave their possibilities into our character.

Courage takes a variety of forms, depending on the kind of threat one faces. Three overall forms of courage are relevant to our efforts to understand the perfection of energy: (1) courage in response to a threat of injury or death; (2) courage in the face of despair and loss of purpose; and (3) courage as an everyday act of overcoming timidity and fearfulness in life. Cultivating courage, we develop the energy to stand and face challenges of these three kinds.

The first kind of courage that comes to our attention is that through which great danger is faced—the subject matter of heroic stories from all over the world. In Buddhism, the paradigmatic story about fear is the Buddha's own confrontation with Mara, the Indian mythic image of embodied evil. This traditional legend stands at the climax of the Buddha's quest for enlightenment. Meditating under the bodhi tree, the bodhisattva was approaching the moment of liberation. Sensing this danger to his regime of suffering, Mara dispatched an army of fierce demons to frighten the bodhisattva out of his concentration. Slicing down through the sky, vicious creatures whirled their weapons and threatened the meditating saint. In response, the Buddha maintains his composure in meditation, mind unflinching. The basis of his ability to overcome fear is the liberated understanding that stands as the grounds of the Buddhist tradition. The Buddha sees the "true nature of all things," including himself, and this vision undermines the shortsightedness that gives rise to uncontrollable fear. At that point, the Buddha sees beyond life and death, so the threat of death, although very real, does not hold the power over him that it does the rest of us.

This story features a dimension of courage that derives from a comprehensive understanding that subsumes the human dimension by placing it in an even larger context. On this point, it is interesting to note that in Aristotle's account, courage is the ability to control one's fear by means of attention to an ideal more important than the issue of one's own life or death. This is important. The courageous person is not fearless—that would simply be a lack of perception or understanding. Instead, courage is the ability to be fearful in proportion to the actual danger that exists, while still being able to overcome it through the depth of one's character and commitment to higher ideals.

Facing situations of true fear, a great deal is revealed to ourselves and others about who we are. There is no hiding from this revelation of oneself in extreme life situations, and what is revealed is more than anything else the kinds of self-cultivation through which we have become who we are. Courageous energy, the capacity of strength to move forward and to confront struggle and suffering, is developed through processes of strengthening that are in certain ways analogous to physical strengthening. Physical exercise is a training of body and mind, a way of voluntarily undergoing some degree of pain in order to raise one's capacities to a higher level. It requires concentration of will and a focus of purpose. Similarly, training in the perfection of energy intensifies concentration and spiritualizes desire by altering its focus and orientation. More than anything else, it requires the practices and accomplishments made available in the fifth and sixth perfections, meditation and wisdom. Practicing awareness of choice, practicing imaginative variation on the ordinary, we sculpt into ourselves greater capacity for energetic courage. Only through practices of concentration and imagination are we able to envision ourselves in the transformed mode that the perfection of energy makes possible. Lacking intentional effort, courage and energy of mind remain as underdeveloped as muscles that have not been flexed and used.

Courage as the ability to face danger steadfastly is the form best known to us. We hear and read tales of it almost daily—valiant firefighters facing an inferno, brave parents risking their lives for their children, athletes "playing through" an injury in order not to abandon their teammates, and much more. Although this dimension of courage is important, a second form of courage is even more vital to the perfection of energy.

Distinct from the capacity to confront life-threatening situations, a second form of courage is the capacity to avoid the depths of despair when circumstances appear to offer little hope. The waning of energy in life is something experienced by everyone, often alternating in patterns of highs and lows. But there are times in almost everyone's life when the disappearance of energy is momentous, when a turning point in our existence is reached from which we may or may not manage to recover ourselves. At these crucial junctures, despair—the sense of being without hope—is a real possibility, as well as a distinct temptation. Having experienced loss of many kinds, having failed to do or have what we had hoped, we are tempted to surrender altogether, refusing to be open to new chances and refusing to allow this to matter. Despair is the disappearance or surrender of hope, the release of all desire directed at the good in life, and functions psychologically to protect us from the possibility of further pain and more failure. In the twentieth century, versions of this same experience have come to be called "depression," a motionless urge for seclusion, invulnerability, and closure.

The possible causes for the disappearance of life's energy are numerous, sometimes monumental and sometimes seemingly insignificant, sometimes mostly the result of our own careless choices and sometimes attributable to forces far beyond our control: a major injury, a sudden loss of health, chronic pain, the loss of someone on whom we depend, or a failure just beyond what we can bear, given our capacity and what we have already endured. The possibilities are obviously endless, and all of us have experienced at least some of these. The crossroads to which these events may bring us put us to the ultimate question: Can we gather the strength and energy to revitalize our lives, to continue energetically in life or, discovering the pointlessness of the particular quest we were on, to make a new beginning?

There are times when we can see that under the pressure of these circumstances, some people fall into despair and lose the capacity to get out of it. Suffering at this threshold, they find themselves unable to withstand the pain of a new beginning, opting instead for unconscious strategies of self-protection. We all know the fear of being wounded, but when pushed to this extremity, we find ourselves willing to give up altogether rather than face it again. Mahayana sutras refer to people undergoing this extreme experience as "those intimidated by fear of the world," those "terrified by fear of life."²⁹ Under certain circumstances, this fear can be so overwhelming that we are tempted to concentrate our minds on the loss suffered, to focus over and over on possibilities now beyond our reach, and to cultivate and harbor injury or resentment over our losses. Under the power of these temptations, a new start is extremely difficult to make, often impossible because the mode of self-understanding necessary to get out of it has been undermined—the capacity to continue to think of ourselves as free agents capable of choosing.

   To someone in this situation—terrified, in despair, and depleted of sufficient energy to do anything about it—it is not helpful to recommend the practices enjoined in the perfection of energy. These practices, as we have seen, are training for someone already well endowed with the capacity for energetic striving; it is training intended to prevent the occurrence of extreme despair by providing both purpose and the energy to stay with it. Energy to engage in practice, not to mention motivation and purpose, is precisely what those in terror and despair lack. In such a predicament, Mahayana sutras often recommend devotional exercises— prayer, chanting, and ritual. Here is how it is put in the *Vimalakīrti Sūtra*, a text that is otherwise entirely focused on practice and conception at the level of the most discerning bodhisattvas. Manjusri, the bodhisattva of wisdom, poses a question to Vimalakīrti, the sutra's most exemplary image of wisdom:

> Manjusri: To what should one resort when terrified by fear of life?
> Vimalakīrti: Manjusri, a Bodhisattva who is terrified by fear of life should resort to the magnanimity of the Buddha.³⁰

   The magnanimity of the Buddha is the Buddhist image of compassion and grace. In situations where we simply lack the power to pull ourselves up out of a lifeless despair, only "outside" help remains. "Outside help" would include theistic grace, medical and psychological assistance, the kindness and concern of family and friends, and more. The fundamental teachings of Mahayana Buddhism preclude conceiving of these as truly "outside," however. "No-self" means simply that the lines separating inside from outside are porous, temporary, and always open to erasure by way of the confluence of community interaction. When one person is saved or revived through the compassionate agency of others, the community heals itself.

A third kind of courage is perhaps most important to the perfection of energy because it stands at the basis of the first two. All of us, to the extent that we are alive and active, manifest this type of courage to some degree. This is a courage that enables us to overcome pervasive but unconscious fear in everyday life. No matter how confident and brave we are, no matter how privileged and well-off, well-being in our lives is never fully assured. We are all vulnerable; we all face risk. Awareness of this truth about our finitude is never far from the surface of our minds. We all sense the dangers we face, not just the dangers of accident and disease but also those of embarrassment, humiliation, loss, and failure. Some of us are more vulnerable to this basic fear than others, and we can see this difference in the various ways we address our lives.

The difference is evident if we look at the extent to which we pull back from life in fear or expectation of harm or press ahead with energy and courage. Some of us respond to the world as though it is a profoundly dangerous environment. In hypersensitivity, we perceive the reality around us as deeply fraught and inevitably harmful. In such a life situation, we become habituated to fear and the presence of danger, and the long-term effects of this perceptual habit are debilitating. Although only a few are paralyzed by the perception of harm, all of us allow ourselves to pull back from life in proportion to our perception of the threat. To some extent all of us numb our minds to the sting of this potential pain, but often the effect of this is increasing inability to take risks, to be innovative, to feel deeply, to think autonomously. Fear in daily life can render us more or less passive even when we avoid full paralysis.

There are religious forms of this retreat in life that a contemporary perfection of energy would strive to avoid. They become manifest in a contrived humility, a humility that derives from fear and is therefore distorted by its cause. Religious passivity in the forms of patience and tolerance are also common forms that this failure of energy can take. Fear is not a worthy source for any of these virtues, even when it is disguised as the admirable effort to extinguish egocentricity. The ideal of the perfection of energy would lead us in the opposite direction, where humility, patience, and tolerance are generated from sources of power like insight, understanding, and deep compassion. In this setting, courage is the capacity of body and mind not to allow the fear that we all face to hold

sway over our thoughts, emotions, desires, and activities. It is the everyday courage to expand and change, to feel joy, to experience beauty, and to
love both the world and our own existence in it in spite of all the ways that
our lives are endangered.

When we are attentive to these forgoing examples, we can see how
courage is more than a rare capacity for self-assertive daring and bravery
that emerges in occasional crises. We recognize courage as an ingredient
in all of our personal ideals at every level and in all of the Buddhist
"perfections." Authentic generosity, morality, and tolerance all presup-
pose some element of courageous freedom. Moreover, it is important to
see that in its Buddhist forms courage is the effect of wisdom and
compassion, the result of having moved beyond conventional self-interest
to get a glimpse of a goal that is worthy of the possibility of substantial
self-loss. Acts of courage, as we learned from Aristotle, are characterized
by a willingness to set aside the interests and concerns of the individual
self in deference to something greater, something that clearly transcends
the self.

No matter how daring, a sacrifice made for the sake of personal
advantage is typically not considered courageous. The courageous participate in something beyond themselves, something of greater worth for
which they offer their sacrifice, whether this "greater" is a principle like
truth or justice or one's family or one's community. In choosing to risk
their own personal well-being, however, courageous people are elevated
instead of diminished, ennobled rather than demeaned—no matter what
the loss—and this paradoxical turn of events is at the heart of the perfection
of energy. Courage presupposes some level of selflessness, a generosity of
spirit that is self-effacing in view of what is greater than the self.

An authentic act of courage includes within it some degree of submis-
sion to the possibility of suffering. Courage is the capacity to face risk, and
what we risk overall in an act of courage is suffering. Hoping to be
spared, hoping that we might be immune to suffering, we dodge the
recognition that what matters most in life is the quality of the confrontation and who we become as a result of it. Everyone, of course, hopes for
and focuses on success, a good outcome. But only the one who has trained
in courage can set that concern to the side in order to concentrate on the
more encompassing good that is always sought through the integrity of
courageous confrontation.

Something like faith or trust is implied in every act of courage and, in
some sense, courage must be grounded there. Faith or trust of this kind is

not a simple optimism, the assumption or hope that things will turn out
well. Nor is it a sense that we deserve to have things go well. Things may
go badly, and there are no cosmic forces assuring us otherwise. But it is
faith or trust that empowers us to use that realization in the process of
generating energy. Part of this power is what psychologists have called
"basic trust," the sense, developed early in childhood, that risks can be
taken and that overall well-being is at least possible. This kind of trust is
initially more a given than a conscious achievement. To a great extent it is
either given to you by your parents through genetics and environmental
conditions or it is not, and you will either give it to your children or you
will not. When we either receive it or do not, we are too young and too far
from self-conscious agency to do anything about it.

Once we are aware of the potent reality of trust, however, there is an
important dimension of it that can usefully be cultivated, and the degree
to which we are able to be courageous in life is fully dependent on success
in this venture. Lacking a deep sense of trust, we are subject to debilitating fear or disengaged alienation, both of which undermine anyone's
ability to live well. Cultivating trust, we acknowledge and address our
lack of control, all the ways in which our agency is limited and at times
completely overshadowed by the magnitude of the reality surrounding us.
Trust of this kind enables us to accept that truth. It places us in a position
to move confidently in that space of inevitable uncertainty toward goals
that we ourselves have chosen.

Larger Spheres of Energy

Finally, it is incumbent upon any Buddhist interpretation of the perfection of energy to recognize the narrow scope of these reflections. For
energy is, of course, not just a human phenomenon. Seen from a broader
and more comprehensive perspective, energy far transcends the human
sphere as the essential element in all things. If our reflections here focus
narrowly and self-servingly on how human beings might maximize their
powers in the pursuit of collective awakening, it must be worthwhile in
conclusion to step back from that limitation to notice that the energy that
channels through us is the same energy that races through all atomic
particles and that gave rise to the universe in the first place.

It seems clear that if there were a Buddhist metaphysics conceived and
written in our time, it would be a metaphysics of energy. Metaphysics is
the philosophical effort to understand what there is, finally, in the

broadest and most all-encompassing sense. From a Buddhist point of view what that would be, finally, is not things or substances or atomic particles, but energy. Energy surges through all things, giving rise to them, sustaining them, and transforming them into something else. What remains beyond the birth and death of all things is the energy that bounds forth into new forms upon the demise of the old.

Several of the most fundamental Buddhist concepts took shape in accordance with a worldview designed along these lines. Buddhists claimed (1) that everything is change, and this flux is without beginning or end, (2) that all things arise and pass away dependent on the force of energy surging forth from other things, which themselves were similarly generated, ad infinitum, and (3) that therefore there is "no-self" or essential unchanging core to anything, since all things are temporary formations of energies that are simply passing through their current states.

No traditional metaphysical system, whether religious or philosophical, comes as close to prefiguring modern physics as the Buddhist one. Contemporary physics works out of an understanding of energy as the generator of all things. Energy is thought to take a broad range of forms—from nuclear energy, gravitational energy, electrical energy, heat energy, chemical energy, kinetic energy, elastic energy, radiant energy, to mass energy. We are told, by no less a source than Albert Einstein, that matter *is* energy—that the two are essentially interchangeable. The various theories of creation in contemporary physics all point to the energy required to give rise to the universe. The leading theory—the Big Bang—sees the cosmos resulting from a primordial explosion of energy that is still expanding into increasing complexity. Nevertheless, we are told, the amount of energy in the universe is constant. It never changes, even though the forms it takes are constantly changing. The energy of an exploding star is the same as that of a boulder tumbling down a mountain, which is the same as that stored in a carrot, released in the spin of Einstein's mind or the play of a small child.

Buddhists were, on occasion, tempted by this basic principle to move in this metaphysical direction philosophically. On two sides of the Buddhist tradition were sophisticated influences that encouraged them to do so. On one side, Brahmanical or Hindu metaphysics in India attained noteworthy success in its efforts to think through the implications of a worldview that interprets everything as a manifestation of a primordial divine energy, thereby giving full consideration to the ultimate unity of all existence. On the other side, Daoist metaphysics understood the unity and change of all reality through the concept of *qi* or *ch'i*, a primordial energy at the foundation of all things human and nonhuman. And when Buddhists took those influences seriously, they thought brilliantly along the cosmological lines of the *Avatamsaka sūtra* and the *Hua-yen* school of Buddhist metaphysics.

Nevertheless, most Buddhist thinking resisted this metaphysical line of thought, insisting instead that for human beings the most important questions had to do with human becoming rather than with other forms of it. Buddhist philosophy is astonishing in the extent that it sets metaphysics to the side and focuses intently on what it means to be a human being and how it is that we can live this life in noble ways. Thus, when energy is the topic at hand, it is human energy and the perfection of it that is foremost in Buddhist minds. And in that arena, the culminating image is of bodhisattvas overflowing with energy from sources beyond themselves, buoyant and radiant to the point that this energy passes through them and onto others who receive it energetically as the outflow of grace. It is with this image in mind that traditional Buddhist writers claimed that "where there is energy there is enlightenment."[31]

THE PERFECTION OF
MEDITATION

TRADITIONAL BUDDHIST IMAGES OF
THE PERFECTION OF MEDITATION
(DHYĀNAPĀRAMITĀ)

Thinking globally, we might want to begin this important chapter by acknowledging the debt that the world owes to India for its astonishing cultural creativity in the domain of meditation. The practice of meditation has already proven to be one of India's greatest gifts to the larger world, perhaps the greatest contribution among the many that come down to us from the vast heritage of Indian culture. Many cultures that include some version of meditation practice in their religious and philosophical repertoire have borrowed the conception behind it and the particular methods of its practice either consciously or unconsciously from Indian culture.

Today the English word "meditation" is practically synonymous with the styles of meditation that were engendered and developed in India. Meditation is the quintessential Indian religious practice, and our own images of it reflect those cultural connotations. But since "meditation" is an English word branching back through medieval Europe into classical Latin and Greek roots, it is important to recognize that the reason this word was chosen to translate and name Indian spiritual practices was that those practices bore significant similarity to Western practices. We have "meditations" from Marcus Aurelius and René Descartes, and medieval Christian monasteries taught a variety of meditative arts to innumerable practitioners over many centuries. Therefore, because there are traditions of meditation in European culture and in other cultures around the world, we will want to think broadly about meditation beyond the specifics of Buddhist practice.

Although at first glance the philosophical meditations of Marcus Aurelius or Descartes may seem fundamentally different from many of the best-known forms of Buddhist meditation, those differences may be

deceptive. Meditation in all these Western contexts was a spiritual practice, and its diverse forms were intended to alter the practitioner's vision
and way of being in the world. These practices were thought to require
the utmost in concentration and commitment and were considered to
have far-reaching spiritual implications for practitioners. Moreover, as we
will see, Buddhist philosophy was positioned within the domain of
meditation. Philosophical meditation was one of several forms that meditation could take, and certainly not the least important of these.

Even considering the central role that meditation has played in Buddhist
cultures, however, we might still be surprised to see it among a list of
personal virtues, the fifth of six perfections. Being generous, moral, patient,
energetic, or wise may seem categorically distinct from meditation. Meditation is an activity, a practice, while the others may seem more like qualities of
human character. But this contrast is deceptive, and shows the weakness in
our current understanding of meditation. To be meditative—thoughtful,
contemplative, imaginative, and calm—is to possess a set of personal qualities, traits of character that can be cultivated through meditative practices.
From Buddhist points of view, there is no structural difference between this
fifth perfection and the others. Each of the six is a characteristic or quality of
an enlightened person as well as a set of specifically designed practices meant
to engender that quality. Words for meditation in Buddhist languages
capture that complex relationship between the practices you undertake
and the effect these practices have on your character.

Besides the generic Sanskrit word *yoga*, probably the broadest and most
widely applicable word for meditation in the early Indian repertoire is
bhāvanā, which means cultivation or development, the art of bringing
something into existence and tending to its fulfillment. Meditation is thus
conceived in Buddhism as an effort to develop and cultivate certain states of
mind that are conducive to enlightenment. This effort requires a rigorous
regime of spiritual exercise—training (*śikṣā*) in mental experiences that
differ qualitatively from ordinary forms of awareness. Linguistic images
that give us a sense of how this training was conceived show a strong
tendency toward restraint and discipline. The meditator, says Ārya Śūra,
"should repeatedly harness the mind with applied mindfulness."[1] Śāntideva
adds: "the mind should be watched with all one's effort, so that, bound to the
great post of reflection on the Dharma, it does not break loose."[2]

Changing the patterns and content of one's mind in any fundamental
way was seen to require enormous strength and energy, and in this way it
makes sense that this fifth perfection—meditation—follows immediately

after the perfection of energy. These two were understood to be closely linked, neither truly possible without substantial progress in the other. Therefore Śāntideva begins his chapter on the perfection of meditation by connecting it to the just completed passages on energy: "Increasing one's energy in this way, one should stabilize the mind in meditation, since a person whose mind is distracted stands between the fangs of the defilements."[3]

Raw energy needs guidance, however, and the last two perfections were designed to provide it. Meditation and wisdom, the final two Buddhist perfections, have historically been separated from the first four as the culmination of the sequence and as the personal powers upon which the entire structure is founded. All the others point toward and lead up to meditation and wisdom, and these two guide the others along from the very beginning.

Equally revealing as a distinction between the first four perfections and the last two is that all discussion of merit that accompanies the first four perfections disappears in the context of meditation and wisdom. At these final two stages, no lure into the practices is necessary beyond rewards intrinsic to meditation and wisdom. But of these two, and among all of Buddhist virtues, meditation is the most unusual from a modern point of view, and it is often the most readily misunderstood. In an otherwise excellent early book on the Mahayana bodhisattva, Har Dayal could only begin his section on the perfection of meditation in perplexity and condescension. He writes: "Dhyāna-pāramitā. With this Perfection, we enter the realm of asceticism and abnormal psychological phenomena, and the Mahāyana now begins to be anti-social and unintelligible."[4] No doubt early modern encounters with Buddhist meditation could not help but find it "anti-social and unintelligible." In the meantime, however, grounds have been laid for a widespread and deeply appreciative understanding of this practice.

The Purpose of Meditation

Early Buddhist texts are insistent on the necessity of meditation in the quest for Buddhist enlightenment. Without this kind of intense and deliberate discipline, various forms of human diminishment were considered very likely to prevail. Early sutras name the "three poisons"— greed, aversion, and delusion—that were thought to dominate human minds. The kinds of calm, focused mentality formed in meditation were considered the most effective remedies for the "three poisons" of human life. When human greed prevails, we pull the world toward ourselves. When aversion dominates, we push the world away, and when delusion obtains, we are oblivious of our true circumstances, or hide in denial. The goal of meditative practice, therefore, is to eliminate the oppressive force of these obstructions so that the truth that is otherwise hidden from us is open to our minds. Particular meditations aimed at each of these poisonous obstructions were designed so that cures would be as appropriate as possible to the particular ailments they were meant to alleviate.

Moreover, it was through meditation that Buddhists thought it possible to understand the workings of our own minds—reflexive awareness. Knowing one's own mind through meditative introspection was considered the single most productive knowledge that anyone could hold. Only through such meditative self-awareness was it thought possible to overcome the interior mental hindrances that so often yield pervasive suffering. The "five hindrances" (nīrvarana), for example, are not external problems that we face out in the world.⁵ They are interior states of mind that obstruct the human capacity to see how things really are—sensual desire, ill-will, tiredness and laziness, elation and depression, and doubt. Buddhists claimed that the hindrances were powerful, universal forces working against human efforts to live good lives, and that only through meditation could we see ourselves clearly enough to keep them in check.

Although meditation was traditionally considered the most effective means of evading these hindrances, traditional Buddhists never assumed that just anyone in any set of circumstances would be able to avail themselves of its liberating power. There were prerequisites. Buddhists typically thought that without a basic level of moral aptitude, a certain degree of innate or conditioned mindfulness of others, and "good friends" or teachers and co-contemplatives, it was highly unlikely that anyone would undertake these difficult meditative practices, much less progress in them.⁶ Those too far under the sway of the "hindrances" and "poisons" would be both unable to admit the need for change and unable to imagine the possibilities of enlightened existence.

The Basic Division of Buddhist Meditation:
Calming and Insight

Buddhist sutras show that very early in the history of this tradition there were two different styles of meditative practice. These two styles developed alongside each other, at some point linked as two essential components of one overall strategy of spiritual practice. These two styles are "calming" (*samatha*) and insight (*vipassanā*).

The first of these is *samatha*, "calming," a meditative practice that functions to stabilize and focus the mind, while at the same time initiating a process of nurturing certain desirable mental qualities such as friendliness, compassion, and equanimity. This kind of meditation typically begins with "mindfulness in breathing" (*ānāpāna-smrti*), a central practice throughout the history of Buddhism. Engaging in these exercises, practitioners are instructed to pay close attention to the inflow and outflow of breath, sometimes counting each of these movements and preventing other thoughts and sensations from disrupting single-minded focus on respiratory processes. This simple practice—which is anything but simple once you begin to attempt it in earnest—initiates a movement toward "composure of mind" and "onepointedness of mind." Similar practices also select some other object as the focal point of attention. This is literally training in mindfulness, the ability to focus resolutely, to pay attention without allowing the mind to slip away into ordinary diversions. Ārya-Śūra calls this "silencing of human noise," which is accomplished through the "power of mindfulness."[7]

The state of high-level composure and focus achieved through calming meditation is called *samādhi* or concentration. Although most human thinking goes on without concentration at this level, Buddhists claimed that thinking characterized by wisdom is always grounded in *samādhi*. Concentration at this level generates a stillness and composure against which the "poisons" and "hindrances" of mind cannot gain ground. States of mind characterized by *samādhi* were often called *dhyānas*, spheres of meditative concentration. Four such spheres were distinguished, each one an attainment of greater purification of mind. They move from a purified form of reflection or thinking at the lowest level to nondiscursive awareness, deep mindfulness, and equanimity.

In fact, the term *dhyāna* is the word chosen to name the perfection of meditation. It is *dhyāna*, a profound state of concentration, that is to be perfected in this fifth dimension of the *pāramitās*. But the later meaning of *dhyāna*, associated as it is exclusively with calming meditation and not with insight meditation, is too narrow, and classical Mahayana authors like Śāntideva show their recognition of that fact by including the teachings of "insight meditation" under *dhyāna-pāramitā*, the perfection of meditation.

In contrast to the concentration of consciousness required of calming meditation, insight meditation (*vipassanā*) entails the cultivation of thinking, specifically those thoughts capable of giving rise to enlightened wisdom. Buddhists traditionally understood wisdom to consist in a profound realization of "the way things really are," that is, the way reality is present to the human mind when greed, aversion, and delusion no longer obstruct it. For this reason, insight meditation is structured in terms of the early Buddhist teaching of the three characteristics of existence—perhaps the most basic doctrinal statement in Buddhism about "the way things really are." These three are that existence is "impermanent," "lacking in a self or inner essence," and "unsatisfactory." In the process of this meditation, the practitioner undertakes an analytical investigation of the perceiver himself or herself and the perceived world by following meditative formulas associated with each of the three characteristics. One's life and the world are investigated in terms of their impermanence, selflessness, and suffering.

Insight meditation, therefore, was designed to follow the example and patterns of the life of the Buddha by attempting to recognize how reality is structured apart from the meditator's desires about it, and it proceeds, like the Buddha, through questioning and testing ideas in relation to real experience. The sutras articulating insight meditation techniques instruct the practitioner to "produce the thought that..." or to "view things in this way...." Contemplative meditation directs the mind to contemplate the world in ways that would slowly alter its basic orientation. Meditative thinking was taken to be a rigorous practice, not one that is brought to fruition without deep concentration and enormous energy. One Mahayana sutra has the Buddha instruct his disciple, Subhuti, that the goal of enlightened wisdom is impossible to attain if one "is unpracticed, ... dull-witted, ... not eager to learn, or unwilling to ask questions."[8] The kind of radical transformation of human consciousness imagined in Buddhist enlightenment would require a highly sophisticated practice of contemplative thinking (*vipassanā*) in conjunction with an equally developed exercise of calm nonthinking (*samatha*).

One of the most common meditative themes in Mahayana Buddhism is the bodhisattva's compassion for all beings. In his chapter on the perfection of meditation, Śāntideva undertakes a lengthy meditation on compassion through what he calls the "exchange of self and others." This meditation serves to deepen reflection on the Buddhist doctrine of "no-self" and the moral virtue of unselfishness that accompanies it. Śāntideva begins: "At first one should meditate intently on the equality of oneself and others as follows: 'All equally experience suffering and happiness. I should look after them as I do myself.'"[9] Four stanzas further he writes:

- I should dispel the suffering of others because it is suffering like my own suffering. I should help others too because of their nature as beings, which is like my own being.
- When happiness is liked by me and others equally, what is so special about me that I strive after happiness only for myself?
- When fear and suffering are disliked by me and others equally, what is so special about me that I protect myself and not the other?
- Therefore, just as I protect myself to the last against criticism, let me develop in this way an attitude of protectiveness and of generosity toward others as well.
- Therefore, in the same way that one desires to protect oneself from affliction, grief, and the like, so an attitude of protectiveness and of compassion should be practiced toward the world.
- Whoever longs to rescue quickly both himself and others should practice the supreme mystery: exchange of self and other.[10]

Then, suggesting that the reader/meditator challenge his own mind, Śāntideva writes:

- "Hey Mind, make the resolve, 'I am bound to others'! From now on you must have no other concern than the welfare of all beings."[11]

One frequently employed meditative technique to accomplish that "exchange of self and other" is a concentrated inward effort to "irradiate the entire world with a mind associated with friendliness," and the practice of imagining oneself "providing the necessary conditions" for others to engage in the Buddhist practice of the perfections themselves.[12] The connection between meditation and the possibility of far-reaching compassion for others is frequently and carefully made. In a brief reflection on the perfection of meditation, one sutra claims: "When he matures any sentient beings by meditation, he matures them by having an undisturbed mind, his mind not straying outside and having no mistake of mindfulness. By not being sidetracked though he act for a long time or speak for a long time, he protects and matures their minds. This is the Perfection of Meditation."[13]

Teachers of meditation and authors who write on it frequently assign meditation topics in accordance with their suitability to differences between people. Differences in age, gender, and in extent of experience in meditation were obviously important distinctions that had to be taken

into account. But even more basic than these was the tendency to divide
meditation teachings in accordance with different character types, on the
thought that different people have very different shortcomings, different
problems of mind that would need to be addressed by very different
contemplative methods. For example, in describing the bodhisattva as one
who is skillful in teaching according to the forms of suffering experienced
by different people, the *Large Sutra on Perfect Wisdom* says: "He encourages those who have distracted thoughts to the practice of trance,
and . . . those who course in greed he encourages to meditate on the
unlovely, those who course in hate to the practice of friendliness, and
those who course in delusion to meditate on conditioned coproduction."[14]

As the Buddhist tradition evolved, relations between the two basic
types of meditation were worked out in considerable detail. Calming
meditation came to be regarded as a necessary condition for advancement
in insight meditation, because it gathers the mind out of distraction,
teaches it the powers of concentration and focus, and enables the mind
to forgo the pleasurable distractions in which the rest of us are frequently
engaged. Similarly, insight meditation came to be regarded as a prerequisite for advancement in calming meditation, since only in reflection on
the *dharma* does the rationale for the pursuit of enlightenment
become cogent and clear. In insight meditation, the Buddhist worldview
is articulated and cultivated to the point that it becomes a part of the
mental makeup of the practitioner. Each type of meditation supports the
other and provides conditions making the other possible. Therefore, one
frequently mentioned image of the relation between these two practices is
that they are the "two wings of a bird." Only with both wings functioning
fully and simultaneously does the bird ascend into the heavens, and only
with the progressive development of both kinds of meditation will the
practitioner advance along the bodhisattva's path.

From the very beginnings of the Buddhist tradition, and even prior to
that in earlier Indian traditions, some degree of detachment from society
was thought to be a requirement for serious advancement in a meditative
life. Perhaps the primary argument for detachment from the social world
was that desire had to be overcome, and society invariably served to
develop and extend personal desires rather than to help control and
eliminate them. Śāntideva, although intently focused on the bodhisattva's
compassion for all living beginnings, nevertheless advocates temporary
and occasional withdrawal from the world in order to seek detachment
from desire. He writes: "These sensual enjoyments are the cause of

suffering here in this life through the fact that one seeks out worldly objects. One should not desire them."[15]

In spite of this rejection of "sensual enjoyment," the meditative existence Śāntideva imagines is not devoid of pleasure. Instead, pleasure is channeled through other forms of mental experience, each of which occurs in meditation. The bodhisattva is "the one who tastes the pleasure of meditation," although "the undertaking is not for the aim only of his own pleasure."[16] A higher pleasure, in other words, resides in the life of the contemplative mind that Buddhists sought. Śāntideva calls it "pleasure born from the joy of *samādhi*."[17] Similarly, when the *Large Sutra on Perfect Wisdom* asks: "How does the bodhisattva, who courses in perfect wisdom, fulfill the perfection of meditation?" The reply is: "Detached from sense desire and other evil and unwholesome dharmas he dwells as one who has entered on the first trance, which is applied and discursive thought, born of detachment, full of rapture and ease."[18]

It is interesting that many of the practices we have encountered in the early perfections were meditations that could be done in solitary isolation, even though they were often reflections on the communal and social dimensions of life. The practitioner would meditate on the act of giving, for example, on the thought that such meditation would eventually give rise to spontaneous desires for actual giving. Similarly, one would meditate on compassion even though the required setting for the meditation entailed isolation from others. Meditative work on the self was thought to require unusual conditions, and only upon those results would any significant work on behalf of others be possible.

A final topic is important in describing the traditional Buddhist understanding of meditation, that of the miraculous powers that were commonly thought to result from extensive meditation practice. The meditator who pursues these practices to the end is thought to have attained five powers (*abhijñā*): the divine eye through which the bodhisattva can see suffering beings far away as well as activities in other worlds; the divine ear through which the bodhisattva can hear calls for assistance as well as the *dharma* being preached anywhere in the universe; knowledge of other minds; remembrance of previous births; and magical powers. Unlike earlier traditions of Buddhism, Mahayana texts often encourage the use of these powers on behalf of the *dharma* and in aid of others' enlightenment. Some sutras, like the *Vimalakīrti sūtra*, imagine a bodhisattva's use of these powers in a wide range of beneficial methods for enlightening others. Bodhisattvas in this sutra take on a variety of forms in order to help suffering beings get skillful access to enlightening wisdom.

It is easy to see how these traditions of projecting magical powers onto the bodhisattvas arose—they led extraordinary lives and were therefore assumed to be capable of extraordinary achievements. If, as one Mahayana sutra puts it, "the bodhisattva approaches perfect wisdom, apperceives it, enters into it, understands it, reflects on it, examines, investigates, and develops it—with acts of mind that have abandoned all deception and deceit, all conceit, the exaltation of self, all laziness, the depreciation of others, the notion of self, the notion of a being, gain, honor, and fame, the five hindrances, envy and meanness, and all vacillation"—then we can see why such a person would be thought capable of almost anything.[19] Compared to these achievements in the domain of character, the magical powers imagined are not so impressive!

CRITICAL ASSESSMENT:
A CONTEMPORARY
PERFECTION OF MEDITATION

What we are discussing in this chapter is precisely what we are doing. We are engaged here in a mediation on meditation. In fact, this entire book has been a meditation on the six perfections, but only now do we direct our attention to what we have been doing all along. Since meditation is a mental exercise—an exercise in consciousness—we experiment in this chapter by adopting as a framework for our reflections on meditation the three most basic forms that human consciousness takes. Forms of meditation found in cultures with sophisticated traditions of contemplative practice can be usefully aligned with basic structures of human consciousness, the three levels of complexity that we can identify in the human mind. All types of meditation cultivate and focus on the development of at least one level of human mentality.

What are these levels or structures of human consciousness? We can think of human consciousness—as some modern philosophers have—as composed of three layers or levels of awareness. At the most basic level is immediate experience, direct awareness of some appearance, internal or external. We hear sounds in our environment; we see objects, movements, shades of light, colors; we smell fragrances, taste flavors, and feel the tactile character of our world. We encounter the world around us through the full variety of our senses. But we are conscious of much more than what the senses provide. We are aware of feelings of various kinds that pass by without our reflecting on them—elation, gratitude, frustration, anger. We understand the situations, stories, and relationships that surround our lives. We are host to ideas and narratives that pass consciously and semiconsciously through our minds; we entertain daydream images. We are even conscious during segments of our sleep, since dream images continue mental activity while our bodies lie dormant. Immediate experience or direct awareness is simply having some experience, any unscrutinized, unself-conscious experience.

Consciousness at this level is not a distinctly human phenomenon, of course. Animals show signs of profound degrees of awareness, sometimes with an acuity far beyond our own. Although their experience is nonlinguistic, nonconceptual, and because of that differs significantly from ours, animals are nevertheless acutely conscious. Dogs can hear sounds with far greater sensitivity than human beings can. Eagles can see the smallest movement at enormous distances. Even the most primitive creatures respond to touch, demonstrating that they are aware of contact with something beyond themselves. Every form of life maintains different kinds and qualities of consciousness, each sculpted through evolutionary processes to enhance their capacities for survival as that particular form of life. At this first level of consciousness, we include any form of unreflective and unself-conscious experience and seek to examine what it means to be meditative in relation to our most basic consciousness of the world.

A second layer of human consciousness—reflective thinking—goes beyond direct awareness. In thought we step back out of immediate awareness in order to inquire and reflect on some dimension of it. When engaged at the reflective level of consciousness, we raise questions about what we have experienced, we deliberate, and make judgments: Is this really what it appears to be; is this tool really the best one for this purpose; does this activity conflict or cohere with my moral or political convictions? By employing the mental tools of critical thinking, the reflective level of awareness enables broader and more nuanced understanding. This expansion of consciousness makes deliberate choice among alternatives possible, and its cultivation enhances our capacity to make sound decisions. Many forms of meditation work within the parameters of this level of consciousness, and part of our task will be to explore what it is to engage in them.

The third form or level of human consciousness is self-awareness, or reflexive consciousness. At this level, the mind bends back in awareness of itself. Beyond the objects of our awareness at the first level and our thinking about them at the second is the self-awareness of the one whose experience this is. Whereas the things of experience and our thoughts about them can become objects of reflection—we can get them in front of our mind's eye in order to contemplate them—the one who does this cannot be similarly objectified. This is so because every time you attempt to step back to look at yourself or your current engagement in any activity, the one who steps back to look is the one at whom you hope to look. I cannot see myself as subject—my subjectivity as such—in any direct way because I am always the one doing the seeing.

Furthermore, the more "I" understand "myself" in deeper and deeper self-awareness, the more I realize that, in Buddhist terms, there is "no self." To say that there is "no self" is not to say, absurdly, that I do not exist. It is instead to say that the more profound my self-understanding becomes, the more aware I am of the kind of existence I live. Given deep enough meditation, my existence reveals itself as impermanent and interdependent with a wide variety of other beings, all set within frameworks that are metaphysical, physical, and social. This is, of course, a crucial form of meditation in the Buddhist tradition, and we will want to explore the contemplative possibilities of this third dimension of human consciousness as carefully as possible.

These three levels of consciousness constitute the structural options of human awareness, at least so far in human evolution. In immediate experience we are aware of the world. In reflective experience, we step back out of immediacy to question or ponder this world. And in reflexive experience, we encounter or get a sense of the one whose experiences these are. Since everything we experience falls within one of these three domains of awareness, or some combination of them, it is helpful to think of meditation as developing the skills and insights associated with each of these levels.

Although there is an ascending relationship between the three—each one adding further complexity onto the basic kinds of perceptual and sensual awareness we share with animals—this does not always mean that the forms of meditation associated with each level become increasingly difficult. In fact, because at this point in human history we reside so frequently at the second, reflective level of thought and judgment, this is the form of meditation that often seems most natural to us and is often the easiest to practice. Although we are not always skillful at it, critical thinking about issues in our lives is what we do with our minds much of the time—we worry, we plan, we hope, we think, but only rarely are our minds free enough of these activities to be mindful of immediate awareness, to really see or hear anything.

By contrast to reflective practice, meditative engagement in the first level of consciousness requires a temporary suspension of thinking in order to reengage with the most basic level of experience, and this suspension is very difficult to master. We only occasionally pay "attention" to the sounds we hear during the day or to the taste of our food. Residing so frequently and so single-mindedly at another level of consciousness, we are distracted from the immediacy of experience to the point that it only occasionally becomes the focus of attention. And although the third level of awareness requires no such bracketing of our thought processes, its difficulty comes from the enormous abstraction required of anyone who hopes to get meditative perspective on the "I" who lives and works at the center of my experience. In reflexive experience, we sense the mysterious "empty space" from which both immediate experience and thinking arise.

All three levels of experience can be differentiated and understood qualitatively. That is the point of meditation. All three forms of consciousness can be cultivated to a higher level of function and insight. You can be either skillful or unskillful in your capacity to be directly aware of the world right in front of you. You can be either reflectively probing, insightful, and imaginative—or dull and unskillful in all these ways. And you can develop a profound sense of your own subjectivity and its place in the world or be largely oblivious to your own reality. The point of meditation is, first, deepening awareness at all three levels and, second, integration of functions between the levels. An adequate contemporary "thought of enlightenment" will need to take both of these challenges into consideration.

Meditation at the First Level of Consciousness:
Immediate Experience

It takes something like the practice of meditation to show us just how active and complicated our minds normally are. Throughout the day, and even much of the night while sleeping, our minds maintain a wide range of engagements, always on the move from one focal point to another: I see and hear a car drive by; the sound of a siren displaces the car in my mind; I fear trouble; I recall a troubling movie scene; I smell the ripe fruit at the fruit stand; I feel hungry; remembering the morning newspaper, I think famine; I realize that I forgot my reading glasses; I reverse course, and on and on and on throughout not just my day but my entire life, each experience asserting itself on and in relation to the others. All of these experiences are "immediate"—at the moment of their occurrence they are not mediated through reflective thought or reflexive self-awareness. They just come and go in the always moving stream of consciousness, without critical judgment or anyone in charge.

Buddhist meditation theory begins with a critique of the quality of this immediate lived experience. Although the critique is articulated at the reflective level of human thinking, what it aims at is an enhancement of the quality of prereflective immediate experience. The quality sought is undistracted mind, the mental capacity for focus and concentration. This is a state of mind that maintains its focus in the present, that does not leap from one image to another, from past to future, from inner to outer, but that can reside in profound awareness of the situation at hand. Unmeditative, we do not notice this state of distraction. We do not notice both because it's our habitual state of mind and because that is what distraction is—unawareness, a state in which we simply do not notice. Left to its own natural tempo, my mind moves rapidly from one focal point to another. I have no say in the matter and just follow the scenes as they unfold.

Recall that in classical Buddhism, the most basic form of meditation, the one best equipped to focus or concentrate the mind, is *samatha*, meditative exercises of mental "calming." In "calming meditation," Buddhist practitioners learn how to rein in the mind's frenetic activity so that calm focus and deep concentration are possible. This requires both a suspension of the activities of thinking and an exercise in mental convergence and fixity. The point of this contemplative exercise is to slow down and temporarily stop the frantic racing of the mind from one experience to another. It is a practice of silence, a stilling of the mental noise that prevents calm states of focus and steady awareness.

In many forms of Buddhism, this practice is initiated by concentrating on the respiratory process, the simple exercise of "mindfulness of breathing." Typically, we are not mindful of breathing. Although we have been breathing for as long as we have lived, we are almost never aware of it. Like digestion, the respiratory function of the body proceeds on its own without our attention. But respiration differs from digestion and other physiological systems in that we can perform it consciously; we can exert control over it. Meditation of this sort, therefore, is simply the practice of conscious breathing, whether consciousness simply pays attention to the effortlessness of customary rhythms of respiration or attempts to deepen and improve its effectiveness.

Although we can get by without being conscious of respiration, there are very good reasons to be mindful of it. Conscious breathing is a practice that has a deeply calming effect; it brings about a tranquil, relaxed attentiveness that is extraordinary. The ideal is a mental balance of relaxation and alertness, two qualities that may seem at odds with one another. Several factors make this balance possible. One is physiological. Paying attention to the depth and rhythm of air as it enters and departs from the body has the effect of supplying more oxygen to the blood stream at a more constant pace. Oxygen stimulates and awakens all the cells of a human body including, or especially, brain cells. This wakes us up, makes us alert, while at the same time evoking deep relaxation. There is a direct, physical link between quality of respiratory function and state of mind. Composure and mental clarity follow from deep rhythmic breathing.

Another factor behind the meditative balance that can be achieved between relaxation and alertness is the training in concentration that occurs in the practice of "conscious breathing." Concentration on any-thing is mentally beneficial, but when this focal point is the respiratory process at the physical center of our bodies, the effect is extraordinary. Although the metaphor of "centering" often sounds too clichéd to be useful, in this case its meaning is virtually literal. Supplying oxygen to every cell in the human body, respiration is at the very center of bodily function and its cultivation does yield that stabilizing, centralizing effect.

Buddhist *samatha* meditation includes much more than mindfulness of breathing. In every type of *samatha*, however, concentration is the goal. Some forms of this meditation take a simple object as the focal point for mental concentration and build focus up to the point where the mind can maintain its concentration on that object for long periods without waver-ing. This training in concentration is preparatory for other forms of reflective meditation that require the ability to remain attuned to a subject without letting go. Developing powers of concentration enhances capa-cities in every other area of mental endeavor, from hunting and mating to computer programming and literary composition.

Whereas this form of calming meditation entails a contraction of mind—absorption into a single mental space—another form of meditation at the level of immediate experience strives to maintain focus on the contents of consciousness without judgment or intention. This form of mindfulness meditation allows the mind to do whatever it does while attending to that process through clarity of observation. In this exercise you teach yourself to be more thoroughly conscious of whatever it is that enters your awareness—to become aware of awareness. Noticing whatever comes to mind, you practice inclusivity, allowing the mind to proceed without any disruption other than observation. Simple observation and enhanced awareness are the goals of this discipline, and the ideal is to develop the ability to realize what it is that your experience encompasses. This is a heightened sense of consciousness we ordinarily do not have, and it is transformative in several ways. For one, heightened awareness focuses the mind. The hyperactivity of ordinary states of mind slowly winds down of its own accord simply by virtue of observing its processes, and gradually concentration replaces both the frantic mental activity and attention deficit. Another effect is that we see how frenetic and distracted our minds really are, giving us resolve at the reflective level to harness this flailing energy by providing guidance and direction to the mind.

Calming types of meditation also make possible a renewed attention to bodily experience. There is a continuity of mind and body that is always in effect regardless of our lack of awareness, but meditation opens the possibility that this continuity can be consciously developed and enhanced. Meditation makes it clear to us how much influence the body has on the mind, and how significant a role the mind has to play in our physical lives. When the integration of mind and body is cultivated, there is heightened experience of both.

In India, there is a long-standing cultural practice of conjoining physical *hatha* yoga with the mental yogas of concentration and philosophy. The conjunction of these impressive practices hints at the kinds of education we might encounter in the sphere of mind/body integration. Yet all traditional religions, Indian ones included, have more than occasional tendencies to be disdainful of the body, and the challenge for contemporary thinking, Buddhist or otherwise, is to make constructive use of these realizations about mind/body integration in contemporary life. Facing this challenge will require a meditative reeducation, a conscious effort to understand all the ways in which body and mind are now conceivable in coordination and unity.

Although the idea that meditative practices strive to focus the mind on immediate experience is somewhat common, the understanding of immediate experience that is articulated here differs from the one most commonly found in modern discourse on Buddhist meditation. So it is important at this stage in the discussion to clarify. Some theorists of Buddhist meditation consider immediate experience to be fully "preconceptual," "prelinguistic," and "precultural." They claim that in meditation at the level of immediate experience practitioners penetrate through ordinary conceptual and cultural structures of mind to the "raw data" of experience untouched by cultural learning. This theory, however, has become more and more difficult to maintain in view of developments in cognitive science and the philosophy of mind, and now seems less fruitful as a way to understand meditation. By contrast, in the conception of meditation suggested here, practitioners do penetrate down beneath rational thinking and self-awareness, but not to a level beneath the functions of language and concepts in our minds. Immediate experience thus entails the immediacy of understanding. For the most part, we understand whatever we experience without having to think about it. When I see a tree, I understand immediately that I am seeing a tree. No mediation of reflective thinking is required to arrive at that understanding.

Understanding, which functions through language and concepts, is built into perception. We understand what we perceive as whatever it appears to be when it makes its appearance—we understand this sound as laughter; that visual object as a tree—without reflection. Unless there are hindrances to perception, we do not need to think about whether that is a tree or not; we just see it as what it appears to be. Immediacy, therefore, is neither prelinguistic nor preconceptual. Language and concepts are, at this stage of the development of human consciousness, built into perception by way of the immediacy of understanding.

If this sounds counterintuitive, which it may given current philosophies of meditation, just experiment. Try experiencing anything without experiencing it "as" something in particular. Try separating "raw perception" from the activity of understanding it for what it is. It does not matter whether your initial understanding turns out to be correct or not, or whether you could ever decide that or not, the fact is that understanding is always built into your experience. You experience everything as something in particular. Imagine that you experience something out in front of you as your friend's dog, her collie, Dorado. If it's a clear perception, you can't see it otherwise—it just is Dorado. But perhaps you're less sure that it's hers and you experience it simply as a collie, or lacking even that certainty, just as a dog. No matter what the level of specificity, if it is an experience at all it will be identified *as* something— as an animal, as animate and moving, as brown, as something you just saw just two minutes ago, as an illusion of mind, as a mental projection, as a completely mysterious experience.

The fact that we always experience everything *as* something shows the link between percepts and concepts. Wherever experience does not take linguistic or conceptual shape as something, then no experience has occurred. Whatever form an experience takes, concepts are there in the mind shaping the way the experience is received. At no point in the experience is it fully "prelinguistic" or "preconceptual," because these elements are inextricably woven into human experience. This does not mean that we are always engaged in rational thinking, or that there is no immediate experience. It just means that direct awareness for humans is always already linked with past experience by way of language and its conceptual structure. The process of understanding is simultaneous to perception rather than requiring an additional step of mediation.

The point of this digression is to explain why it is best to avoid thinking, as some contemporary writers do, that in meditation on immediate experience we return to a form of consciousness altogether prior to the linguistic and conceptual structure that forms the basis of human culture. In fact, meditation itself takes advantage of heightened levels of human culture, and through sophisticated techniques we cultivate all dimensions of consciousness at our disposal. Rather than moving backward through the evolution of mind in meditation, we move ahead.

Similarly, meditation on immediate experience is sometimes taught in such a way that reflective levels of consciousness are denigrated. But this orientation to the subject does not take account of the fact that many of the most important forms of Buddhist meditation are themselves reflective. When this perspective is taken, prereflective forms of meditation are emphasized, and the spontaneous, intuitive character of immediate experience is valorized as the most enlightened mode of consciousness. Although there is often a legitimate point behind claims like these, they are profoundly misleading. To see why, consider how any claim about the superiority of one mode of consciousness over others is necessarily articulated at the level of reflective thought, even where reflective thought thinks its own weaknesses. Only at the level of reflection can you compare forms of consciousness, and only in reflection can you engage in qualitative judgment about the character of immediate experience. Only in reflective thought can you see that immediate experience varies greatly depending on the kinds of reflective guidance that have shaped it. Immediate reactions can be either aggressive or peaceful, either caring or self-absorbed, greedy or generous. There can be and are enormous differences in the quality of overall orientation in life—how we react to the world "immediately" without having planned or decided anything about that particular matter.

This is the point of one of the most important forms of Buddhist *samatha* meditation, one designed around the "four immeasurables." In reflection we can see that human lives are greatly improved when they exude the qualities of "loving kindness," "compassion," "sympathetic joy," and "equanimity." Thinking this thought at the level of reflection does not in itself bring about the transformation in character that it conceives. That occurs when these four qualities are woven into one's character at the level of immediate experience so that they have become natural inclinations rather than ideal aspirations. Hence the importance of meditations at the immediate level of consciousness. Nevertheless, it is important to recognize that all meditations are conceived, designed, articulated, and carried out at the reflective level of consciousness— even when their design targets the development of immediate consciousness. So although there are many reasons to engage in meditation to cultivate sensibilities at the level of immediate consciousness, it is a serious reflective mistake to think that dwelling at that level of consciousness could ever be sufficient to lead a life of human excellence.

Reasons for getting out of obsessive critical consciousness and returning to mindfulness at the level of immediate experience are many—to cultivate enjoyment at that basic level of experience; to halt incessant activities of thinking that are unproductive and pointless; to provide the calm that always accompanies wisdom; to develop focus and concentration for sustained periods of time; and to instill enlightened habits of mind at the level of intuition and spontaneous activity. But mindfulness at the level of immediate experience is not enough precisely because that level of mindfulness depends on the kinds of cultivation that occur at the other two levels. Coordination between this and other forms of meditation is essential.

Moreover, it is not the case, as sometimes claimed by theorists of meditation, that deep meditation within immediate experience is essentially all you need to live an enlightened existence. Attaining deep levels of attention, mindfulness, and meditative concentration, some people believe, naturally gives rise to compassion and wisdom. But if we reflect on several examples to the contrary, it is easy to see how mindfulness, although very important, is not enough. Attentiveness, mindfulness, the ability to focus and not stray are very useful attributes; they make anyone significantly better at what they do. But if this is the only level of meditative development, ideal practitioners would include not just race-car drivers and poker players but also burglars and pick-pockets.

A skillful burglar has developed deep powers of concentration; he is fully attuned to all sounds, can be so quiet as to escape notice, and senses everything going on in his environment. His level of attention and mindfulness are exemplary and, just like meditators, the more he uses these skills the better they get. But nothing would persuade us that he is therefore an admirable person, much less an enlightened one. His skill of concentration is very specific, and it accompanies activities that show the otherwise perverted character of his life. Although mindfulness is one feature of character that we would certainly include in our description of meditative excellence for human beings, unless it is cultivated in relation to a larger reflective framework of ethical existence, the attained results will be correspondingly limited. The ideal bodhisattva will be maximally perceptive and always attentive. But unless, through reflective medita-tion, such a one also becomes generous, moral, tolerant, energetic, and wise, nothing more will have been achieved than the capacity to concen-trate, and that will not be enough to persuade us that a life of human excellence has been attained.

Meditation at the Second Level of Consciousness: Reflective Practice

A second way to be meditative aligns with the second, reflective level of human consciousness. At this level, meditation consists in reflective thinking, and the majority of traditional forms of meditation in Bud-dhism are located here. The difference between the first and second level is not that there are no thought processes engaged at the level of immedi-ate experience. The mind is engaged when we think that "there is a lake" or that "I'd like to buy those pastries." But there is an important differ-ence. At this first level, my mind immediately understands the object or situation it encounters. At the second level, my mind stands back from that immediacy in doubt and questioning—"Am I right that this is a lake, or is it really a bay, or just a mirage?" Or, "given my diet, the inflated price, or the workers' strike against the bakery, do I really want to buy those pastries?" Reflective experience focuses not just on the thing before us but on the complex relation between my mind and the thing. In immediate experience, subjectivity is projected into the objective world without our awareness. In reflective thought, we are aware of the projection and, by thinking critically, begin to recognize the conjunction of subjectivity with the objective world that occurs in our experience.

At the first level, I just think or do whatever comes to mind; at the second I ask myself whether I ought to think or do that. At the reflective level, we learn to think critically, questioning the way things make their appearance to our minds. At the first level, we are aware of lakes, and pastries, and desires, and so on. At the second level, we are aware of the relationships that our minds or emotions have to these things, and this step back overcomes the naïveté of immediate awareness by adding the power to question what otherwise seems self-evident. Beyond the immediate focus on objects of experience, we come to recognize that we have the power to ask ourselves whether what appears to us in immediate experience really is what it appears to be, and whether we really do want whatever it is that appears to be so desirable.

We saw that one basic form of Buddhist practice is mindfulness meditation, an attentiveness that simply observes sensations, thoughts, feelings, and images as they pass through the mind. When, going one step further, the meditator attempts to describe and classify mental experience, we enter the domain of reflective meditation. In modern philosophy, this exercise of focused subjectivity is called phenomenology, the effort to study the contents of consciousness systematically by analyzing their different appearances and the effects they have on our minds. Practitioners of Buddhist meditation have been conducting phenomenological analysis for slightly over two millennia.

In a tradition of meditative writing called Abhidharma, Buddhists honed their skills of concentration and focus to the point that they could describe the inner contents of their own minds with unsurpassed sophistication. *Dharmas*—moments of awareness—were described in detail, classified into experiential categories, and judged to be either healthy or unhealthy and therefore worthy of cultivation in a positive or negative sense. Meditators taught themselves to recognize when different forms of experience have taken hold of their minds, experiences like blame or resentment or learning or gratitude. They taught themselves to be profoundly aware of mental change and to resist the temptation simply to identify with whatever state has come to mind.

Recognizing when a particular mental state has occurred, knowing how each of these experiences differ, and understanding the effects that each has on our lives were basic dimensions of Abhidharma meditation. Reading these Buddhist meditation texts, we realize how little we know about our own mental behavior. Does any of us know whether we spend more mental time engaged with past memories or with future plans? Do we know the exact extent to which daydreams occupy our minds, what narrative structures our daydreams follow, and what effects they have on our lives? To what extent do we observe and evaluate our moods, or do we simply suffer them unconsciously? We can answer these questions only to the extent that we have ourselves engaged in reflective, phenomenological meditation. Lacking such meditative practices, we really do not know what goes on in our own minds.

The practice of mindfulness and phenomenological-style descriptions of mind formed the basis on which Buddhist ethics could develop as a conscious, meditative shaping of mental processes. We step fully onto this reflective level of meditative practice when we consider the Buddhist practice of *vipassanā*. In describing this form of Indian Buddhist meditation, we called it "contemplative thinking" because, in contrast to most *samatha* or calming kinds of meditation, *vipassanā* cultivates thinking in the service of enhanced awareness and wisdom.

In traditional Buddhism and in contemporary meditative practice, *vipassanā* meditation takes several forms. But in each case the practice entails focusing thought on an idea or a series of ideas. In one form, the particular ideas are internalized, committed to memory. In another form, the teachings are spoken to the practitioners in the midst of meditation. Very frequently, however, the ideas upon which meditation dwells are absorbed in the act of reading. In Buddhist monastic settings, reading is among the most prominent forms of meditative practice. Although somewhat different in appearance, these practices aim at roughly the same effect—they entail working an idea or set of ideas carefully through the mind with the intention of internalizing them, or coming to embody them. The advantage of internalized teaching is that no prop is needed, and focus can dwell entirely on the matter at hand. The advantage of reading is that the depth and breadth of the teachings under consideration can be significantly greater, since the limitations of memorization are not a restriction. Both are effective, and both have been practiced throughout the history of the Buddhist tradition, as well as in other traditions.

An example we examined in describing this kind of meditation in Mahayana Buddhism was Śāntideva's meditation on the Buddhist teachings of "no-self" and "compassion" called the "exchange of self and others." This meditation entails reasoning along with Śāntideva, the author of the meditation text, as he considers a series of ideas. He asks meditators to realize how all people are worthy of respect and how privileging one's own well-being over others is simply out of accord with the social reality in which we live. The text has us meditate on how much we dislike suffering, and then has us ask ourselves whether that is only true of ourselves or whether it is equally true of others. It then goes on to draw the appropriate conclusions about how we should treat the suffering of others. Meditators simply work the teachings through their minds, over and over, until their impact begins to be felt. Substitute any other Buddhist teaching or text, and the practice proceeds in essentially the same way.

Being meditative in this way is designed as a spiritual exercise in which the practitioner strives to absorb the orientation of the teachings into his or her character. This form of engagement differs from the typically modern activities of reading or thinking in that it is not a pursuit of information or knowledge. Instead, as a meditative praxis, its point is to alter and shape the character of the reader. This requires that the practitioner join the spirit of the practice through full involvement and some degree of self-abandonment. Rather than thinking of oneself as a spectator or analyst standing outside of the idea under consideration, the meditator opens himself or herself to the idea in hopes that it will take root within.

Taking a position of trust within a tradition, meditators assume the validity of the teachings at the outset and hope that through practice they will come to understand them fully. They adopt a position of belief at the outset in order eventually to develop understanding (as the Augustinian Christian formula puts it, "I believe in order that I may understand"), and they seek understanding in order to be transformed in its light. Understanding presupposes being resituated in the world in some new way, and the meditation has succeeded to the extent that the quality of one's participation in the world is transformed as a result of the meditation.

Perhaps even more important than training in ideas or thought is the role that meditation can play in shaping emotions. Many *vipassanā*-style meditations strive to cultivate particular feelings that correspond to transformations achieved in thought. Emotions function to give an over-all orientation to human experience. They attune us to the world in particular ways and encourage us to interpret events and situations in light of this orientation. This implies that emotions have cognitive signif-icance and that emotional orientation neither is nor could be separate and subsequent to rational judgment. Emotions give us a particular disposi-tion toward things by putting us in touch with some dimension of the world that we would not sense otherwise.

Thus the cognitive significance of emotions is that they direct our understanding and shape it in correspondence with a certain orientation to the world. This is not always a good thing, of course, as we know when we are angry or resentful or envious. The point of contemplative medita-tion is to give direction to emotions so that emotional inclinations are cultivated along lines that we have chosen. Enlightened emotional re-sponses do not just happen accidently. They need to be cultivated through mental disciplines in order to make their spontaneous emergence at the right time more and more likely. Buddhist meditations that focus the mind on compassion or gratitude or sympathetic joy serve to make responses of compassion, thankfulness, and joy more prominent in the mental repertoire of the practitioner and therefore more readily available to everyday experience. The hope is that over time they become a second nature, well-honed tendencies of character.

Enlightened habituation of this kind is important because the goal of meditative practice is not always to be meditating. It is, rather, to have so integrated the content of the meditation into one's being that the concepts themselves need not be conceived explicitly in every situation. In this way of imagining the meditative person, he or she is able to respond to situations in the world by way of the meditative wisdom, now embodied and instinctu-ally available, without needing to step back from every one of them in order to think critically. Spontaneity and simplicity are among the long-term goals of reflective meditation and are achieved when reflective values have become instinctual and embodied at the level of immediate experience.

PHILOSOPHICAL MEDITATION

Due primarily to our modern Western separation of philosophy from religion, it is counterintuitive for us to think that philosophy is related to meditation, which we take to be religious. Nevertheless, in the Buddhist tradition, as well as in classical and medieval European traditions, philosophy *is* meditation, and the momentum of its careful practice is thought to propel the practitioner toward "enlightenment."

Although, given Western classification schemes and the particular historical evolution of Western culture, this juxtaposition of meditation and philosophy may still seem odd, it is not difficult for us to see the logic of their union. Both "philosophy" and "meditation" are extraordinary cultural practices, activities that suspend the ordinary, everyday flow of life. In both philosophy and meditation we withdraw from the surge of ordinary, worldly experience, temporarily stepping back in order to gather ourselves, and through a transformative cultivation of the mind, to prepare ourselves to reenter ordinary life with greater perspective, vision, and efficacy. Moreover, wisdom is the primary goal of both practices. Meditation and philosophy, conceived as two forms of a larger comprehensive sphere of mental practice, have been understood in Buddhism to work in conjunction, both active in the service of human emancipation.

The "split" between "theory" and "practice" that occasionally surfaces as a vexing problem in Western cultures is only occasionally visible in Buddhist contexts. Theoretical reflection is a practice, one that is essential to the maintenance of all other practices. If you do not think about your practices and their goals in comprehensive, theoretical terms, they will remain undeveloped, unsophisticated, and, in some sense at least, ineffective. Philosophical practice is therefore conjoined with other practices and serves them by clarifying and honing their connection to life. Like other practices, theoretical thinking aims to transform daily life by bringing insight to bear on it. Of course, this is not always successful. But when it is not successful, we should understand this not so much as a deficiency inherent in theoretical practice as a sign of poorly executed practice.

Philosophical meditation is not easy to learn; it requires concentration and discipline. For this reason, Buddhists considered "calming" types of *samatha* meditation to be preparatory for reflective meditation. They assumed that insightful understanding of oneself or the world depends on the state of mind of the thinker. They saw a direct relationship between the level of reflective understanding and the interior state of the person who seeks to understand. When the mind lacks concentration, or when it is dominated by resentment, envy, anger, or greed, the ideas projected by it reflect those particular deficiencies. A mind that lacks clarity and breadth will experience a world lacking clarity and breadth.

Self-centered thought projects a cramped, self-enclosed world. Similarly, a relaxed, concentrated, and selfless mind peers through the "self" into larger dimensions of the world. Open, far-reaching vision encounters an open, far-reaching reality.

So what is philosophical meditation? Etymologically, "philosophy" is a friendship with or love of (*philos*) wisdom (*sophia*). Ideally, a philosopher is someone who cultivates profound vision or insight into reality by pursuing it without compromise. The metaphor of "vision" here implies an understanding that is comprehensive, broad, and far-reaching. One well-known modern way to think of philosophy is that its aim "is to understand how things in the broadest possible sense of the term hang together in the broadest possible sense of the term."[20] Insight into how things "hang together" is initially generated through wonder and, following that, the power of open questioning.

The open questioning of philosophy differs to some extent from the kinds of reflective meditation that Buddhist monks typically practice in *vipassanā*. How so? In *vipassanā* meditation, Buddhist practitioners reflect on the fundamental teachings of the tradition. They absorb the tradition by pondering impermanence, causation, the self, and other foundational issues identified in traditional Buddhist texts. Practices of this kind are reflective meditation, but they are not necessarily philosophical meditation. Whether they are or not has to do with the extent of "open questioning" involved in them.

In discussing *vipassanā*-style meditations on the teachings, we noted that this practice typically assumes the truth of the teachings and, through meditation on them, aims to internalize these ideas into the practitioner's character by asking how or in what ways they are true. Practitioners begin with intellectual acceptance of the teachings and hope that through meditative practice they might come to understand them at a deeper level. They follow the instructive path of the meditation text, trusting that the tradition's wisdom assures its suitability and truth. Although this trust is often well placed and the meditation that follows it is often transformative for the practitioner, this is not yet philosophical meditation.

Ideally, philosophical reflection proceeds on the principle that nothing need be assumed and that everything stands open to critical questioning. So, whereas a typical practice of *vipassanā* might meditate on the ubiquity of "impermanence," a philosophical meditation would need to ask whether that fundamental teaching of Buddhism is, in fact, true, or whether that particular way of guiding our thought about the world is misleading in some way.

Returning to our example of Śāntideva's meditation on the "equality of self and others," we can see this difference between the reflective practice of *vipassanā* and philosophical meditation from another angle. Think of the difference in practice between the many meditators who have followed the text of Śāntideva's meditation and Śāntideva's own creative act of achieving the insight behind it in the first place. In following the text and placing themselves under Śāntideva's influence, practitioners gradually learn how to understand the world in the new ways he suggests. But this learning does not necessarily involve the full force of critical questioning. Philosophical meditation is open inquiry, inquiry that is willing to depart from the tracks laid by others by submitting everything to a process of questioning that is truly one's own. This is what sutras say the Buddha did, as did every other Buddhist philosopher since then, including Śāntideva. And whenever we inquire in a thoroughgoing way and follow these questions wherever they go, we too practice philosophical meditation.

The essential requirement of this practice is that meditators engage in critical questioning. Indeed, one of the most important paragraphs in the early sutras has the Buddha disclaiming his authority as the guarantor of Buddhist truth. He says, essentially, "don't take my word for any of this; engage these issues in your own philosophical meditations and see where the process of questioning will lead you."[21] Each practitioner is invited to engage in critical thinking in order to test the truth of Buddhist ideas for himself or herself. Lacking this experimental posture, practitioners retrace the conclusions reached in previous thinking, but do not put themselves into the necessary position of testing its truth on their own. Open questioning entails reaching out beyond the given, the already understood, and probing on one's own for something beyond it. Neither the Buddha nor anyone else can do this for us.

"Critical questioning" is sometimes understood in a limited way to mean criticizing an idea, interrogating it to see what might be wrong with it. When we do this, we challenge the ideas that others champion by showing where they have gone astray. But this is far too limited a conception of critical thinking, because it leaves out the most important challenge that authentic thinking places on us. Understanding the limitations of ideas put forth by others, the challenge to us is to push beyond those ideas to an alternative conception that *does* appear to meet the ideal we find lacking in the criticized account. Having seen what is wrong with that way of understanding an issue, it is now up to us to place another way of looking at the matter on the table for critical consideration. Thus the negative task of critique is merely preparatory for the positive dimension of critical questioning in which we put our own vision up for interrogation, risking the possibility of rejection in the same way that the person before us has done. The risk, however, is not what it seems. "Being wrong" is simply another opportunity to advance meditative inquiry. Every occasion of being wrong provides hints about the direction that thought might more fruitfully take.

Philosophy as a form of Buddhist meditation does have an overarching rationale or aim. Theoretical practice is considered most worthwhile when it aims to improve the quality of life. This practical, ethical orientation in Buddhist meditative thought can already be seen in the early parable of the "poisoned arrow."[22] In this parable the Buddha poses a rhetorical question: Would the person struck by a poison arrow be well advised to pose speculative questions about the archer, his background, his motives, the quality of the shot, and so on? Or would he be best off attending to the practical question of how to deal with the situation at hand—the poison—in such a way that one's life is preserved? Similarly, questions unrelated to the quest for "awakening" were thought unwise, irrelevant to the one issue that really matters. Questions aimed at transformative vision were considered to be the essence of philosophical meditation.

One of the most important functions of philosophical meditation is that this is the practice within which the conception of the Buddhist goal is engendered, honed, and articulated, and the means through which that conception becomes a reality in one's daily life. "Conception of the goal" here means what Western philosophers have meant by the "concept of the good" and what Buddhists mean by the "thought of enlightenment." This thought, and the realization that there may be forms of life clearly superior to the one I am living, when taken in their full force, lead to the practice of meditation on ideals.

We might ask, though, how conscious a practitioner must be of these conceptual ideals achieved through philosophical meditation. Is it not possible for someone to have internalized the essential content of "an idea of the good" without having engaged in the kind of abstract philosophical practice envisioned here? Are there not, in the long history of Buddhism, accomplished and admired Buddhists who simply are not reflective thinkers? The answer to these questions is, of course, yes. It is certainly possible to live in accordance with worthy ideals without being able to articulate them conceptually. Someone may have internalized enlightened instincts in life well enough to follow them effectively without being able to render them in a discursive form. And not all forms of human excellence require reflective awareness. Nevertheless, examples of these achievements are the exception, not the norm, and the extent of the excellence they embody will always be limited by the absence of reflective skill and enhanced self-awareness.

The quality of a person's actions depends on several factors, but the most important of these is their overall conception of who they are and what they are doing. The more articulate someone can be about that conception, the more developed and precise their daily actions will be, and the more likely we would be to admire their achievement in life. The attainment of reflective depth or insight in Buddhism corresponds to the ability to see beyond the surface appearance of things and events in oneself or the world. Meditative analysis penetrates into the depth dimension of something whenever it comes to be understood in its complex movements and relationships rather than in simple isolation. The greater the depth of insight, the larger the unified vision within which something is seen. Hence the definition of philosophical meditation given earlier as the pursuit of a comprehensive understanding of how everything "hangs together."

This criterion for profundity of insight is most clearly articulated in highly evolved Mahayana meditations on "emptiness" (*śunyatā*). Meditations like these enable one to see reflectively what cannot be seen at the level of immediate experience—how it is that all things are what they are only temporarily and only in relation to all the conditions that make their particular existences possible. Such exercises are perhaps the most potent forms of reflective meditation available in our time, whether Buddhist or not. They open up the depth dimension of whatever is under consideration, whether that is the global ecosystem, world economics, or the intricacies of the human mind. Wherever this kind of contextual, historical, and transdimensional thinking is underway, reflective meditation at the second level of consciousness is in good order.

Meditation at the Third Level of Consciousness: Reflexive Awareness

A third level of human consciousness—reflexivity or self-awareness—has evolved from the resources provided by the first two. At the first level, we maintain direct and unmediated awareness of the world. At the second level, we exercise the capacity to step back out of that immediate awareness to question whether what appears immediately to the mind really is as it appears. And finally, at the third level of consciousness, we get a glimpse of the point of view from which all this takes place, the "I" whose immediate awareness and reflection this is. Meditation at this third level strives for self-awareness and self-knowledge, and traditional Buddhist meditation practice has attained impressive sophistication at this most highly refined level of consciousness.

The "self" of subjectivity is profoundly elusive, however. Whenever each of us says the word "I," we know exactly what we mean. But as soon as we attempt seriously to consider what it is that this word names, we are at a loss. Subjectivity is at once the most obvious and the most invisible phenomenon, making the ancient philosophical exhortation to "know thyself" the most difficult task.

By its very nature, the subject cannot become an object of experience or reflection in any comprehensive way precisely because it is always the one doing the experiencing and reflecting. Although the subject can consider itself retroactively—looking back to examine its character during a previous moment of experience—it cannot ever get its own here-and-now act of experience into view. Buddhists recognized this truth about subjectivity very early in their history. The fact of impermanence—our immersion in the movement of time—means that the "self" is ungraspable.

This realization constitutes the grounds upon which Buddhists articulated their distinctive theory of the self, the counterintuitive claim that in the final analysis there is no "self." This is neither a denial of subjectivity nor an avoidance of the individual's responsibility in the world. What is it that is being denied in the theoretical claim of "no-self"? If by "self" we mean a permanent center of subjectivity, something fixed, self-established and independent of the world around it, something fully in command of its own existence and knowable as such, then careful observation leads to the conclusion that there is no such entity at the heart of human subjectivity. That single realization became perhaps the most important focal point for Buddhist meditation, and the sutras challenged practitioners to examine and test its truth in introspection and philosophical analysis.

The "no-self" claim is not the end of Buddhist reflection on this matter, however. In fact, it is just the beginning. If there is no self in the sense of a permanent soul, an independent entity whose experience this is, then who am "I"? Buddhist answers differ substantially depending on by whom, when, and where the question is posed. But one early and enduring articulation attempts to divide what appears to be a unified "self" into operating divisions or functions. Human beings, they claimed, are composed of five always impermanent components that are observable most directly from within but also in some way from the outside. These are the five *skandhas*, five components that make human experience what it is. They are (1) a body whose five senses make contact with the world; (2) various feelings of approval and disapproval in response to perceptual stimulus; (3) conceptual thinking that classifies and manages perceptions and feelings; (4) volitional forces that guide our movement through particular wishes and desires; and (5) self-consciousness that holds all of these components together as a relatively unified subjectivity in the world.

Different Buddhist texts and different translations of them divide these components up in different ways. But the important point is that, from a traditional Buddhist point of view, no one element constitutes the soul or self—the one you really are. Instead, human existence is imagined as a loosely configured movement in and among these various components as they shift and change over time. Hence, from their point of view, in any substantial sense, there is no self, and no meditation was thought to be more enlightening or productive than those focused on this central point. Nevertheless, claiming that there is "no-self" in the senses named above does not eliminate the necessity to responding to the challenge to "know thyself," and that effort constitutes much of the energy of Buddhist meditation at the level of reflexive consciousness.

In Western cultures, two primary positions on the "self" are dominant today, as they have been for well over a century. The first, the older of the two, takes many forms, but today it is generally called "dualism." Whenever the self or the soul is conceived as independent and detachable from the human body, this twofold division constitutes a form of dualism. Dualist positions are not all alike, but soul theory in many forms of traditional Christianity is dualistic, as is the Cartesian mind/body theory that defined early modernity in Europe. There is also a significant structure of dualism in all religions that feature a theory of reincarnation or rebirth, including Buddhism. Although Buddhists reject the substantial, permanent "soul" in principle, many Buddhists nevertheless hold that after death they will be reborn as individuals in another life. To the extent that they imagine the new life to be "theirs," Buddhists too are dualists, since their fundamental identity, sometimes identified as consciousness, is detachable from the body and brain in which they currently reside. Not all Buddhists, traditional and modern, accept such a theory of rebirth, but many have and still do. So whereas the Christian soul is separated from the body at death to reside permanently in heaven or hell, the reborn Buddhist "soul" is imagined to be reborn in another life with yet another body/mind identity. All dualists maintain that the true self is detachable and separable from the apparent self that we see in our bodies and minds.

Contemporary scientific materialists reject traditional and modern dualism. They claim, as a handful of philosophers before them did, that human beings are material in ultimate identity and that consciousness is no more than a product of the physical brain. In this way, we are animals all the way down, with no mental or spiritual remainder. In the Darwinian theory that dominates all biosciences today, neither souls nor disembodied minds have a role to play. It is assumed that everything necessary to explain the development of human consciousness either has been or will be found within our biological material identities. Due to the success of bioscience and neuroscience in allowing us to understand dimensions of our identities that were previously unfathomable, there is strong contemporary plausibility to this view. Evolutionary theory is obviously compelling, and no current philosophical position on these matters can afford not to follow its lead at least in part.

One assumption supporting this view is that since science has been so thoroughly successful in explaining the origins and nature of the natural world, it will be just a matter of time before similar explanations will be provided for human consciousness. But this assumption may assume too much. Consciousness may require an explanation of an entirely different character from those that have been so successful in explaining the material world. It is not at all clear that methods useful to discover the principles behind other aspects of ourselves and our world will be applicable in the case of consciousness. The difficulty of these issues becomes clear when we recognize that the kinds of introspective awareness that show us consciousness are very different from the "extrospective" tools of scientific analysis. No amount of brain research has given us access to consciousness as it manifests internally to each one of us. In fact, knowing everything that we know about the brain would never lead us to posit consciousness as its product if we were not simultaneously aware of consciousness from the inside of experience. Scientists can test and analyze evidence of consciousness in many ways but can never see consciousness itself from the outside. The gap between internal and external views of consciousness is, at least so far, an unbridgeable one.

This difficulty with contemporary materialism does not, however, make dualism a better option. Consciousness does not just accidentally occupy human brains; they are inseparable. The brain is clearly the foundation of consciousness, and the latter is not currently conceivable without reference to the former. Dualism splits consciousness too radically off from the brain and fails to take into account all the ways in which the first necessarily depends on the second. Honest reflection on this issue now makes some kind of genetic relationship between the brain and consciousness look like the most plausible position, even when we do not know how or why that relationship prevails. At the same time, however, scientific humility requires that we acknowledge that the explanatory gap between the brain and the mind is enormous, and that we currently have no way to cross that divide. It may be that we must await a paradigm shift in understanding before we can begin to unravel this relationship. We just do not know. But lack of understanding on the issue of how the exterior, empirical findings of brain science are to be correlated to the inner, reflexive findings of contemplative meditation does not prevent both of these disciplines from carrying on with rigorous, worthwhile practice.

There is a reflexive dimension that is engaged whenever Buddhists take meditations on the concept of "emptiness" far enough to encompass the subjectivity of the thinker. This has long been important in the history of Buddhism, but now constitutes a significant contribution to the history of human consciousness. Here is a summary of how the "emptiness" of all things encompasses the "self" in such a way that we can get a glimpse of "the one who is right now reading this." Recall that "emptiness" can be handily defined in terms of three basic Buddhist principles—impermanence, dependent arising, and no-self. Things are "empty" of their "own-being" insofar as they are always subject to change and insofar as the change they undergo is caused and conditioned by change in other things upon which they depend. All things lack a "self," therefore—a permanent, self-caused identity that always makes them exactly what they are.

Meditation on this universal predicate—that all things are empty— eventually attains a reflexive dimension when it returns to encompass the one who predicates "emptiness"—you or me as subjects. What would it mean to understand through prolonged meditation that "I" am "empty?" There are two important dimensions of realization that emerge from this meditation, one concerning the universal "emptiness" of all selves and another focused entirely on "the one right now thinking"—the here and now act of subjectivity.

The first of these entails the realization that what is true of all other things—that they are "empty" of their "own-being"—is also true of me. Like all other things, the being that "I" am is interdependently embedded within a physical world, a social world, a cultural world, a linguistic world, and so on. I am who I am only in relation to these larger encompassing spheres. All of the beings that I assume to be other than myself are actually at this very moment making me exactly who I am—the air I breathe, the food I eat, the tools I handle, the political and economic worlds in which I live, the neighbors and coworkers with whom I speak, the loved ones with whom I partially identify, and much more. Meditating on that thought of fundamental interconnection, I begin to see myself more clearly. The more I see these truths at the basis of my own subjectivity, the more I realize the reflexive dimension of "emptiness."

The reflexive dimension of "emptiness" helps us see the impersonal background to the wide variety of feelings and thoughts that constitute personal experience. There is a universal and a personal dimension to this realization. When I realize that all human beings are interdependent with the worlds around them, I understand something that is universally true. When this realization focuses on the specific elements of dependence that right now shape my own thinking and feeling, then I attain the full extent of the reflexive dimension. Work any example through, and you can see the connection and the difference between these two dimensions. Universally I realize that the food a person eats affects who they become, or that the kind of job someone spends their time performing has a significant bearing on who they are as human subjects. To carry this mediation through reflexively, however, I need to make the universal particular to my own subjectivity. How is the food I have been eating or the job I have been performing right now affecting the kinds of thoughts that I am writing? What conditions in the background of my composing these words have made them possible? What conditions of weakness in my background right now prevent me from seeing truths significantly more profound than the ones I am right now entering into this computer? As I fill in the answers to these questions with concrete realizations about my here-and-now experience, I engage in reflexive meditation. You do the same when you use the same word "I" to refer to your here-and-now engagement in subjectivity. In each case, that subjectivity becomes aware of its own "selflessness" when it considers the extent to which its "own-being" is really constructed out of relation to all of the other beings in its contextual world. That is the reflexive meaning of "emptiness."

This realization makes us profoundly aware of our embeddedness within larger worldviews, languages, cultural contexts, and historical epochs. The words I right now write, for better or worse, have been conditioned and made possible by the fact that I was raised in this particular language, at this particular moment in its evolution, as honed by this specific set of educational institutions. Had any of those been different, so would these words. It is not so much that these are not therefore *my* words, it is rather that my words are the words of these particular conditioning contexts. Well-attuned historians, looking back at this book one or two hundred years from now, will be able to indentify the intellectual contexts from which this book emerged. They will not mistake what has been written here for the thinking of eighteenth-century England or nineteenth-century New England. The ideas conceived in this book became possible only recently and only in this setting, for better or worse, and that is also true of your act of subjectivity in reading this book right now, regardless of whether you approve or disapprove of what you are reading.

Although we might be tempted to conclude from these realizations that freedom has thereby been eliminated, in fact, the opposite is true. "Emptiness" is the meditation that yields freedom, whether this meditation is performed in Buddhist or non-Buddhist terms. If you do not understand how the choices you make are conditioned by your background and the context within which you face them, you will have very little freedom in relation to these conditioning factors. If you do not understand that your political views are largely a function of the particular influences that have been exerted on you from early life until now, you will have no way of seeing how other worldviews give justification to other views just as yours does for you, and therefore no way of even beginning to adjudicate between them except by naïvely assuming the truth of your own.

If you do not realize that what seems obvious to you seems that way because of structures built into your time and place and the particularities of your life, you will have very little room to imagine other ways to look at things that stretch the borders of your context and imagination. You will have no motive to wonder why what seems obvious to you does not seem obvious to others in other cultures or languages, and to wonder whether you might not be better off unconstrained by those particular boundaries of worldview. The extent to which you are limited by your setting is affected by the extent to which you understand such constraints both in general (anyone's) and in particular (yours). The way you participate in your current given worldview shapes the extent to which you will be able to see alternatives to it and be able to reach out beyond it in freedom.

"Emptiness" and similar non-Buddhist meditations on the powers of interdependence and contextuality are among the most fruitful means of generating sufficient freedom to live a creative life. Reflexively aware, we are more and more able to see and act on alternatives that would never occur to us otherwise. In reflexive meditation, we come to embrace the finitude of all acts of thinking as a way to liberate us from dogmatism and certitude. Understanding the uncertainty that is constitutive of our human mode of being, we develop the flexibility of mind necessary to be honest with ourselves about our own point of view.

It was the importance of self-knowledge that led Socrates to declare, famously, that the unexamined life was not even worth living. Although a Buddhist perspective would also attribute great importance to meditative examination of one's own life, it would also see how Socrates may have been guilty of overstatement. It is not that an unexamined, unself-aware life is not worth living. All of us have known people who without much reflection or self-consciousness nonetheless manage to lead good and relatively happy lives. The point is rather that self-knowledge makes possible an enhancement of life experience beyond what is possible without reflexive awareness. Meditative awareness of one's own motives, one's desires, and of the qualities of one's actions deepens the experience of life and sets the stage for seeing one's life as a path of self-transformation and enlargement of vision. Reflexive meditation puts the tools of self-knowledge at one's disposal and orchestrates change in patterns of living that would not have been possible otherwise.

Every level of consciousness brings with it greater and greater spheres of freedom. In immediate consciousness, we feel the freedom to move and act in the world. In reflective consciousness, we ask ourselves whether what appears to be so really is, and thereby attain powers that prevent our being fooled so often by the world at the level of immediate consciousness. At the reflexive level, we can learn who we are, how to avoid fooling ourselves, and how we might extend and enlarge ourselves in imaginative life.

Meditation and the Imagination

"Imagining" is a more important and frequently employed mental activity than we often assume. Whenever we are not focused on the here and now, our imaginations are engaged in some way. In imagination we construct images of the past and the future, because otherwise these vital dimensions of time lack presence. And since we can only be in one place at a time, mental engagement with any place other than where I am requires the imagination to perform its work of transportation.

Our joint effort in this book has been one of imagination. We have sought to imagine how the ideals stated in the Buddhist six perfections would need to be construed in order to be considered truly ideal in contemporary circumstances. We have sought to ask ourselves what our own ideal would be in each of these dimensions of life. In considering the fifth perfection—meditation—our question now comes to this: What roles might the imagination play in the mental life of a truly admirable person? What forms of imaginative life should we set before ourselves for the purposes of aspiration?

The imagination has played an important role in Buddhist meditation from the earliest stages of that tradition. In meditation, practitioners sought to imagine some state of affairs quite other than the one currently in effect. They imagined their bodies as corpses, and their anger, greed, or envy cooled by breezes of calm, selfless serenity. They imagined the character and content of the Buddha's enlightenment and tried to form images of what their own lives would look like if they pursued those ideals. As the tradition evolved into more complex forms, so did the role of imagination in meditative practice, coming to fruition in a wide variety of visualization exercises in Mahayana and Tantric practice. Many of these practices can be conceived as meditations on some aspect of the "thought of enlightenment." By dwelling on an imagined state of human perfection, practitioners have sought to weave some small degree of that perfection into their minds and characters. Exercises of the imagination were imagined to be powerful tools for human transformation.

Acts of imagination open up the mental space in which we envision possibilities, gazing beyond what is toward what could be. Attending to possibility enables us to form an image of a better world, a better community, a better self, a better anything. When we imagine, we picture something other than what currently prevails. We go beyond the actuality of here and now into what is not yet but might be. In that sense, the power of imagination is a basic condition for the possibility of human freedom. Freeing us from the dominance of the present world, the imagination opens the space of alternatives to the present. In imaginative acts, we submit "the given" to questioning by envisioning what might come to be in its place.

Although our tendency has been to regard imaginative mental capacities as secondary or less important in the overall operation of our minds, on close examination this turns out not to be true. When we are uncertain how to understand or explain something before us, we imagine how it might be, form plausible hypotheses, and then seek to confirm or falsify them. When faced with a problem, we imagine possible solutions and test them for their potential efficacy. When we need to know what to believe, we imagine plausible accounts of the issue and what might count as evidence in their favor or against them. Imagination functions in an astonishing range of human activities, from basic problem solving through the creative acts of art, music, and literature, to our own efforts to imagine ideals that are worthy of guiding our personal lives—the "thought of enlightenment." By cultivating this central, meditative capacity, we open up dimensions of our lives we were previously unable to access. Those who do this skillfully position themselves in a more experimental relation to life, a posture less susceptible to dogmatic closure and open to a wider set of possibilities.

In the process of asking ourselves how the imagination would function ideally as a form of human excellence, it is helpful to consider its deficit—what happens when life is unimaginative, when the capacity for imagination is deficient? Living in unimaginative states of mind, we hardly notice, and in that sense do not experience any lack at all. The reality we are currently living is experienced simply as "reality," and we cannot imagine it being any other way. When we encounter complex situations, fraught with dangers or fruitful possibilities, we simply do not see these complexities. The situation appears simple to us, and we proceed through it unaware of perspectives on it beyond the one that currently holds us in its grip. The consequences of life lived in oblivion are not attractive, however. Without the freedom and openness of imagination, life is severely diminished and confined.

The simple lack of imagination is one form of human diminishment, but intentional, fearful inhibition of imagination and the possibilities that it presents is another, more deadening form. Here we picture a life of avoidance and fear, a tendency to hold tight to already known desires, thoughts, and habits that have come to dominate our lives, even though others well worth considering are available to us. Avoiding alternatives, we increasingly settle into set patterns of perception, conception, and action, making ourselves unable to entertain possibilities beyond those. Fearful living of this kind diminishes its practitioners; it shrinks the range of possible experiences and limits one's freedom. Lacking spiritual imagination, we constrict our mental horizons, ignoring and denying what could be in preference for a small segment of what already has been.

Meditative cultivation of the imagination is the best way out of these forms of mental closure. It intentionally opens the question of "the good" or "the better" in our minds and energizes particular disciplines of image formation. Cultivating a profound sense of the possibilities that are actually available to us in our own setting, we force ourselves to question our lives and look ahead. One way that this is frequently done—without calling it "meditation"—is by acquainting ourselves with other forms of human life through literature, history, and the study of other cultures. Immersing ourselves in a wide range of models for life, we come to understand that the conventional possibilities initially available to us do not come close to exhausting the full range of options. As we consider lives in other cultures, in other historical epochs, and in other occupations and interests, the breadth of our imaginative considerations grows dramatically. Enlarging the imaginative field, our possibilities and our understanding of them deepens and along with them the scope of our lives.

It is often the case that in the midst of our daily lives we find ourselves fantasizing, lost in captivating daydreams. Although the movement from a meditative discipline of imagination to the fantasy of pleasant daydream images is quite natural, the distinction between them is important to maintain. In fantasy, we may entertain possibilities, but they are not *our* possibilities. Fantasizing, we can remake ourselves into whomever we want and entertain these images internally without any serious thought about whether or how they might be actualized. Even though these daydreams may evoke powerful emotional resonances, they have little or nothing to do with our actual situations in the world. I can fantasize a life for myself as, for example, the greatest athlete in the world, even though in reality I have neither skill nor potential in that domain. Fantasy is fully imaginative and profoundly entertaining, but it lacks that vital ethical function that, at its best, the imagination can have. Moreover, it often proves to be a distraction. Fantasizing illusory possibilities, I evade reality and prolong the habit of ignoring the real possibilities that are actually available at various moments in my life.

The meditative development of imagination is distinct from fantasy. When it functions creatively, it stays attuned to our actual possibilities and shows us what could be at stake in cultivating one or more paths that might right now be open to us. In this sense, imaginative meditations are based on authentic self-knowledge rather than the unconstrained desire of fantasy. They take as their point of departure thoughtful appraisal of who we are, what we might conceivably be able to do or create, and work energetically toward actualizing some element of authentic ends.

One way to understand the difference between the meditative use of imagination and the kind of free-form fantasy that we experience in daydreams is as the difference between an activity that is voluntarily engaged and an involuntary act that proceeds under the direction of unconscious impulses. Meditative imagination is a discipline, an intentional activity through which we explore possibilities that we take to accord with the actual situation in which we reside. Although fantasy is certainly a conscious activity, it is something that simply happens to us beyond our will—neither chosen nor voluntary. Intentional and unintentional imaginative acts are both creative activities through which we create images, but the dimension of our minds that is thus engaged is very different in each case, the difference between intentional functions of mind and unintentional ones.

Imagination, in its most creative and productive forms, is a discipline, a practice, and this is what qualifies it as a form of meditation. Our most imaginative acts, thoughts, and products do not just happen; they emerge when we train our imaginations on a particular idea or sphere. Discipline is required in the first act of forming images and then in subsequent acts of reenvisioning through which the object of imagination is honed to perfection. This meditative discipline calls for scrupulous attention, imagination cultivated as a mental discipline. Our minds need to be trained to stay on the task until we get it right, until the act has been pushed through to its highest order of potential. This meditative discipline entails careful experiment, where one mental test after another is performed to examine the image in its various dimensions.

The discipline of imagination also presupposes a commitment to the truth conditions that shape our lives. All imaginative acts are constrained by the particular contours of the situation in which we reside; we cannot just make things up. To get it right, we hone our images in conformity to the realities that contextualize our world. This requires patience and a commitment to push beyond complacency to an imagined account of things that really does fit the situation in which it has been formed. Although we are freed by our imagination from certain constraints of the past and present, the imagination performs its work in connection to these same conditions that show us which images are really worth pursuing.

The imagination as a meditative discipline is inherently creative, a discipline of change rather than conservation. Its goal is always transformation, breaking through the weaknesses of previous orders and pushing toward something extraordinary and new. In this sense, products of the imagination are often counterintuitive. They run against the grain of our previous ways of understanding ourselves and the world. Our measure of them is the degree to which they open up new dimensions of reality to our mind. But sometimes this "opening" takes time to see or to feel. This is especially true of the most imaginative acts. Imaginative acts are most transformative when they are directed not toward a product that has been conceived in advance—where we already know clearly what we want. Instead, the imaginative acts that are most useful lead us to see and desire something that we could not have conceived or desired before that moment in time.

And, of course, given inevitable impermanence, whatever was transformative for us in the past may not remain so. Everything is always open to further acts of imaginative attention. It would be hopelessly dogmatic to believe that the current form of anything—Buddhism, the six perfections, this book—has achieved its highest possible stage of cultivation. When we cling to the past and present in this way, we acquiesce to dominant practices and conceptions and close down the powers of the imagination. Holding onto the familiar in this way, we conclude that history has run its course and that the work of spiritual imagination is over, thus artificially constricting the future of human enlightenment.

Recognizing this pattern of fearful clinging, it would be foolish to think of meditation as an already finalized set of practices from the past. If we were able to look closely at the practice and conception of meditation through its long and interesting history, we would see that how it was understood, how it was practiced, and the effects that it has had on people have changed through time in accordance with changing conditions and circumstances. If we were able to get our minds beyond thinking of meditation as a timeless cultural practice, we would see that meditation is itself open to become something beyond what it has been. It is through imaginative meditative excursions out beyond the ordinary that future possibilities for meditation will be revealed to us.

Imagining a Meditative Life

Throughout this chapter, we have worked back and forth between two different orientations toward meditation. The first of these conceives of meditation as a practice, something you do with purpose and discipline. The second takes its bearings from the several qualities of mental character that are meant to result from the successful practice of meditation. Thus truly meditative people would embody certain personal character-istics; they would be calm, focused, insightful, and profoundly aware of the world in which they dwell. In the first sense, meditation names a set of practices and disciplines that suspend daily activity in order to cultivate the mental orientation behind all other activities. Its goal is to alter who we are in relation to everything else we do.

If, over time, this transformation is successful, the result is a mental orientation and a form of life that we would describe as meditative. The ideal of this fifth perfection is to live in a meditative frame of mind regardless of whether we happen to be meditating. The goal, therefore, is not always to be meditating, always to be practicing a preparatory activity, but rather to live in the spirit of composure and insight that the practice has produced. This is the second orientation to the topic of meditation.

In Zen Buddhism, it is widely thought that the ultimate goal of the practice is neither to be engaged in *zazen* (seated meditation) nor to achieve *satori* (the sudden disclosure of reality) but rather to embody in everyday life the vision that *zazen* and *satori* have made possible. In that sense, "meditation" is not the intentional activity so much as it is the quality or depth of mindfulness that you bring to any activity. Thus, depending on which orientation to meditation you take, you might say with equal truth that an awakened human being no longer spends much time in meditation (in the first sense) or that in fact such a person is virtually always in a meditative state of mind (in the second sense).

It is to the second of these senses—a way of being meditative—that we now turn. How should we imagine a meditative life that in our own judgment has achieved excellence? In what ways can human conscious-ness really be made more profoundly conscious than it already is? In order to frame our reflections on these questions coherently, it will be useful to identify the transformation of consciousness that takes place through meditation at the three levels of mind that we have described. Ideally, mental function and capacity will have been expanded first at the level of direct awareness of the world, second at the level of reflection or thoughtfulness, and third at the reflexive level of self-awareness.

At the first level of immediate experience, a meditative person is directly aware of the surrounding world. With a steady eye of observation, ears attuned to the immediate environment, and other senses in sharp focus, we can imagine a meditative mind attentive to the environment in ways that we are not. Such a person notices things and movements in the surrounding world that escape our attention. Alert and focused, mindfulness and perceptiveness have become natural ways of being in the world.

Having come to embody the repercussions of meditation, the attentive person has learned to breathe deeply. Depth and steadiness of respiration arise out of a learned but now natural desire for the calming, clarifying effect of oxygen circulating through all the cells of the body. More oxygen wakes us up, brings energy, and makes us alert. Further, meditative capacity at this level of consciousness enhances mindfulness of the body. It makes us uncannily aware of the miracles of our physical existence, the smooth functioning of all bodily systems and the incredible coordination between them that gives us physical singularity and presence.

One dimension of this coordination is the ease with which emotions can be woven into the whole of direct awareness. A person fully experienced in the meditative arts can allow emotions to take their course without self-conscious fear of their impropriety. This is attributable not to their magical alignment but to the work that has been done at the reflective level on the integrity of character through various dimensions of ethical cultivation. On this basis, enjoyment takes a more central position among daily experiences. Finding joy in sights, sounds, and tastes, in plants, stones, and the sky, in buildings, events, and art, and in friends, neighbors, and communities becomes a daily possibility, something within that is no longer so difficult to access. This ease of enjoyment includes sense of humor, an artful taste for joyful hilarity, and the confidence to let oneself go into an unexpected burst of laughter.

Attributes such as these must proceed from some advanced level of equanimity, a well-focused, relaxed presence that is not embattled over unfulfilled desires or anxious self-consciousness. Very often relaxed rather than tense or anxious, the meditative person feels naturally at home in the world. At ease and with minimal sense of insecurity, we would imagine a natural humility that is simply an absence of the common urge to assert our own priority. Not clinging for security, letting oneself go in the world would not be so difficult. This ability to overcome anxiety derives from a profound trust, not trust in something particular so much as an open trust that whatever happens will be worthy of wonder and amazement for those who have eyes to see it. Alert and relaxed in such a state of trust, the meditative person would be open to and able to wait for whatever it is that will be revealed in time.

It is important to notice that all of these possible qualities of meditative life at the level of immediate consciousness are not necessarily brought about by meditation at that particular level. Immediate consciousness will be honed by what we do reflectively and by the extent of our self-awareness. Each level of meditation has effects at every level of human consciousness.

Imagining meditative excellence at the second level—the level of reflective contemplation—we would expect to find someone disciplined in analytical observation. This discipline gives rise to clarity in grasping the situations we face and makes skill in discernment and sound judgment possible. Enhanced critical facility includes the ability to see through illusions that commonly entrap the rest of us, and such a person would be less susceptible to flights of fantasy that evade realities that we are better off facing.

Skill in the realm of critical reflection requires a willingness to question deeply without fearing the conclusions that this process might yield. It includes the steadiness of mind to inquire in a fundamental rather than a rhetorical way. To do that, a meditative person must be able to reside with some degree of ease in the state of "not knowing," waiting for the most insightful orientation to emerge. A reflectively mature meditator also senses that the boundaries of the known are only temporary limits, and that stretching those limits is always worthwhile, always possible. In that sense, the reflective person lives in pursuit of insight, with a passion to break through current complacencies and illusions.

Reflective skill includes experience in the discipline of imagination. Expanding the limits of understanding requires imaginative probing, but so does the expansion of the possible. At this level, the meditative person is experimental and enjoys testing the possible to see what new forms of life it might yield. Reflectively meditative people are attuned as much to the commonplace as they are to the extraordinary. They see that you do not have to look far away to find wonder and profundity, and that "the extraordinary" very often results from a distinctive and imaginative take on the ordinary. Reflective people can find just about anything interesting. They are mentally awake, not lulled to sleep by the repetitive character of every day life and the numbing effects of too much "common sense."

At the third and highest level of consciousness, a meditative person is self-aware. This awareness is not objective—it does not come from empirical investigation, even though it will often incorporate whatever elements of self-knowledge objective perspectives offer. Instead, reflexivity is direct awareness of subjective activity from the inside. Unlike critical reflection on the "self," reflexive consciousness is a vivid, first-person sense of the one who right now understands these words. The more meditative people become at the reflexive level, the more their experience at all levels gains presence and clarity. Learning to be reflexively meditative, vision is enlarged to encompass a sense of the point of view from which vision proceeds, and as that occurs, awareness and perspective are enriched.

The more effectively self-aware someone becomes, the more honest the self-knowledge they practice and exhibit. Self-awareness includes understanding in advance the mistakes to which they are prone. Having learned from the unintended desires and errors of judgment that they have made in the past, they are increasingly adept at compensating for them. In this way, meditators well versed in self-awareness know their strengths and weaknesses. Their reactions to their own failures and disappointments are not debilitating, as they sometimes are for others. Seeing who they are, they manage to dampen the destructive effects of despair and self-pity. In this respect they practice integrity, a balance of character in the midst of turmoil with a strong coherence between desires and larger goals.

People of integrity are not in hiding. They are not afraid to appear to be the awkward and uncertain beings that all of us in fact are. This eclipse of fear derives from seeing their true place in the cosmos, and it yields a profound degree of equanimity and ease. The effects of reflexive awareness carry down through reflection to immediate experience. Those who have sat long enough with themselves in reflexive awareness can relax and smile while the rest of us grimace. Residing immediately in themselves and opened out to the world, they have a presence that others in their unself-consciousness lack. At this level, however, the meditative results that we are describing pertain to what Buddhists prefer to call "wisdom," and it is to that final perfection that we now turn.

THE PERFECTION OF WISDOM

TRADITIONAL BUDDHIST IMAGES OF
THE PERFECTION OF WISDOM
(*PRAJÑĀPĀRAMITĀ*)

The last of the six perfections, *prajñā,* is the perfection of wisdom. Wisdom is the heart of the Mahayana Buddhist tradition of thought and practice. The sutras that communicate the Mahayana teachings are justifiably called the *Perfection of Wisdom Sutras* because throughout this impressive body of literature wisdom is the primary topic of discussion. In the mythology surrounding the tradition, wisdom is the "mother of Buddhas," since it is wisdom that gives birth to enlightenment and it is wisdom that nourishes and sustains the bodhisattvas' compassionate involvement in the world on behalf of all beings. The *Wisdom Sutras* repeatedly set forth the attractions and benefits associated with the practice of wisdom. One says: "So greatly profitable is the perfection of wisdom of the bodhisattvas, the great beings, as productive of the supreme enlightenment! A bodhisattva should therefore train in just this perfection of wisdom."[1]

The perfection of wisdom is pictured as more than just the highest and most exalted of the bodhisattva's virtues; it is the one that brings the others to fruition. The first five perfections are initially practiced at ordinary levels of understanding and then nurtured to the level of perfection when wisdom is applied to them. Therefore, the *Perfection of Wisdom in Eight Thousand Lines* says: "For this perfection of wisdom directs the six perfections, guides, leads, instructs, and advises them, is their genetrix and nurse. Because, if they are deprived of the perfection of wisdom, the first five perfections do not come under the concept of perfections, and they do not deserve to be called 'perfections.'"[2] Wisdom is also said to encompass the other five perfections: "It is thus that the bodhisattva, the great being who trains in this deep perfection of wisdom, has taken hold of all the six perfections, has procured them, has conformed to them. And why? Because in this deep perfection of wisdom all the perfections are contained."[3] The image of encompassing the other practices of perfection leads the *Large Sutra on Perfect Wisdom* to claim that "when the bodhisattva trains in perfect wisdom, he acquires all the accomplishments which he should acquire."[4]

What, then, defines wisdom in Mahayana Buddhism? Although wisdom is understood more in terms of a certain comportment, a particular way of being in the world, than it is in doctrinal or conceptual views, ideas are nevertheless the essential starting point for the practices of wisdom. Therefore, the *Heart Sutra*, the most compact version of the *Wisdom Sutras*, begins by claiming that those who wish "to practice the profound perfection of wisdom should view things in this way:"[5] The implication of this passage and many others like it is that there is a certain way to "view" the world that leads to wisdom. This view is not itself wisdom, because holding it as an intellectual position or belief does not necessarily make you wise. But, they claim, this is the point of view that will get you there. What is that view?

The view in question is *śūnyatā*, the Mahayana principle of "emptiness" to which we have alluded at every stage in our reflections on the six perfections. Wisdom is the capacity to envision and work with the "emptiness" of all things. Therefore, the sutras maintain that the bodhisattvas' "home is deep thought on the meaning of emptiness."[6] "Emptiness" is a universal predicate in this Buddhist tradition, a claim about all claims, a view about all views, a position with respect to all positions you might hold. The bodhisattva dwells on the concept of emptiness, hoping eventually to embody its meaning at a more profound level than the conceptual.

What "emptiness" means is best explained in terms of what it is that things are empty of. All things are "empty," the texts claim, insofar as they lack their "own-being." "Own-being" is a technical term (*svabhāva*) for the quality of being self-generated, self-possessed. *Tzu-hsing*, the Chinese translation for *svabhāva*, literally means "self-nature," the immortal self or immutable nature of a thing. Things in possession of their "own-being"—things with "self-nature"—are not subject to conditions, influences, and change. They just are what they are without respect to other things or time. The central insight of "emptiness," then, is that all things lack this characteristic—nothing generates itself, nothing stands on its own, and nothing just is what it is forever. If nothing controls its "own-being" in this way then, in Buddhist terms, all things are "empty." Claiming that all elements of existence are "empty" in this sense, Mahayana Buddhists took the word "emptiness" to name the character of reality overall.

What reasoning leads Buddhists to the conclusion of pervasive "emptiness"? Essentially the same line of reasoning and life experience that had generated the Buddhist tradition in the first place. Three early Buddhist principles are brought together to help define the Mahayana concept of emptiness: "impermanence," "dependent arising," and "no-self." In the following passage from the *Large Sutra on Perfect Wisdom*, wisdom is defined in terms of "emptiness," and "emptiness" is defined by way of these three early Buddhist concepts: "When he thus surveys dependent arising, a bodhisattva certainly does not see anything that is being produced without a cause, nor does he review anything that is permanent. . . . He reviews nothing as a self, a being, a soul, a creature."[7] All things are "empty" insofar as they "arise dependent" on other things, insofar as they are "impermanent" and subject to change, and insofar as they therefore lack a permanent essence, an independent soul or "self." Wisdom is the ability to see how all things are "empty" in this sense, and to transform one's relationship to everything accordingly.

The *Perfection of Wisdom Sutras* are best conceived as extended meditations on this single theme worked out in as many nuances and implications as the authors could imagine. Page after page they ponder the "true nature" of all things—that they have no fixed, nonrelational nature. They examine things in the world and find them to be "empty" of such a nature. They examine human beings, both in their totality and divided into their fundamental components—perceptions, feelings, concepts, volitions, self-consciousness—only to discover that they are all "empty" of unchanging, independent characteristics. They consider their own concepts about all these things, only to discover that they too fit the same pattern—concepts are fundamentally relational and always subject to change. Nothing appears to stand on its own. Nothing has its "own-being" because the being of all things depends on other equally relational things and is, on account of that, always contextual and always in motion.

As the reader advances in understanding, other, more sacred objects come under the scrutiny of the concept "emptiness." Enlightenment, the Buddha, and even "emptiness" itself are all declared to be "empty" of "own-being"—they "arise dependent" on factors beyond themselves, they are impermanent and change along with everything else. They therefore lack a permanent, independent essence or nature. Even these principles of Buddhist thought and practice are thoroughly "empty." Wisdom is profound insight into this universal state of affairs. In that light, here is how one sutra meditates on the "emptiness" of "perfect wisdom" and of the bodhisattva who seeks it: "It is because of this fact,—i.e., that just as perfect wisdom is empty . . . so also the bodhisattva is empty . . . —that a bodhisattva arrives at the full attainment of enlightenment."[8] You approach the wisdom of enlightenment, in other words, as you come to see that like everything else, enlightenment is "empty."

The sutras seem to flaunt the negative connotations of the word "emptiness." Contemplating this idea is meant to undermine the persistent tendency to reify things, to consider them more substantial, independent, and permanent than they could possibly be. In spite of the negative connotations of the word "emptiness," however, it is important to recognize, in the quote above and elsewhere, that "emptiness" defines *how* things exist—relationally and impermanently—and is not therefore the assertion that things somehow do not exist at all. What does not exist is a fixed essence to anything, a center that always remains the same, a condition independent of all conditioning. Nothing, the sutras claim, possesses its "own-being" in this sense. And yet things exist just as they are.

The point of stating these matters so strongly appears to be twofold. First, this conception of the nature of things—that they lack a fixed nature—was the account of things that seemed to be true. Early Mahayana Buddhists found no exceptions to the rule of "emptiness." Everything changes, and everything is what it is in relation to other things. Contemplative evidence seemed to support a strong assertion of "emptiness." Second, however, because a world of impermanence and interrelations implied the impossibility of a permanently true and comprehensive conception of things, the authors of these sutras and the Buddhists who followed their teachings were most interested in a transformation in the way people relate to things in their daily lives. That is, Buddhist monks sought self-transformation above and beyond their search for a conceptual picture that corresponded to the way things really are. They sought a fundamental transformation in the way they lived their lives by means of awakening from unenlightening ideas, habits, and practices.

One vital element in this transformation was the practice of nonattachment that had been cultivated in Buddhism since its inception. If wisdom is the insight that nothing has a fixed nature and that all things are in process, that would suggest cultivating just enough detachment from things, ideas, and people to accept that they would all change and finally pass away. Wisdom meant letting go to some extent, releasing one's grip on what would inevitably pass away on its own. Meditating on "emptiness" was meant to cultivate a certain degree of nonattachment by showing practitioners how it is that things continually appear, change, and disappear.

This line of reflection had been basic to Buddhist practice already for hundreds of years by the time the *Wisdom Sutras* were composed. One element that these sutras added to the tradition was concentrated reflection on the necessity of nonattachment to specifically Buddhist ideas, especially those that would have constituted the very basis of monastic life. So the sutras spend considerable time asking how, for example, "the thought of enlightenment might become a source of attachment."[9] Holding onto this thought for one's own spiritual security, fixing it in one's mind as though "enlightenment" possessed its "own-being," was a mental error that could be just as unhealthy as other less subtle forms of attachment. Therefore, the sutras expose a wide range of "bases" upon which someone might become "attached," and attempt to demonstrate their "emptiness." The text claims that the Buddha would go on to teach "other, more subtle attachments," and how to get loose from them.[10] "Perfect wisdom" is, of course, one of these. Thus, the *Large Sutra on Perfect Wisdom* says: "But if it occurs to the bodhisattva, the great being, that 'I course [train] in perfect wisdom, I develop perfect wisdom'—if he perceives thus, then he moves away from perfect wisdom. . . . If the bodhisattva even perceives the perfection of wisdom, then he has fallen away from it."[11]

So, if you seek a kind of wisdom that is unchanging, an eternal wisdom that exists in and of itself, something that just is what it is without reference to context, relations, and time, then you seek it unwisely. The sutras recommend instead that you engage in the quest for wisdom without objectifying any of the elements in it—the seeker, what is sought, and the search are all "empty." Each of these becomes what it is through particular conditions and changes along with alterations in these conditions. The mental demands of this quest are obviously extraordinary, and from various common-sense points of view, lead to baffling and paradoxical consequences.

The *Wisdom Sutras* do not hide from these consequences. In fact, they revel in them as a way to push practitioners through ordinary states of mind to the extraordinary domain of wisdom. So, in the *Large Sutra on Perfect Wisdom*, a dialogue between the Buddha and his disciple, Subhuti, gets to the point where Subhuti can only say in exasperation: "Is, then, enlightenment nonexistent?" Fearing this paradoxical conclusion, and hoping to be given a straight and uplifting answer, Subhuti only gets from the Buddha the answer he dreads: "So it is, Subhuti, so it is, as you say. Enlightenment also is a nonexistent."[12] The concept of enlightenment that you hold in your mind is just as "empty" as anything else. It takes the mental shape that it does dependent on other elements of understanding in your mind, your culture, your historical epoch. When they change, so does "enlightenment," and vice versa. Becoming dogmatically attached to your current vision of enlightenment, therefore, is unwise. It is just another way to be stuck in place, another form of fearful grasping for security.

In another section, the *Large Sutra* has the disciple Subhuti respond to the Buddha's claim that "the perfection of wisdom is empty of the perfection of wisdom" by proclaiming that "this is the perfectly pure demonstration of the perfection of wisdom. No one has demonstrated it, no one has received it, no one has realized it. And since no one has realized it, no one has therein gone to final Nirvana."[13] This is obviously very unusual spiritual discourse. Wherever practitioners want something solid and secure to stand on, the mental rug is pulled out from under their feet. No ultimate foundation is offered, because this kind of spiritual training is intended more to raise transformative questions than to provide easy answers.

Contemplating the unnerving realization that wisdom is "empty," Subhuti goes on to ask the Buddha the obvious question: "Will not bodhisattvas, who have newly set out on the quest for wisdom, become apprehensive and regretful when they hear this exposition, will they not tremble, be frightened, be terrified?" In response, the Buddha agrees without being bothered by that prospect: "They will tremble, be frightened, be terrified, if, newly set out on the quest, they course in perfect wisdom while still unskilled in means, or if they have not gotten into the hands of a good spiritual friend [that is, a master teacher]."[14] The training entailed in the perfection of wisdom is pictured as extraordinarily difficult, not just conceptually but also psychologically. As the sutra says: "A doer of what is hard is the bodhisattva who, while coursing [training] in perfect wisdom, does not lose heart when the perfection of wisdom is being preached, and does not mentally turn away from it, who persists in making endeavors about the perfection of wisdom and who does not turn back on the supreme enlightenment."[15]

Wisdom, therefore, is the ability to face the truth and not be un-nerved or frightened. It is the capacity to be disillusioned, but not disheartened. It is the ability to consider the contingency and the groundlessness of all things, oneself included, and not turn away from that consideration in fear. Wisdom means setting aside illusions about oneself and the world and being strengthened by that encounter with the truth. It entails willingness to avoid seeking the security of the unchanging and to open oneself to a world of flux and complex relations. This includes, as the *Vimalakīrti Sūtra* puts it, "overcoming the habit of clinging to an ultimate ground."[16] One way to say this is that bodhisattvas—those who seek wisdom and open transformation throughout their lives—can be distinguished in terms of how much truth they can bear, how many illusions of comfort and security they are willing or able to set aside. With something like this in mind, the *Large Sutra* says: "if when this [perfection of wisdom] is being expounded, the thought of the bodhisattva does not become cowed, stolid, or regretful, and if his mind does not tremble, is not frightened or terrified, then that bodhisattva courses in perfect wisdom."[17]

Developing the capacity to see the relationality and temporality of all things and not wince or turn away from that vision requires the bodhi-sattva to engage in training. The sutras do not hesitate to state clearly that the vision required of the bodhisattva is unusual, and would therefore call for an unusual discipline aimed at an unusual transformation of mental powers. They assume that it would take years of training to redirect the mental habits of one's past and one's culture, to reorient oneself toward a more complex and demanding vision of reality. Wisdom was thought to entail a thoroughgoing transformation in one's relationship to oneself and to the world. Here is the *Perfection of Wisdom in Eight Thousand Lines* summarizing what the quest for wisdom would require:

> If the bodhisattva approaches perfect wisdom in this way, apperceives it, enters into it, understands it, reflects on it, examines, investigates, and develops it—with acts of mind that have abandoned all deception and deceit, all conceit, the exaltation of self, all laziness, the deprecia-tion of others, the notion of self, the notion of a being, gain, honor and

fame ... —then it will not be hard for him to gain the full perfection of all virtues.[18]

One dimension of the training in wisdom featured in these sutras is the willingness to probe dimensions of experience that we normally just assume without question. This is the capacity to ask *real* questions. Repeatedly the sutras admonish those who fail to inquire, who want to be told rather than to think themselves. So in one, the Buddha says: "It is hard to gain confidence in the perfection of wisdom if one is unpracticed, ... not eager to learn, unwilling to ask questions."[19] To ask is to open oneself to the possibility of a change or deepening of mind, to put oneself into a posture from which far-reaching transformation may be irresistible. So the sutras stress that practitioners should ask "questions and counterquestions," "take nothing as a basic fact," and persist in inquiry, not yielding to the conventional views that dominate most human minds.[20]

According to the *Wisdom Sutras*, one of the reasons that profound questioning is required is that the practice of inquiry brings us to an awareness of the role of language in our experience of the world. These sutras, along with other Buddhist texts, are extraordinary in the extent to which they have engaged in penetrating reflection on language. The bodhisattva is pictured as understanding what few of us ever encounter, the connection between what we experience and our language about it. Although these can never be entirely separated, bodhisattvas are pictured as able to see the bearing one has on the other and to avoid mental mistakes that arise from assuming their identity. In teaching, therefore, bodhisattvas show others where language is blocking rather than enabling insight. They realize that the language in which the perfection of wisdom is articulated can either prevent or evoke the dawning of insight.

In order to call attention to the role of language in shaping human experience, one sutra has Subhuti say: "To call it 'perfection of wisdom,' that is merely giving it a name. And what that name corresponds to, that cannot be got at."[21] In another place, a sutra says that bodhisattvas refer to the ideas in their mind as "notions, agreed symbols, and convenient expressions," but not as the true nature of things.[22] The Buddha is pictured as proclaiming: "Beings are supported on words and signs, based on imagination of that which is not. It is from these words and signs that the bodhisattva, when he courses in perfect wisdom, sets them free."[23] Bodhisattvas realize, the texts claim, that the tendency to assume the solidity, the permanence, and the independence of things is grounded in the familiarity of language, all the ways language is largely invisible to us. The ability to stand back from language on occasion in order to understand its role in the constitution of experience provides greater flexibility and skill in daily practices. It is one factor enabling wisdom in life.

These abilities—to question, to see the effect of our language on our minds—are considered part of what Mahayana Buddhists called "skill-in-means" (*upāya*). Skill in handling the means through which awakening might occur is essential to the practice of the bodhisattva. This skill is closely linked to the perfection of wisdom. One sutra says: "But the skill in means of the bodhisattvas should be known as having come forth from the perfection of wisdom."[24] Another says: "The bodhisattva should train himself in the skill in means contained in this perfection of wisdom."[25] Skill comes forth from wisdom and skill is contained in wisdom; developing one is simultaneously cultivating the other. One cannot be skillful without a profound realization of the "emptiness" of all things, and one cannot realize the "emptiness" of all things without the development of "skill-in-means." The link between them is so tight that the *Vimalakīrti Sūtra* says: "Wisdom not integrated with skillful means is bondage, but wisdom integrated with skillful means is liberation. Skillful means not integrated with wisdom is bondage, but skillful means integrated with wisdom is liberation."[26]

One way to understand this would be to say—as the sutras do—that the perfection of wisdom "contains" and "controls" the other five perfections. Wisdom holds the criteria upon which the others can be called perfections at all. So, for example, one sutra says: "The perfection of wisdom does the work of the other five perfections, and the five perfections follow it and revolve around it. When they do not lack in the perfection of wisdom the five perfections get the designation of 'perfections,' but not so when they do lack in it."[27] Another says: "the five perfections are embodied in the perfection of wisdom; they grow supported by the perfection of wisdom; and as upheld by the perfection of wisdom do they get the name of 'perfections.' So it is just the perfection of wisdom that controls, guides, and leads the five perfections."[28]

These sutras often use the first perfection—the perfection of generosity—to demonstrate this relationship. Wise giving is perfect. Giving that is based on the donor's conception of his own interests in the transaction or on a condescending idea of the recipient's incapacity cannot fulfill the criteria of perfection, even if it is still generous. Only in the realization that "gift, giver, and recipient" are "empty" of independent, permanent standing are we sufficiently mature in understanding to give selflessly and in the spirit of true generosity. Giving can be truly generous only when it encompasses the wisdom to see through our common motives and to recognize the larger horizons that frame an act of generosity. Therefore the *Large Sutra* says: "Someone who has fallen away from the perfection of wisdom is not capable of consummating the perfection of giving."[29]

These are the grounds upon which the sutras distinguish between what they call a "worldly perfection" and a "supramundane perfection," the two levels on which the six perfections can be practiced. A worldly practice of perfection is a typical quest for human achievement. You undertake the effort in order to achieve something good for yourself— human excellence. You engage in generous acts, for example, in order to be a good person, one known for the quality of generosity and respected as a contributor to the common good. Describing this level of practice, the *Large Sutra* says:

> The bodhisattva gives and gives liberally. . . . It occurs to him, "I give, that one receives, this is the gift. I renounce all that I have without any niggardliness. I act as the Buddha commands. I practice the perfection of giving. Having made this gift into the common property of all beings, I dedicate it to the supreme enlightenment." Tied by three ties he gives a gift. Which three? The notion of self, the notion of others, the notion of a gift. To give a gift tied by these three ties, that is called the worldly perfection of giving.[30]

By contrast, the "supramundane" perfection of giving is based on a full realization of "emptiness" as the nature of all things. Neither the giver, nor the recipient, nor the gift is conceived as a separate, independent entity, as permanent and fixed in what it is. As a giver, you would sense your own dependence on a multitude of factors beyond your own efforts. You would know that you live only on the basis of vast gifts that brought you into being and that have sustained you throughout your life. Having emerged in the world from causes prior to your own choosing, you would understand that you are not a permanent, independent entity; you would realize that there really is "no-self" in the nonrelational way that common sense assumes. You would know that, while you may be able to activate this gift, it is not really yours to give. Things circulate in the world forever, taking this form now and endless other forms at other times. You would understand the quaint and limited sense in which there really is ownership at all in life. You would also sense that while the recipient of your gift is very much in need, that fact is contingent on a whole array of conditions that might have been otherwise. The bodhisattva thus understands that people come to be who and what they are in larger contexts of influence; their identity is dependent on who their parents are, their friends, their teachers, what opportunities happened to come their way, what education was available to them, as well as the extent to which they were able to take responsibility for their own acts and determine their own future.

All of these structural elements in the act of giving are "empty" in that sense—they are all dependent on multiple factors, subject to change at all times, and therefore have no fixed essence upon which a permanently established picture of giving could be based. Here is how the *Large Sutra* puts it:

> The supramundane perfection of giving, on the other hand, consists in the threefold purity. . . . Here a bodhisattva gives a gift, and he does not apprehend a self, a recipient, or a gift; also no reward of his giving. He surrenders that gift to all beings, but does not apprehend those beings, or himself either. And, although he dedicates that gift to the supreme enlightenment, he does not apprehend any enlightenment. This is called the supramundane perfection of giving.[31]

At the highest level of Mahayana Buddhist imagination, the bodhisattva is pictured as so enveloped in profound understanding of the "emptiness" of all things that none of this needs to be conceptually articulated. The bodhisattva just sees things as they are and acts accordingly, without needing to plan or scheme. This is the attainment of "effortlessness" through which a bodhisattva gives selflessly and wisely but without apparent effort, simply on account of an enlightening vision of how all things really are in the world.[32]

From points of departure in ordinary mentality where most of us reside, it was widely thought in Mahayana Buddhism that an initial faith is required to begin this practice of wisdom. As the *Large Sutra on Perfect Wisdom* defines it "Faith here means the believing in perfect wisdom, the trusting confidence, the resoluteness, the deliberation, the weighing up, the testing."[33] Without some faith that these practices are worthwhile, that exerting oneself in them would be a healthy engagement of time and effort, no one would or should take them up. But the sutras imagine, sensibly, that in the process of engaging in these practices, on the basis of that initial faith, what at first requires faith because it seems so foreign and unnatural later becomes a second nature, internalized on the basis of experience. At some point the practitioner "knows" something, feels something strongly, based on what has already taken place. The more deeply ingrained the practices of perfection become, the less discipline is required and the more one is able to perform a wise act spontaneously out of a profound sense of what is right under the circumstances.

Where the early Mahayana sutras distinguish between two stages in the pursuit of wisdom—worldly and supramundane—later philosophical texts outline a more nuanced doctrine of stages through which movement from one position on the path to another can be conceptualized. When seen as an ethical movement from unenlightened forms of life to more enlightened forms, these practices assume a gradual unfolding of wisdom through a multitude of levels that are not imaginable from the perspective of the point of departure.

At exalted levels—images of character that appear to embody wisdom—the bodhisattva is pictured as selfless in energetic acts on behalf of the community as a whole. The comportment of compassion and communal concern is thought to arise from a deep realization of "emptiness" through which the bodhisattva experiences the interconnectedness of all elements of reality, himself or herself included. Whereas the bodhisattva continues to find ample reason to act, there is no more reason to act just on behalf of himself than there is on behalf of others. That distinction is "emptied" of the force it carried in earlier embodiments of self-understanding.

At earlier stages of "self-" cultivation, where one hopes to achieve something for oneself, the merit and progress accrued in virtuous acts is very important as motivation. But by the time the sutras work up to the perfection of wisdom, all talk of merit and individual accomplishment disappears in the texts. Wisdom entails overcoming the isolation of the self, not just for the self but on behalf of a larger collective reality beyond the self. It imagines stages of self-cultivation where self-concern is no longer the focal point of the activity, where doing what is right, doing the good on behalf of all members of a community are the images of perfection. At this stage, there is very little point in calling it "self-"cultivation because all attention is now focused on a set of concerns that go far beyond the individual.

This evolution beyond the "self" is symbolized in the sutras in the practice of dedicating one's own merit to another (*parinamāna*). Meditating on the act of giving one's positive merit to someone else begins the process of learning how to take the lives of others as seriously as we are able to take our own. Thus one sutra says: "That the bodhisattva wishes to make that ease of nonattachment, that ease of freedom, that ease of the Blessed Rest [enlightenment] common to all beings, and therefore dedicates his store of merit to the supreme enlightenment of all beings, that should be seen as his magnanimous resolution."[34] Achieving that ability, however, one no longer dwells on merit at all, and the symbolic, preparatory gestures of meditative giving can be set aside in preference for actual giving—work on behalf of the enlightenment of everyone, oneself and others. At this level, wisdom and compassion are functionally synonymous.

Finally, it is instructive to consider how the perfection of wisdom came to be mythologized in Mahayana sutras. This final perfection was thought so exalted, so perfect for the emancipation of all beings from lives of suffering, that it came to take a variety of mythologized forms. Some texts suggest that, given the power of the perfection of wisdom to transform lives, it must have life-saving properties. Thus, the sutras claim, anyone studying these sutras would not be vulnerable in battle to "weapons hurled at them."[35] Having provided that image of supernatural power and divine protection, however, the sutra immediately demythologizes the passage by turning its meaning back on the reader's practice of self-cultivation: "coursing in the perfection of wisdom, they vanquish the arrows and swords of their own greed, of their own hate, of their own delusion."[36] Moreover, the sutras suggest that the perfection of wisdom is so exalted that merit accrues to anyone who would "honor, revere, and worship the perfection of wisdom."[37] Again, following this passage, the text immediately takes the occasion to say that whatever merit would be earned by honoring or worshiping the sutra would be not nearly as great as the merit accrued by studying and putting its wisdom into effect.

Written during a period of growing devotion to the Buddha, the *Perfection of Wisdom Sutras* were eager to take up the question of the benefit of devotional practice. Although very careful not to denounce or denigrate this religious tendency, one of the reasons authors of the sutras raised the topic of the worship of the Buddha was to demonstrate how it is that the ethical practice of the perfections, especially wisdom, is simply better. So, in the following passage, the Buddha raises the question: If you were given a choice between many sacred relics of the Buddha or a copy of the *Perfection of Wisdom Sutra*, which one should you choose? The author of this sutra has the respondent say: "The perfection of wisdom. And why? It is not that I lack respect for the relics of the Buddha, and it is not that I am unwilling to honor, revere, and worship them. But I am fully aware that the relics of the Buddha have come forth from the perfection of wisdom and that for that reason they are honored, revered, and worshipped; I am aware that they are saturated with the perfection of wisdom, and for that reason they become an object of worship."[38]

The logic generating these passages appears to be this: Yes, the Buddha is enlightened and worthy of great respect, even worship. But how did he become so exalted a being? Through practice of the perfection of wisdom, not, primarily, through acts of worship. Therefore, in asking yourself what practice you should undertake, follow the example of the Buddha. The practice of wisdom is wiser than the worship of those who engage in this practice. It is better to be one of them than to worship them.

CRITICAL ASSESSMENT: A CONTEMPORARY PERFECTION OF WISDOM

In the cultures of our ancestors, both East and West, wisdom has been valued above all else as the greatest human virtue. Today, however, we are not so clear about the status of wisdom, or even what it might be. We rarely use the word. One reason for our lack of clarity about wisdom is that we are doubtful about the terms in which it was previously conceived. Wisdom was the capacity to envision eternal truths, to perceive directly the timeless moral and metaphysical order to which human lives must conform. It is not at all clear to us now that there is such an order or how, if there is, any actual human being could know it. Doubting the very context within which wisdom once made perfect sense, we are not sure how to understand wisdom as a form of human excellence. This doubt, however, and all of the contemporary circumstances that give rise to it, make reflection on the character and possibility of wisdom all that much more important for us today. Wisdom may be the most important stimulus to thought that Buddhism can offer us.

Using a variety of Buddhist principles as they come to be reflected through contemporary thinking, the goal of the remainder of this chapter is to articulate a Buddhist-inspired account of wisdom suitable for contemporary lives and circumstances. Buddhist resources are particularly useful for this purpose because they focus so intently on the complexities of life in the world rather than beyond it. Eschewing emphasis on afterlife as a primary concern, Buddhists have carefully examined the character of human existence, the complex human setting of desire, suffering, impermanence, relativity, and uncertainty, which is exactly the sense we have about the life-world in which we live. Wisdom is needed precisely because we do not know timeless truths, because we do not have direct access to a metaphysical order underwriting the world in which we live.

Understanding this as our situation in life, we acknowledge human finitude, the fact of always being immersed in the world in some particular time and place, and experience the reality around us from that specifically shaped and contoured point of view. To be useful for us, therefore, wisdom must be the capacity not to reach outside of our finitude to a permanent order beyond this transitory one but rather to work effectively within it. Although it is tempting to envision a truly wise person as altogether exempt from ambiguity and limited vision, as earlier traditions have done, that would be a state of omniscience, not wisdom. Accepting finitude as the starting point for these meditations, we begin to contemplate wisdom not as the end of uncertainty but rather as a capacity to face uncertain and ambiguous situations with integrity, composure, and reflective insight. Wisdom, therefore, will need to be reconceived as a quality of character that prepares us to function with fine-tuned ethical sensibility in changing contexts of extensive complexity and nuance, while still acknowledging fallibility.

Several realizations make wisdom more difficult to imagine than the other five ideals we have examined. Wisdom differs from the others in the extent to which it is readily identifiable and noticeable. When we look for acts of generosity, morality, tolerance, energy, and meditation, we know roughly where to look. Acts of generosity, for example, are located in a certain sphere of our lives; they are easily identified wherever something beneficial is intentionally and freely transferred from one person or group to another. But where do we look to find examples of wisdom? Nowhere in particular, or anywhere. There is no specific domain of wisdom. You can be wise or unwise in any dimension of life. Wisdom can be found at work in all of the other perfections and in everything we do, rather than in its own domain. There is wise giving, wise tolerance, wise eating, wise shopping, and so on. Wisdom appears at a more comprehensive level than the other perfections, and this is how it can guide, encompass, and perfect the other perfections.

Another factor making wisdom particularly hard to envision is that it is not a rule-governed capacity. The wise are not wise by virtue of adherence to a set of ideal precepts, even rules about wisdom or about life. It is not that rules are rendered useless in making wise decisions; it is rather that wisdom is what we call on to decide which rules to bring forth at what time and how to apply them. And in this, there are no rules to follow. One act performed twice in the same general situation may at one time be wise, and at another, foolish. A rule about that type of situation may be helpful, but only if we have the wisdom to know whether, when, and how to apply it. Wisdom is the ability to recognize what is and what is not an appropriate guide for dealing with situations skillfully.

For these reasons, living wisely in a wide variety of situations requires skill at improvisation. It is often the case that finding a suitable response to a situation means that we must improvise, avoiding rigid applications of past customs to current circumstances. It is not so much that the rules or guidelines are abandoned in these situations, but rather that they are appropriately extended or revised to encompass a situation that has not come up before. Wisdom, therefore, includes the skill of flexibility, the ability to follow guidelines when they are adequate to the circumstances, and to adjust and improvise when they are not. Buddhists have called this dimension of wisdom "skill-in-means," the wise capacity to find means or methods for action best suited to navigate the divide between the complex situation at hand and the ideals that have provided guidance in the past.

If wisdom is not simply a matter of learning the right rules, it is also not just a matter of knowledge. It is important to distinguish a person who is wise from someone who is knowledgeable. Knowing a lot about a situation is not enough to enable you to act wisely in it. You must also be able to see how the elements of the situation all fit together, how each factor should be weighted in relation to the others, and how this particular situation stands in relation to overarching ideals. A wise person will certainly understand the value of knowledge and seek it constantly. He or she will see its place in the larger scheme of things and understand when and how to put knowledge to use. Authentic wisdom will also lead to the recognition that in most situations we really do not *know* at all, if by "know" we mean having a complete and final grasp of all dimensions of the situation. As the image of Socrates implies, wisdom includes a realistic understanding of the contours of our ignorance.

Moreover, the wise person is more attentive to learning than to knowing. Whereas "knowing" is a fixed state, beyond which one need not go, learning is an ongoing process, one that is never complete. For this reason, wisdom is not so much what is learned as it is the pattern and practice of learning—the exercise of care and thoughtfulness that comprise skillful learning. Wisdom entails an openness to what we can learn from others, from situations, and from experiences that pass through our lives on a daily basis. An experienced person is more than someone who has had a lot of experience. It is someone who has learned a great deal from his or her experiences, someone open to being transformed by what happens in life.

The most important forms of experience transform us. They show us weaknesses in our prior understanding of things and point in some new direction. In that sense, experience disillusions us. It divests us of the "knowledge" that is sometimes so dogmatically held that it stands in the way of learning. Those who are wise undergo a continual process of revision based on life experience. They expose themselves to situations where conceptual holdings are thrown into question and where fundamental reinterpretation of the world might be mandated. In this sense, wise learning is a form of suffering, something we live through at the cost of some disruption and discomfort. The counsel of wisdom, however, is not to avoid this disruption but instead to seek out the transformative powers within it.

One of the dominant images of wisdom in certain types of Buddhism is esoteric knowledge. This image is often given caricature as a secret knowledge that is withheld from the uninitiated in order to cultivate an atmosphere of mystery. A better way to understand these "secrets," however, is to realize that wisdom and most forms of insight can only be entered or received once you have undergone the preparatory cultivation of mind required to grasp them. Indeed, ascending to higher levels of understanding often requires a transformation of who you are as a knower. The "password" allowing access to a deeper sense of reality is much more than a word, a mysterious sentence, or a thought; it is a complex alteration of the perspective from which you seek that depth. In Buddhism, that alteration or "awakening" typically "arises dependent" upon the mastery of meditative practices that function to change the way you experience things, yourself included.

This is the motivation behind various theories of "stages" in Buddhism. Each stage on the path to enlightenment is thought to depend on mastery of practices prescribed at the previous stage of development. There is nothing necessarily mysterious in this. Higher forms of learning in every sphere of culture are possible only after certain prerequisites have been fulfilled. Proficiency at a certain level of mathematics, for example, becomes possible only after previous stages of calculation have been mastered. Nor will you be able to shoot a jump shot on the basketball court until you have already tried many shots with your feet firmly on the ground. Very often, attaining a higher level of proficiency requires initiation by passing through earlier levels of understanding or skill acquisition.

However, "stages on the path to enlightenment" would appear to imply a well-structured ladder, where both "enlightenment" and the steps leading up to it are fixed in identity and set for all people at all times. Although some traditional Buddhist teachers and texts have assumed uniformity in the overall structure of the human quest for enlightenment, it would be unwise for us to adopt that picture of Buddhist or any other kind of self-cultivation. If reality really is "impermanent" and comes to be what it is "dependent upon conditions" that have not yet been determined, then neither enlightenment nor wisdom could possibly be fixed in this way.

Opening our minds to this new but certainly very "Buddhist" way of thinking brings us to see, once again, how the word "perfection" can be misleading. The "six perfections" or the "perfection of wisdom" might easily be taken to imply a set of practices that lead to a fixed state at the end of practice, the final goal of practice—a perfect state. "Perfection" appears to commit us to an image of an established and ultimate level beyond which we cannot go. Wherever Buddhists are true to their principles, however, no such state is asserted. Recall that our word "perfection" translates the Sanskrit *pāramitā*, which implies transcendence, an act of "going beyond." Perfection is the activity of perfecting, the practice of being on the way toward greater vision, greater wisdom. This requires learning to be at home on the journey, because there is nowhere else to be. Engaged in the practices of perfection, you are always in the process of working your way into deeper insight, always moving beyond where you have been, and always opening yourself to the possibility that the insights and practices that have helped you along so far may soon prove inadequate. This open situation in which we live calls for an experimental stance, a flexibility of mind that has developed beyond the expectation that the new always conform to patterns established in the past.

This orientation to wisdom takes ongoing creative growth as the ideal and casts doubt on the traditional ideal of a fixed and timeless goal for all human beings. It opens the way to a path that is not determined in advance for us but unfolds as we move along through a history that simply cannot be known ahead of time. The quest for wisdom, therefore, becomes a process without end. Since it is open-ended, we will not be able to know in advance what kinds of achievements human beings will come to admire and seek in the future.

This understanding of the quest and its goal accords with the image we have of enlightened masters inscribed in classical Buddhist texts. Enlightened teachers do not make claims about having reached the end of the quest. Whatever others have said about them, from their own points of view, they are—as before—fully engaged in the pursuit of greater depth. We might assume that this reluctance to make claims about their own wisdom is simply the humility and modesty of the wise. But that image of modesty is weak. A stronger version regards the wise as having a more highly developed and flexible conception of wisdom, one that understands wisdom as increasingly profound ways of engaging oneself in life. Wisdom in that view cannot be separated from the pursuit of it. The wise are those who have learned always to reach beyond themselves, always opening themselves to the possibility of transformative insight.

Our discussion in this chapter so far has summarized a number of preliminary issues that would be entailed in a contemporary concept of wisdom. As we begin to examine actual images of wisdom, we realize that there are multiple dimensions of human excellence that a contemporary "perfection of wisdom" would need to encompass. At this point in our historical development, wisdom cannot be encapsulated in any single image of excellence. In order to account for these multiple dimensions and to give wisdom a sufficiently comprehensive character, the remainder of this chapter articulates six interlinked dimensions of a Buddhist-inspired contemporary wisdom. We begin where Mahayana Buddhists began.

Wisdom in the Vision of "Emptiness": Breadth
and Depth of Perspective

Mahayana Buddhist sutras are very clear in making a strong connection
between wisdom and the realization of "emptiness" (*śūnyatā*). Wisdom,
they claim, is profound awareness of the "emptiness" of reality. Our initial
goal in this section will be to consider that claim carefully. To what extent
is it wise to ground a contemporary understanding of wisdom in a
metaphysical vision such as this one? Responding to this question, we
describe the basic concept of "emptiness" by reexamining it from three
distinct points of view. In the first instance, "emptiness" is understood as a
theory that guides how we think about individual things in the world—
all things of all different kinds. The second dimension of the concept is
the articulation of a comprehensive vision of the whole within which all
individuals are encompassed. And a third dimension of the concept
concerns the perspectives from which we encounter both earlier dimensions.

The first component of the theory of "emptiness" is invoked in the
sutras whenever something in particular is declared to be "empty." Over
and over these texts reapply the idea of "emptiness" to new entities, new
concepts, new situations—they remind the reader that all things are
"empty" insofar as they are mutable and depend on conditions established by other things. Wisdom is the capacity to see how every
individual thing lacks its "own-being," the quality of being self-established and independent. Relationships, changing over time, provide
the foundations for the identity we experience in things. Given these
"foundations," "empty" things do not have a fixed nature; their most
basic "nature" is to be open to processes of change due to continually
changing relations. Instead of having an intrinsic character that is fixed
and final, things have contexts, conditions, and histories. The discerning mind is aware that things are what they are for contextual and
temporal reasons and is able to trace those reasons skillfully in
the pursuit of insight.

In this first sense, the meditative principle of "emptiness" is a Buddhist
therapy aimed at overcoming the habit of understanding things by isolating them from their connections to the surrounding world and its
history. This is accomplished by highlighting the complex matrix of
conditions and relations within which everything stands. Understanding

that principle in practical detail facilitates living wisely within the moving web of interconnections.

This orientation to understanding the world is thoroughly contemporary. Analogues to these Buddhist ideas can be found in almost all fields of contemporary global thought. These are sometimes called "systems thinking" or "process thinking," but the goal of all of them is to propose models for thinking that are complex enough, subtle enough, and flexible enough to match the reality that they attempt to understand. These contemporary systems of thought often overlap with Buddhist principles so extensively that we could regard some of them as having extended Buddhist thought by its careful application to one particular domain of life.

Evolutionary biology is a good example of this. Like Buddhists, biologists now assume several basic principles in their inquiry: that all forms of life lack a fixed essence, that all living things have come to be what they are dependent upon influences exerted on them by other things, contexts, and time, and that not just individual things but entire species are relatively transitory and always subject to some degree of transformation. Although, to our ordinary experience, giraffes and junipers are two set biological types found in our world, to evolutionary biologists these are simply the most recent outcomes of biological transformations that have passed through countless stages to arrive at this temporary and transitory point of species development.

In a post-Darwinian culture, there are no biological essences, no timeless molds in which life forms are created. All forms of life come into being through mutations in earlier forms of life and then lose their current form through further mutations that incrementally alter each species over time. No outcome is determined or known in advance, because all other forms and processes are similarly contingent and subject to unpredictable movement. Although aspects of these processes may be relatively stable, no form of life generated within them could ever be.

Millennia before Darwin, Buddhists had proclaimed that everything is impermanent and "empty" of fixed essence. But until Darwin, no Buddhist had been able to see that biological species are not permanent, essential structures of organic life, even though their principles would have suggested that possibility. Impermanence, it turns out, and "emptiness" are much more pervasive than Buddhists ever imagined. Darwin had discovered, in a word, the "emptiness" of the "species" of plants and animals—that they are not eternal "forms" that are fixed forever. What

Darwin realized was that not only individual creatures but the models behind their emergence are impermanent and dependent on contextual conditions. Tracing this pattern of "dependent arising" back and forward in time, we realize that this was not just true in the past—the process is right now at work, changing who we are and what life forms there will be in the future.

Like everyone else, Buddhists assumed that known species—plants, animals, and human—are fixed types of things and that although individual specimens vary contextually, the underlying species to which they belong always have been and always will be basically what they are now. This assumption, shared by every culture in the world, would turn out to be false. This means that, in spite of its overall orientation to "emptiness," every aspect of Buddhist thought presupposes that there is a permanent structure called "human nature" upon which human beings have always and will always be modeled. Traditional concepts of "enlightenment" and other key ideas assume this basic level of "essentialism" and would now require adjustment if Buddhists aspire to carry through on the insightful themes that initiated the tradition in the first place.

This lapse in the application of Buddhist "emptiness" is perfectly understandable. Until recently the conditions had not yet arisen anywhere in any culture for anyone to see that all biological species are only relatively stable structures passing through relatively temporary states on their way to newer and newer forms of life, indefinitely. Prior to scientific procedures of investigation, no human being had enough historical perspective to see this truth. What Buddhists got right—from contemporary perspectives—are the principles behind these developments, and in terms of which many more such developments might come to be seen. To whatever extent that things have a "nature," it turns out to be a temporary nature that is defined for them by the contextual conditions in which they have come to be what they are. Of all the traditions of classical thinking in the world, none has come as close as Buddhism to anticipating this important realization in contemporary global thinking. Nevertheless, Buddhists will need to respond to this development by expanding their understanding of these basic principles based on new developments in all fields of contemporary thought.

This is to say that the Buddhist principle of "emptiness" is a brilliant guide to wise understanding in the contemporary world, regardless of how successful Buddhists have or have not been in applying it. Applying this principle not just in formal disciplines of learning like biology and history but in virtually every dimension of our lives, a compelling contemporary form of wisdom is made available to us.

A second dimension of the Buddhist concept of "emptiness" is the vision it offers of the whole of reality. Although each individual entity or situation or perspective is "empty," the largest sphere in which these "empty" things interact is called "emptiness." "Emptiness" in this sense is a view of the whole, not in detail, since all particulars can never be brought together into a single vision, but rather in principle. As a principle, this concept suggests a way of conceiving and experiencing the totality. Individual things are set within local relationships, and those relations are set within larger processes, and those within more encompassing spheres, and on and on until everything conceivable has been included within one all-encompassing system of interdependent movement. Everything interlinks with everything else, some in proximity and some at enormous separations of space and time, and all processes of change together form one overarching sphere of movement. Buddhists call this central vision "nondualism" because the point of the exercise is philosophical inclusivity—the effort to "understand how things in the broadest possible sense of the term hang together in the broadest possible sense of the term."[39] Wisdom is imparted through breadth of vision because the capacity to understand inclusively grows to the extent that we cease to project the heuristic boundary lines in our minds out upon the world.

This holistic vision of "emptiness" encompasses the "empty" character of particular entities in the world by weaving them all together in nondual understanding. When the early Mahayana sutras claim that "form is emptiness and emptiness is form," they contemplate the relationship between individual things and the always moving contexts within which they receive their identity. While the parts make the whole, simultaneously the whole makes the parts what they are. In this way, the second dimension of holistic "emptiness" is ultimately indistinct from the first dimension in which we see the relativity of particular forms, leaving only the third dimension to complete the full circle.

A third dimension of the principle of "emptiness" that has a substantial bearing on a contemporary conception of wisdom concerns the way we position ourselves within the interdependent contexts defined by "emptiness." The primary lesson to be learned in this domain is that, rather then imagining ourselves standing outside of contexts as we examine them, we understand what it means to occupy a specific location in the midst of temporal, spatial, and social contexts. This is the reflexive dimension of "emptiness" that we developed in discussing meditation. Several implications of reflexive awareness are entailed in living wisely, and each will be addressed as we work through this chapter. But the one we highlight here concerns the reflexive realization that "emptiness" brings to bear in our own acts of understanding. The fact that human beings are no less subject than anything else to this matrix of contextual influences shows us that whenever we understand anything, we do so from a position within a particular context, a setting that defines a particular point of view, a perspective. We never stand outside of the world to see it as a whole, but always understand in finite ways from a position within it. Acknowledging this fact about human perspective and taking it into account in the way we understand the work of our minds is an important dimension of wisdom.

One significant aspect of context for human subjects is that we are always historically situated. We understand from a perspective made possible by a particular location in human history, from the perspective of a particular language in a particular moment in its evolution, a particular stage of concept formation, particular economic, political, and social positions, and so on. These contextual facts and many more of much greater specificity set us up to understand in the particular way we do. They enable understanding and in doing so particularize it, making possible one or another angle of vision, greater or lesser comprehension, this or that specific set of relations to ourselves and the world. As we begin to understand what finite human standpoint implies, we recognize that no single description of anything could ever comprehend it because other descriptions from other angles that consider other dimensions will inevitably highlight or reveal some feature that was not fully visible from our original point of view.

The reductive insistence that one single way of describing anything should always prevail over others is what Buddhists call "dogmatism." Failing to sense the depth dimension of the reality in which we are situated, this mental posture reduces everything to a single set of qualities or relations, thereby constricting the greater comprehension that might otherwise be available. "Emptiness" as the reflexive realization of finite perspective counters this tendency to reductionism and dogmatism by enabling us to see where we stand when we understand.

Although that recognition of the significance of standpoint and the overarching theory of "relativity" that it bears are very important, it is vital that we draw consequences from them that are enabling rather than stifling. In our time, many respond to the specter of complexity, relativity, and change by recoiling against the threat of "relativism." This word and the morass of intellectual dangers that it signifies tend to evoke fear and other unhelpful reactions rather than thoughtfulness. When that happens, the two extreme positions mentioned above—blind assertions of dogmatic certainty and hopeless confessions of arbitrary relativism—are common outcomes. Neither response is functional, however. Wisdom demands a more thoughtful conclusion, one that appropriates whatever elements of insight may have motivated both positions, while moving through and beyond them.

The partial truth that lends credence to the reaction of "arbitrary relativism" is that human beings are indeed finite, not unlimited in mental powers, and we do live in the midst of an always changing reality that is shifting in accordance with the complex of relations within it. Our concepts are therefore always articulated from particular points of view and always insufficient to a comprehensive and definitive grasp of what they seek to understand. But to conclude from these realizations that our concepts and decisions are therefore arbitrary is an enormously mistaken response to the issue, one that interprets the "relations" in which we stand as insurmountable barriers to understanding rather than as the very connections that make understanding possible. The dangers presented by that naïve view lead some people to embrace the opposite view since, without thinking carefully, they see it as the only other option. But assertions of dogmatic certainty do not fare any better. They are equally immature attempts to avoid facing the issue directly. Merely asserting that the understanding currently most persuasive to my mind or the perspectives afforded by my culture are absolute and unconditional does not make it so, and such assertions fly in the face of substantial evidence to the contrary.

There are far better options for understanding on this issue, all located on middle paths between the awkward extremes of dogmatic certainty and arbitrary relativism. In response to arbitrary relativism, it is wise to recognize that, in spite of finding ourselves in the midst of an always changing context, our ideas are never arbitrary. We do not just make them up randomly. Concepts are formed collectively through their fit with other concepts and with the world in which we live. That sense of "fit" includes both coherence with the current structure of understanding and correspondence to the world as it is currently conceived and experienced. There is a profound sense of necessity that accompanies every concept in our minds. Understanding the "emptiness" of all concepts does not take that sense of necessity away. What it does do is qualify our assertiveness and conviction, giving us sound reasons to keep our minds open enough to consider the alternatives and improvements that might arise in time, since we can now see that "sense of necessity" is grounded in the specificity of relations and standpoint that provide orientation for understanding.

No matter where we stand, we are always charged with the discipline of truth, the effort to see the world for what it is. This demand of truthfulness is inescapable. We live always under the implicit requirement that we strive to see things as clearly and profoundly as we can, given the circumstances in which we find ourselves. Truth in the modern world is linked to "objectivity," but the objectivity of understanding cannot possibly mean standing outside of the whole of reality in order to look back at it comprehensively. What it can mean instead is that we become increasingly aware that our conceptual positions are contestable and open to amendment in view of persuasive evidence or more convincing alternatives. The wisdom of past experience tells us that no matter how convincing a certain set of ideas currently appears to be, that persuasive force may at some point recede. What seems obvious right now could at some point appear to be patently false, in the same way that the obvious flatness of the earth turned out to be an illusion based on inadequate perspective.

Realizing the inherent limitations of all concepts, however, does not change the fact that things appear to us as they do in fact appear. When we are persuaded, we are persuaded, no matter what we know about the possibility that this appearance may be limited, or temporary, or even possibly mistaken. The mental posture recommended by these realizations, therefore, is a relaxed attachment to the insights that enable understanding. "Relaxed" because, having had to alter our views many times before when more convincing understanding comes into view, we are wise to the limitations of human thinking. But still "attached" because we really do see things the way we do, supported as we always are by reasons and evidence. Although a person's "theory" may argue otherwise, in practice no one can consider their concepts arbitrary. On a day-to-day basis we always live our lives and carry out tasks presupposing the reliability and validity of the understanding in terms of which we move about in the world, whether we have assented to that intellectually or not.

Wisdom calls on us to release ourselves from dogmatic self-assertion, setting aside insecure claims to absolute certainty, while at the same time avoiding the hopeless posture of relativistic arbitrariness that prematurely surrenders the quest for understanding. Wisdom takes functional middle paths between these two unsatisfactory options. Skillfully conceived, it puts us into states of mind that allow considerable freedom, experimental states that seek the truth without being either sternly dogmatic or arbitrarily skeptical. The fact that the ground we stand on—the planet Earth—is always rotating on its axis and orbiting around the sun does not mean that at any particular moment it is not precisely somewhere. It just means that we are always on the move and that our location on the spinning globe affects what and how we will be able to see at any given moment. So it is with our efforts to understand our own acts of understanding wisely.

Wisdom in Enlightened Judgment: Relativity and Compassionate Commitment

One of the places where wisdom is most visible is in the setting of decision making, where it emerges as the ability to choose judiciously. The quality of human lives is often determined by the extent to which decisions made turn out to have been wise or foolish. Choosing wisely requires that many factors be taken into account. In every situation in which we must make a judgment, it is important to seek the relevant facts, weigh and assess them in relation to ideals or values, and carefully evaluate which choices fit both the situation at hand and the kind of world we strive to create.

Evaluations of timing, setting, and circumstance are all crucial to wise judgment. We have all seen how a particular decision or action may be graciously fitting in one setting and problematically out of keeping with another, or how a remark may be helpful and encouraging at one point of time, but discouraging at another. Wise judgment is this sense of the fitting, the skill of harmonizing insightfully with the multifaceted world around us. When we judge skillfully, we slip ourselves into the moment with precision, finding just the right action to effect just the right end.

Cultivating wisdom in judgment, one of the most important practices to have mastered is the habit and discipline of conscious doubt. Doubt is the critical practice of probing the vague feelings of uncertainty that enter our minds. Very often we avoid the unsettling discomfort of uncertainty, and when we do, we fail to elevate the initially vague sense of uncertainty to the critical level of self-conscious doubt. When we doubt explicitly and do not turn away in avoidance, our uncertainties become actual questions, which is the essential point of departure for serious inquiry. When doubt is raised to the level of a discipline, thought processes take on a clarity and depth that they cannot attain otherwise.

There are many kinds of obstacles standing in the way of wise judgment. Many of these resemble the kinds of human weaknesses that restrict the other "perfections"—day dreaming and fantasy, inattention and mindlessness, desires and revulsions, anxieties and fears. Wise judgment entails the steadfastness of mind and purpose to resist these weaknesses by concentrated focus on the most salient issues at stake in our lives. Wisdom is the discipline of looking longer, harder, and more profoundly into the subtleties and complexities of the particular situations we face. But most important, beyond the concentration and skill needed for judgment, is the quality of overarching ideals or values—the "thought of enlightenment"—in terms of which all possible choices can be judged. Without depth in the ideals that give overall orientation to life, no amount of mental dexterity will culminate in wise judgment. Wherever peoples' overall ideals are weak or underdeveloped, their judgment cannot help but be correspondingly weak. The values in view of which we make judgments are at least as important to wisdom as the care with which we engage the process of assessment.

Assessing wisdom in judgment, there are several components that need to be taken into account, weakness in any one of which can lead to faulty decisions. We misjudge when we hastily assemble the facts, leaving important elements out of consideration. We misjudge when we have the right facts, but weigh their significance inappropriately, or when we synthesize them into patterns that are out of accord with the situation before us. We also misjudge when we decide without being mindful of a larger vision for ourselves and our society, when we make decisions that do not align with well-cultivated ideals.

Occasionally, we fail to judge altogether, out of fear of the possibility of misjudgment, and in so doing act unwisely by not acting at all. There are a few occasions, however, when it is wise to avoid judgment, and one of these is out of concern for being overly "judgmental." Those who judge wisely also understand that the freedom of others who act or choose in community with us is vital to our collective quest. They know that the self-respect of others is a vital consideration, and that judgment in the form of blame is rarely helpful. Wisdom in these situations shows us when to forgo judgment, leaving the situation appropriately open for the participation and contribution of others.

How we make judgments is a good test of our character. This is true not just of the results of our judgments but also of how we go about coming to the decisions we do. All of us make judgments in accord with our character. Indeed, we are incapable of making them very far "out of character" because our character shapes how we perceive the situations in which we stand. This overall perception includes among its primary elements how observant we are about the world around us, how sensitive we are to others in our community, how we understand the world and our place in it, and what ideals guide us in overall orientation. Lacking cultivation in these larger issues of character, our judgments will inevitably reflect these same deficiencies.

There is one issue having a significant bearing on the topic of judgment that Buddhists faced in the Mahayana sutras and that we still face today in analogous forms. This issue concerns the overall context within which judgment will be made. In this context, there appears to be a contradiction between the two fundamental roles that we play in the arena of judgment, a polar tension between the perceived necessity for reflective detachment, on the one hand, and the requirement for active engagement, on the other. One pole guides our quest for "the truth" and the other our quest for "the good." Because the demands of each of these appear to come into conflict with the other, wise judgment requires reconciliation between them.

One of these poles encourages us to be certain that the good we pursue really is good. To do that, we stand back from activity in thoughtful disengagement in order to seek the truth about the good, so that what we pursue is more than an illusion of goodness at the level of immediate consciousness. The other pole, by contrast, encourages us not to postpone doing the good in order to engage in further refinement of its conception. The detachment mandated by reflection puts us in danger of failing to act on behalf of the good that we already know needs our attention. On the one hand, overzealous pursuit of the truth can hamper our capacity to do the good, and on the other, overzealous pursuit of the good can blind us to the truth that the good we pursue may not be as it appears.

The tension between these two pursuits became a central concern in classical Mahayana Buddhism. In these sutras, we can see the contradiction that elicited their concern, a contradiction between the quest to understand more profoundly the "emptiness" of all beings and the quest to extend compassionate aid to all beings in order to alleviate their suffering and guide them into enlightened existence. These were

the twin demands on the bodhisattva who was committed to enlightenment in the world, and although it was clear that some kind of reconciliation would be required, it was not at all clear how to accomplish that.
An analogous tension is ever-present in our own lives. This is the tension between analysis and action, between the detached life of in-
depth understanding and the engaged life of compassionate conviction.
We find elements of wisdom in both of these opposing ideals, but
have similar difficulties in trying to reconcile them. Attempting just
such a reconciliation, we take up the issue in contemporary terms while
making frequent connection to the analogous issue in classical Mahayana
Buddhism.

The first pole in the dilemma is the requirement that we disengage
from our immediate convictions and engagements at least long enough to
attain a clear understanding of what it is that we are doing. This is the
demand that through meditative disengagement we seek more and more
profound understanding of the situations in which we must act. For
Buddhists as for us, this means the effort to understand how the circumstances we face in our lives have come to be the way they are. All elements
in our overall situation are contingent; they came into being dependent on
other elements, and all of these multiple factors have always been and will
continue to be in historical motion. Given the complexity of any situation,
understanding clearly would require a significant degree of mental
detachment and a high level of concentration.

The difficulties entailed in acts of understanding become even more
prominent when we attain the level of reflexive self-understanding.
When we understand the dependent and mutable character not just of
things and situations in the world but also of the point of view from
which we understand them, at that point we come to recognize that in
principle the task of understanding is endless. Accepting the "dependent
origins" of our own commitments, convictions, and beliefs, we gradually
come to realize that these might have been otherwise. Had I been born in
another age, into another culture, speaking another language, and raised
to practice another religion or set of values, then many of the beliefs that
I hold to be true and that guide my actions might right now be very
different. This is to say, in Buddhist terms, that the self-understanding
that currently grounds my identity and that I take to be obvious in
immediate experience is actually "empty"; it is subject to a wide variety
of contingencies that are time and context dependent. In this sense,
meditations on "emptiness" have a deflationary effect. Employing

them to refine understanding, we particularize, historicize, finitize, and temporalize everything. More and more we come to see everything, ourselves included, not just in general but as the particular, finite, and historical beings that they are. As self-awareness is brought to bear on understanding, more and more we see that the task of clarity in under standing is ongoing, because there is no necessary end to any act of understanding. If reality is bottomless, our inquiries never hit upon a final ground.

On the other hand, action cannot wait. There are problems that need to be solved now if the good that we envision is ever to be actualized. The second pole in the dilemma of judgment is a commitment to action—to justice, to community, and to the alleviation of suffering—now. A life of wisdom includes a commitment not just to envision and conceptualize the good for our communities but also to engage ourselves in such a way that we help bring that vision of the good into being. This requires that judgments be made, not postponed, and that concrete action be under-taken. From the Buddhist point of view that we have been considering, when we make a judgment and select an action, there are two overriding criteria that govern our choice. One of these is "emptiness, "the first principle of Buddhist metaphysics, which discloses the depth of the reality within which our judgments must be made. And the other criterion is compassion, the "first principle" of Buddhist ethics, which guides all actions toward the good of universal well-being with some sense of urgency.

These two principles are difficult to reconcile, however. They stand in tension with each other. Buddhists have worried that the equanimity inspired by meditations on "emptiness" might be incompatible with the compassionate commitments entailed in alleviating suffering in the world. They were concerned that the critical disengagement required of in-depth reflective insight might be inimical to the immediate convic-tions implied in a life of compassionate community involvement. And so are we. Many of us struggle in our efforts to harmonize our own personal pursuit of "enlightenment" with commitment to community, and we cannot always see how our quest for the truth can be adequately balanced with our pursuit of the good.

A contemporary account of wisdom, however, would require just such reconciliation. When these two roles are in balance, we would practice a form of "critical engagement," "critical" in the sense of having passed prospective actions through the fire of critical, reflective meditation, and "engaged" in the sense of full commitment to activities aimed at the good in community. When one becomes "critically engaged," concerns for the good and the true are brought into balance. A balance of this kind locates the mean between analysis and action by developing an intuitive ability to steer clear of two extremes, both unself-conscious convictions and perpetual delay of action in order to complete critical investigations.

Several factors would be essential to this balance. Timing is one. This image of wisdom implies that there are times when reflective meditation dominates practice and other times when action and engagement would take precedence, so that the two essential roles we play would be intertwined and in balance with one another. Because this is an internal balance that needs to be maintained over time, the role of reflexive self-consciousness would be heightened in order to achieve it. It would be important to be able to see oneself both in immediate engagement and in meditative disengagement in order to keep them in critical perspective and to foster the kind of balance that would be needed between them. Both thoughtful hesitation and engaged conviction would be basic components of wisdom.

In the Buddhist sutras that we have been examining, the reconciliation struck between meditative "emptiness" and engaged "compassion" rests on several basic points of departure. One is that human beings are defined as socially interdependent beings. Engagement in community is by that means considered a fundamental component of human existence, and compassion is the principle guiding that engagement. Another is that when meditations on "emptiness" come to be experienced as thorough interdependence between all elements of reality, its natural consequence is compassion and community involvement. "Emptying the self" in this way is the same as seeing all the ways that your own well-being is intertwined with the well-being of the community as a whole and every individual in it.

Nevertheless, each of these forms of reconciliation in classical Buddhism is open to doubt and to critical deconstruction. From the point of view of the central Buddhist insight, all ideas, even those at the basis of compassion and community interdependence, are ultimately "empty." The most difficult questions continue to assert themselves over and over. Is it possible to stand firm for one's commitments and engagements in the world while at the same time acknowledging their relative validity? Is it possible to practice compassion while recognizing that all convictions—even compassion—are relative to the particular conditions and circumstances that have given rise to them? Is it possible to bear that truth in the way the sutras suggest that it is?

It seems to me that not only is it bearable but it may also be one of the most liberating realizations that we are likely to encounter. There is nothing incoherent about committing yourself to ideals that you understand to have evolved out of particular historical contexts and that in principle you understand to be both mutable and transcendable. Recognizing the "emptiness" of ideals does not require abandoning them. Instead, that recognition simply commits you to understanding them, to evaluating them critically, to coming to terms with their backgrounds and future prospects. It is a mistake to believe that contingent, historical values are not really valuable on account of their contingency and historicity. One philosophical mistake of this kind is called the "genetic fallacy," the common assumption that the value of something is based solely on its origins. But the fact that something comes into being through particular circumstances, all contingent, does not in any sense undermine its value. Indeed, there are no alternatives to this form of origination. Everything that exists arises out of dependent circumstances, and everything is for that reason open to reformation.

In no sense, however, does that contingency make anything "random" or "arbitrary." Everything comes to be what it is through specific causes and conditions; there are reasons for the emergence of everything that comes to be. No arbitrary, unconditioned results are possible, and accurate understanding of causality is always a demand that our lives place on us. Since no commitments come with eternal guarantees, that makes it all the more important to engage in meditative evaluation of their "dependent" grounds and to be sure that sound reasons and evidence support our having committed ourselves in the ways that we have. Even though you understand that your capacity to understand is rooted in culturally dependent, historically impermanent forms of cultural practice, you can still proceed with conviction in the decisions you have made. Indeed, you should be all the more confident in them, knowing that they have not been naïvely and uncritically assumed. Understanding more about the convictions you hold does not diminish their adequacy; it renders them more reliable than they would be otherwise. Wise judgment neither declares that the quest for understanding is complete nor abandons that quest altogether. Instead, it resides in the active space between these two extremes.

Buddhist sutras do not take up the issue of judgment explicitly, and words for wisdom in Buddhist languages tend not to be used in connection with decision making and agency. Although there are philosophical treatises in the Buddhist canon that treat themes related to judgment—knowledge and intention, for example—there are no references in sutras and few in philosophical texts that address judgment as a dimension of practical wisdom in the way that we have here.

Nevertheless, it is clear that Buddhists assumed that astute judgment accompanies wisdom as an integral part of it, even where it was not developed philosophically. Buddhists had spelled out many of the considerations that would be fundamental to wisdom in judgment—"interdependence," "contingency," "impermanence," "commitment to compassion," and more. But they appear not to have addressed this as a separate philosophical topic, as it was addressed, for example, in Aristotle's concept of practical wisdom—*phronesis*—the ability to make an effective transition from the abstract level of ideals to the concrete and ambiguous sphere of worldly judgment, or in Kant's critique of judgment, which seeks to understand on what grounds we are justified in judging something to be good or bad, beautiful or ugly. Noticing these differences, the question of judgment as a component of wisdom becomes an intriguing area of cross-cultural philosophy and, more important, a significant domain of reflective meditation for anyone hoping to come to terms with the contemporary world.

Wisdom as Imagination and Freedom in a Contingent World

There is an important connection to be made between wisdom and freedom. Those who we judge to be insightful and wise demonstrate a higher level of mental freedom, a freedom that consists in the ability to notice and explore possibilities in life that never occur to others. A wise mind sees beyond the solutions and customs that ordinarily define the available options. On occasion, this freedom of mind enables an innovative choice or action that in some respect goes beyond the ordinary conventions that unnecessarily constrain the rest of us. In this open area of freedom, wisdom emerges as insight.

This is not to say, of course, that human freedom and therefore wisdom should be imagined as the removal of all constraints. Like gravity, there are many dimensions of human existence that we are not free to ignore, and others that we ignore only at our own peril, that is, unwisely. Nevertheless, the freedom of mind implied in wisdom makes it possible to see the difference between constraints that currently define our existence and are therefore unavoidable, others that we ought to heed for very good reasons, and still others that need not constrain us at all.

Those who demonstrate imaginative insight are aware that although the established patterns and structures in life appear to be immutable, not all of them really are. Appearances notwithstanding, some are actually malleable to some degree and open to being conceived in some different light. They understand that the particular forms that seem to define human life have come into being dependent upon particular conditions, the conditions of *this* history, *this* mode of understanding, and not some other. Imaginative probing opens the possibility of creative, enlightened exploration of possibilities beyond those already established. Those who embody this imaginative freedom are able to treat their lives as ongoing experiments, testing possibilities wherever greater forms of human excellence come into clear view. By training themselves to imagine a wider range of possibilities, they become more and more willing to experiment whenever the prospects for constructive change justify such innovation. Although the cultural patterns provided by our ancestors and contemporaries are excellent guides, among them one important pattern to learn is flexibility of mind, the ability to imagine both old and new ways of proceeding under current circumstances.

Imaginative people have an acute sense of change. They see that changes under way right now in their environment will open the possibility of reenvisioning other elements of the established order. Imaginative people know that the present is different from the past and that the future will be distinct from both. They do not assume that just because things have been this way that they will continue in that vein, or that they must. Change is a fundamental feature of our life contexts—in the natural world, the social world, and the interior mental world. Imagination is the mental capacity to notice the incremental change unfolding in our life worlds and to work creatively with the implications of that change in order to recognize possibilities for the present and the future as they unfold.

Change is never random. Whatever comes to be does so based on very specific causes and conditions, no matter how complex. Possibilities become actualities only when the conditions are right for them to emerge. Wisdom is the imaginative skill to see causes and conditions hidden behind things, processes, people, and histories. Imaginative people see more than the situation in front of them—they see what conditions brought it into being, what conditions sustain it, and what conditions would bring its demise. Having developed that visionary skill to see everything in context, relationships, and movement, they position themselves to imagine what is possible in the future and to see which of these possibilities are most worthy of pursuit.

Prior to the late nineteenth century, human flight was impossible. Although it was certainly imaginable—human flight had been the subject of fantasy for millennia—what could not be imagined were the intellectual and technological conditions upon which it might become a real possibility. When those conditions had come into being in the nineteenth century, still only a few people had the imaginative vision to see how human flight had, in fact, already become possible. Many intelligent people in the nineteenth century understood all of the technological preconditions necessary for human beings to fly. But only a few had the imagination to see this possibility right before their eyes.

If vision depends on contextual conditions, then the ability to recontextualize things in our minds is one key to imaginative thinking. When we imagine the same thing in a different context, we begin to see more of that thing than we could before. Internal combustion engines reimagined with a propeller and in the context of flight changed how we understood the engine's possibilities. Redefining a troublesome problem, imaginative people find that new solutions rise to the surface of an altered angle of vision. Without the capacity to recontextualize, redefine, and reenvision things, we are prisoners to patterns of perception from the past. When we assume that we already have an exhaustive set of preordained possibilities, we simply choose from that standard list and find ourselves more attuned to past culture than to the present or the future. Fostering the kinds of mental openness imagined here requires practice, the practice of mindfulness to all the ways in which what is there before us has arisen out of conditions in the past. When we are inattentive to the reality of change, fearful of the new, or unpracticed in the skills of imagination, we fail to see the possibilities already present in our own time.

In discussing meditation, we saw that in contrast to fantasy—a mental evasion of the constraints of human finitude—imagination is a component of wisdom precisely because of its strong link to reality. The best scientists, physicians, engineers, administrators, and teachers are among the most imaginative people in our societies. They succeed in their work at the highest level of creativity because they have a solid grasp of the contours of the domain in which they work and the freedom of mind to experiment with them. Although we can fantasize just about anything, when we attempt to see our possibilities imaginatively, we seek real possibilities, possibilities that, because of their strong connection to the evolving structures of our world, really could come into being and really are worthwhile. Only when imagination is grounded in a realistic understanding of who we are and how our world is currently structured can its products be authentic possibilities, possibilities that can be both actualized and beneficial.

The imaginative component of wisdom provides the capacity to be experimental in life, to enlarge the field of possibilities by imagining how things look from a variety of perspectives. Although Buddhists were clearly imaginative thinkers, they did not explicitly acknowledge the role of imagination in their own practices. Nor did classical or medieval philosophers in other cultures. But at this point, it is difficult for us to imagine an admirable account of wisdom that does not include imagination as a fundamental component.

Buddhist resources for a reconceptualization of imagination are excellent, however. Taking them seriously would prevent the reemergence of romantic and individualistic accounts of creativity that locate the source of imagination in the mysterious inner self of ingenious people. A Buddhist account of imagination would take root in images of "no-self" and interdependent movement. From that flexible and unself-centered perspective, imagination would be an open-minded attunement to the relationships and processes within which we live and work, an attunement to the world that finds the sources of creativity neither within the "self" nor outside of it, but rather in the tensions, movements, and interconnections between them.

Wisdom in Simplicity, Composure, and Integrity

When we consider all the factors that go into wise judgment and imagination, we are confronted with the sometimes overwhelming complexity of our position in the world. Both Buddhist thought and many forms of contemporary thought show us how multilayered and labyrinth-like the world really is. They sensitize us to the fact that the multiple components of this complex reality are all in motion, everything moving at variant rates and in disparate directions. These images alone, however, would miss something essential about wisdom—the fact that it also consists in simplicity and composure. How is it possible that wisdom could encompass both a sophisticated capacity to confront complexity and a profound simplicity and ease? One of the ways that wisdom enables sound judgment and imaginative insight is that the wisest forms of intelligence function by recognizing patterns within complexity, structures of unity within diversity. Rather than being overwhelmed by complex multiplicity, skillful minds home in on the salient features of a situation, its central structures and characteristics.

Seeing networks of relations within the plethora of facts, the wise are aware of whole patterns of movement. What they see within a maze of divergence is holistic structure, the contours of underlying unity within which complex particulars converge. Clarity and creativity of vision are made possible by this orchestration and coalescence of the manifold. Simplicity in this sense is far from simplemindedness. Where the foolish are merely simplistic, the wise achieve a unified coherence of the highest order. Although it is true that once the full spectrum of background and relations is taken into account, even simple things are infinitely complex, nevertheless, we should imagine wise vision penetrating through this complexity to underlying patterns from which insightful, imaginative decisions can be made.

Moreover, wisdom in the form of simplicity allows improvisation at the level of immediate experience, spontaneous acts that accord both with the situation at hand and with an overall vision of ideals. In some situations, it is enough simply to trust the background of cultivation through which instincts have been shaped. For highly cultivated individuals, well-honed intuitions are often the best guide. Carefree, but in no way careless, intuitions are the products of long-standing disciplines of self-cultivation and therefore do not require constant inspection and analysis in order to be trustworthy. Simplicity in this sense prevents thinking from becoming entangled in obsessive overindulgence. It playfully mocks the seriousness of hyperintrospection, which is always in danger of losing track of where we are.

Wise simplicity of this sort is deeply grounded in the wisdom that has accumulated through intentional practice and life experience. This is the meaning of wisdom as a "second nature," a natural component of wisdom at the level of immediate experience that has been earned through the discipline of self-cultivation. Having achieved that second nature, the wise are free on some occasions to trust their instincts and release themselves into spontaneous action and response. In contrast to the image of the virtuous person struggling to act against all inner inclination, we should envision highly developed individuals acting with noticeable ease from their deepest inclinations, inclinations that have been honed through the discipline of a mature "thought of enlightenment."

This dimension of wisdom is the one that is often featured in the image of the awakened Zen Buddhist master. Zen masters are said to reside in a state of "no-mind" or "no-thought," a relation to the world that is less hesitant and more immediate than more intellectually sophisticated comportments. Having trained long and hard in the various disciplines of mindfulness, Zen masters live in an intuitive grasp of their circumstances that allows them to function easily and extemporaneously where the rest of us hesitate and falter. With a profound sense of unity—the simplicity behind the complexity of the world—Zen masters are pictured as acting out of an intimate connection to the world that has been earned by following Buddhist meditations on "emptiness" down to the level of embodied, practical wisdom. Manifestations of this character transformation are a sense of ease and fluidity, a sense of being at home in the world, and a kind of spontaneity that features unmediated movement and action.

Each of the foregoing traits—the ability to see patterns within divergence, the sense of ease and fluidity of life lived through cultivated instincts, and the cultivated quality of simplicity—are grounded in a background of peace and composure. Indeed, it is hard to imagine any form of wisdom—not just Buddhist—that does not derive from an embodied state of calm and composure. States of character that are fearful, greedy, anxious, compulsively busy, jangled, or nervous tend to diminish the scope and depth of human vision. They do not provide the conditions under which our minds can gather themselves, stepping back from the throes of activity to see where we are and what is going on. When our minds are in turmoil, we lose track of larger perspectives; we push ahead unaware of all the ways the immediate situation we face is framed in more comprehensive perspectives. Composure and equilibrium make that awareness possible and are on that account fundamental components of wisdom.

For Buddhists, of course, the primary setting for this kind of cultivation is the practice of meditation. Both of the basic types of Buddhist meditation, as we saw, are aimed at the generation of wisdom. But one of them—*samatha*, calming—is virtually prerequisite to wisdom. Without the relaxed composure of this cultivated state of mind, we are subject to the domination of diminished states of mind such as fear and unreflective desire. Breathing deeply to gain composure, we expand the power of understanding to see more clearly into the world around us.

Only in some degree of calm and composure can the various dimensions of our lives be integrated with one another—principles and actions, ends and means, thoughts and feelings, joys and concerns. Composure is thereby linked to integrity, a state of nonconflict with ourselves in which the various dimensions of our lives are harmonized. Integrity, in this sense, is a fundamental ingredient of wisdom. It is the balance, stability, and coherence of character that gives wholeness to life. When integrity is manifest, we gather everything we do under the canopy of the unified vision entailed in a well-cultivated "thought of enlightenment." This unity in life is never given. It is an achievement, an ongoing, lifelong project of integration, always undertaken in the face of forces that threaten disintegration. But wherever this kind of integrated balance has been achieved, there is profound sense of beauty to human lives.

Buddhists are insightful in their claims that desire and fear are the primary obstacles to integrity and composure of character. Desires that have not been chosen, cultivated, and integrated within a larger vision of life hold us under their dominance. In postures of grasping, clutching, envy, and acquisition, we have virtually no reflexive capacity to see who we are or what we are doing. Blinded by disparate attractions, we have no means of gaining perspective. In this sense, "composure" is another name for freedom.

Similarly, being fearful undermines our capacity to enter the comprehensive perspectives entailed in wisdom. When under the dominance of a range of states from timidity to fear, our overall bearing is defensive. In this demeanor, our actions function primarily to shelter ourselves. Focused on self-protection, we risk nothing and open our minds to very little. Fearful states of mind tend to overestimate obstacles to well-being, leading us to close down and practice avoidance. Exaggerated awareness of vulnerability undermines the basic trust required to feel at home in the world and to risk living. Composure that has been consciously cultivated through religious conviction or contemplative training helps develop this basic trust. Trust of this kind enables ease, composure, and freedom, the freedom to assess our situation honestly and to risk being open to the world around us.

Buddhists are right that the composure and peace always in the background of wisdom can be cultivated in contemplative exercise. Nongrasping, nondefensive forms of mentality are, like everything else, the results of practice and conditioning. Everything comes into being, Buddhists claim, dependent upon prior causes and conditions. Both the artificial self-enclosures that fear and desire generate and the balanced wisdom produced by perspective and composure have their roots in what we do in our lives. Every state of character, every form of life, has a path of daily activity and practice that leads directly or indirectly to it.

Lacking life practices conducive to such a state, it is unlikely that we could ever come to feel at home in the world and at peace with our being here. Those who are wise attain this peace by practicing peace, rather than by hoping that it comes on its own. They cultivate composure, flexibility, and resilience, and use these personal powers not to control the world so much as to control their own tendencies to close down and diminish themselves. To whatever extent these skills are embodied, wisdom is clearly visible in an balanced life of integrity and peace.

Wisdom in Selfless Irony and Ecstatic Humor

That an individual achieves the status of "enlightenment" or "wisdom" is attributable to that person's individual effort only in part, because achievements of this kind depend on the particular forms of human excellence that have been imagined and sought in the larger culture within which self-cultivation takes place. The wisdom of one exceptional human being—one bodhisattva, one Mozart, one Mother Teresa, one person of excellence in any sphere of culture—is the outcome of centuries of striving in the culture as a whole, through which that state of excellence has become possible. Although it might seem at first that this individual has gone far beyond others in the society, in a larger perspective we can see that the exemplary individual is more adequately understood as the tip of the culture's iceberg, as a surplus of excellence extending out from the society's collective work over long stretches of time.

This is why the heightened success of one member of a society brings pride to the community as a whole. He or she, the great one in some dimension of culture, is in large scale effect their work of art. This expanded vision, which is cultivated in Buddhism by bodhisattvas reflecting on the complexities of "emptiness," forces us to reconsider the individualistic understanding of "enlightenment" that we tend to assume at the outset. Those who ascend to something worth calling "wisdom" have accomplished a significant shift in orientation. They shift from understanding enlightenment as their own personal advantage to understanding enlightenment as a larger advantage for the culture over-all. Through this kind of spiritual transformation, expanding and enlarg-ing their sense of "self" and relations to the world beyond them, they overcome the illusions of individual self-interest that at earlier stages of development seemed to provide motivation for striving. Enlarged vision brings with it more expansive sources of motivation.

The sense of expansiveness entailed in this enlarged vision enables release from prior confinement, an ecstasy of—literally—standing out beyond oneself. In such moments of ecstatic clarity, there is profound irony visible in all habitual acts of self-enclosure that prevent awareness of our own ultimate "selflessness" within the larger spheres of reality that encompass us. In wisdom there is irony, and in irony, the possibility of the selfless release of humor. Indeed, it is laughter that provides some of our finest experiences of heightened lucidity. Humor is one of the most important cures for our habits of self-absorption—it gives us the freedom to laugh at the world, at our meager understanding of it, and at ourselves. When we take ourselves too seriously, humor lightens our load, and in the process gives us the pleasure of release. The wise sense wisdom in laughter, in themselves and in others. Indeed, there are times when laughing may be the wisest thing we do. Without humor, we lack the lightness of touch and clarity of vision that give depth to wisdom.

Comic wisdom celebrates human finitude by making fun of it. Sensing our own inevitable folly, we can either bemoan being human or release the gravity and severity of that state into lightness and laughter. Humor puts everything in perspective. It pokes fun at our pretensions of self-importance and our limited comprehension. In laughter we do not eliminate the seriousness of our lives; we just see it for what it is. Laughter provides disillusionment, undermining preciously held illusions about our-selves and releasing us temporarily from the bondage of self-deception. By highlighting our sometimes morbid seriousness, humor gives us a moment of joyful lucidity. When laughing, we see the truth about ourselves, and if we do not simply evade its biting point, we learn to appropriate that truth in the form of insightful selflessness.

When we "crack up" in laughter we open up to the world, breaking the suffocating sense of confinement in ourselves that separates us from others and the rest of the world. Laughter provides a glimpse of freedom from our self-containment and through that insight gives us the gift of flexibility and resilience. In humor, the wise celebrate human existence, finding joy in our collective existence. Momentarily taken out of themselves, they experience their freedom as pure enjoyment. The wise know that laughter is not a trivial matter, and hoping to liberate us, poke fun at those of us who think it is.

The point here is not that seriousness is unwise. Indeed, we all know the difficulties in life that are caused by insufficient seriousness. Humor cannot replace seriousness, but it can bring it to completion by purifying it in the light of irony and more encompassing points of view. While seriousness is committed and earnest, humor moderates these somber states by providing insight and release into alternative perspectives. Humor makes it possible for us to interpret ourselves and the world from different points of view. It offers a moment of liberation by forcing us to shift mental expectations, to alter our mood, and to see the incongruities always present in our minds and characters. There is tension, of course, between serious concern and the joyful release of laughter, but it is precisely in that tension that wisdom resides.

The *Perfection of Wisdom* literature frequently cited in this book had an enormously powerful impact on Chinese culture. Although initially perplexing, as the translations of this literature became more and more sophisticated, their popularity boomed. What seems to have been most intriguing to Chinese audiences were junctures in the texts where carefully reasoned lines of argument culminate in paradox. When the perfected wisdom of "emptiness" is juxtaposed to ordinary understanding, contradiction jumps to the surface of the text. Chinese readers saw brilliance in this and reveled at the similarities they could see to their own indigenous tradition of Daoism, where paradoxical reasoning is savored and taken to ecstatic conclusions.

When you place these two traditions of philosophical literature next to each other, you notice that one element that is prominent in the Chinese but missing in the Indian is humor. While the Indian sutras push relentlessly on the paradoxical implications of the quest for wisdom, the Daoist *Zhuangzi* guides similar realizations to a breaking point where laughter vaults the reader or hearer into ecstatic release. Once Chinese Buddhists got to the point of making a connection between these two traditions—as they did in the indigenous Chan or Zen tradition of Buddhism—humor reemerges right where you might least expect to find it: in the otherwise stiff and serious context of Buddhist monasteries. In Chinese culture, there is an important connection to be made between wisdom and humor, and the Zen tradition is the segment of Chinese Buddhism where we see it most prominently developed.

So what is it that joins wisdom and laughter in Zen? Zen stories use humor to break through the sometimes nihilistic tyranny of religious and philosophical seriousness. At just the point where serious thinking begins to turn sterile, Zen humor digs in. Wherever seriousness succumbs to rigidity and lack of imagination, a Zen master might rupture that stultifying atmosphere with ironic humor. Humor breaks through conventional boundaries, undermines dogmatism, and shows how everything can be turned upside down and examined from an altogether different point of view. In a moment of laughter, we feel a temporary release from the narrowness and inflexibility that typically structure our relations to the world around us.

In one Zen story circulating orally among practitioners, a Zen master sits bored and half asleep listening to a doctrinal debate between two senior monks. The scene is one of unadulterated tedium, the two monks lost in their own scholastic labyrinth. A novice monk enters the room to serve tea and when he bends down to place the refreshment in front of the two debaters he dislodges a high volume fart. Immediately the Zen master awakens from his half-slumber and in uproarious laughter, bellows: "You two bores are dismissed. At last someone steps forward to bespeak the truth of Zen."

In this story irony generates laughter, and laughter evokes insight and release. Entrapped by narrowness of vision and too much self-seriousness, humor puts the fallibility and finitude of all human enterprise out in the open to be seen. Where rigidity once stood, suddenly there is flexibility of mind. When the world is dull or painful, humor somehow extracts pleasure by altering perspectives just enough to see what is usually hidden from us. Zen humor targets self-absorption in its many forms—arrogance, dogmatism, inattentiveness to the world around us. It recommends laughter as a possible cure for the common habit of self-inflation. When we take ourselves too seriously, humor inspires deflation, and in so doing gives us the pleasure of release.

Laughing at our paradoxical situation in life is not a matter of denying it but rather of refusing to be crushed by it. In laughter we refuse to accept the pain and frustration of life as only painful and frustrating. Laughter provides a shot of relief, a glimpse of freedom from ourselves. Although not easy to articulate, Zen humor and laughter help complete the sophisticated conceptual structure of the classical Buddhist tradition by pointing out a liberating escape route from its tightly woven structure of paradox. It is in this same sense, I think, that contemporary Jewish humor, in all its brilliance, makes it possible to continue to take *Torah* and *Talmud* seriously. When unable or unwilling to release itself into humility—to let go in laughter—a tradition of wisdom risks loosing the critical edge that brought it wisdom in the first place.

Wisdom in Humility and Reverence

There is no more visible sign of wisdom than humility. Humility is a rare and exceptional trait, one that very few of us truly embody. This is so because nothing characterizes our lives more than the desire to be exceptional, a desire so common that it makes all of us who practice it seem quite ordinary. Wisdom entails several realizations that render the wise person humble. First, wisdom is grounded in a realistic understanding one's own limitations. The ability to engage in one's endeavors in view of that understanding shows the skill and dexterity of this wisdom.

Similarly, in accord with the image of Socrates, wisdom includes a realistic knowledge of our own ignorance. When we do not know, it is wise to acknowledge that we do not know and not delude ourselves. These two realizations give rise to a natural humility. Third, however, wisdom entails a finely tuned sense of the vast scope of the reality in which we live. When our vision opens wide enough, we can see that the enormity of space and time overwhelms the proportions of our small lives and world. Small is too big a word to describe the sensation we get when insight shows us something significant about our true place in the cosmos. Living in view of that awareness, the wise are humbled in a way that those lacking a profound sense of proportion are not.

Humility of this kind is much more than the shy habit of self-effacement, which is often just as deluded as the most blatant forms of ego assertion. Instead, picture humility as a form of freedom that comes from a contemplative, disciplined overcoming of self-absorption and from an awe and respect for the scope of reality beyond one's own small part in it. A wonderful irony can be seen in the fact that this wise humility cannot be produced by narcissistic fine-tuning of one's own character in self-cultivation. Indeed, excessive preoccupation with your own character development is a sign of misguided proportion, a deluded sense of significance. In contrast, humility derives from a meditative appreciation of dependence on realities far greater than our own. Acknowledging these sustaining realities—everything from one's family history, one's civic and cultural heritage, the earth, air, fire, and water that sustain us, to the unity of being itself, we get a glimpse into the meaning of "no-self" and the foundations of true humility.

As a dimension of wisdom, humility includes a profound sense that we did not create ourselves and that we owe our existence to larger, more enduring processes that encompass and sustain us. Although this sense is often deeply religious, there are wise people who demonstrate this comprehensive awareness in their daily lives who do not participate in traditional religions. Better, therefore, to call it a deeply human sense, a sense of the truth of our origins and of our ultimately dependent condition. The wisest and most appropriate responses to this sense are awe and wonder, and beyond that a profound gratitude for the gift of our existence. Whether explicitly religious or not, wisdom culminates in reverence for being itself, for everything that grounds our existence.

Conscious that our lives are embedded within realities far greater than our individuality, reverence includes an awareness of our own dependence and fragility. Contemporary habits of mind resist acknowledging this absolute dependence. Our various declarations of independence undermine the grounds upon which reverential moods arise, and insofar as that occurs we lose the capacity to sense the magnitude of the reality that encompasses us and to be taken up in profound feelings of awe. There are several good reasons for this resistance. Some traditional religions identified reverence with fear, teaching that the wrath and terror of divinity determined the true condition of piety. Often the culture of fearful religiosity encouraged steadfast resistance to change and cultivated the mistaken sense that human creativity was blasphemous.

We should not lose sight of these important forms of cultural resistance. Indeed, we should develop an understanding of what it is that we resist in them. Ideally, we would resist any tendency to cultivate fear or to ground human understanding in it. Wisdom is ultimately fearless. Fear of the Lord is *not* the beginning of wisdom, nor is it, in our time, the best way to motivate human action. Moreover, we ought to resist all of the ways that human beings can be ridiculed, belittled, and condemned. These methods of developing religious sensibilities are harmful and mistaken. No one should be taught to cultivate a self-understanding of greater dependence than is actually true in their lives, and the pride of human achievement should be encouraged rather than disdained.

None of these important realizations, however, stands as a legitimate criticism of reverence. An authentic sense of reverence derives from a simple recognition of the truth. We are, in truth, dependent beings. We are, in fact, miniscule within the vast scope of the universe. Reverence is an open and honest human response to the depth and magnitude of reality. When we allow ourselves to come under the sway of this feeling, awe and wonder open our minds. Although in reverential moods we feel how small and fragile we actually are, this is very different from a sense of being belittled or ridiculed. On the contrary, it is an awareness of enlargement by means of a profound feeling of connection to all of the dimensions of reality that transcend, encompass, and support us. The feeling of reverence is an internal and silent celebration of the depth of being itself. The sensibilities that accompany it are awe and respect rather than fear and separation. Joyful reverence celebrates our being embedded within the whole of reality in a clarity of mind that overcomes fear.

In an ironic turn of language history, we find uses of the word "irreverence" as a virtue as, for example, when an "irreverent" literary review or film critique exposes a pompous or pretentious work of art. In this use, "irreverence" is a tool in opposition to false reverence. It becomes a synonym for honesty, courage, and independence of thought in an effort to expose shallowness wherever a presumptuous proclamation of importance or depth is falsely made. Reverence expands to encompass ironic humor of this kind wherever the truth is so served. There are times when the most truthful act possible is a discursive gesture deflating arrogance and pretense. In such times, honest "irreverence" may be the only form of reverence available.

Although sometimes an "irreverent" critique exposes hollow ritual or presumptuous ceremony, it is as true today as in earlier cultures that ritual and ceremony function socially to cultivate the feelings necessary for reverence, even when we do not use those particular words. If reverence is a range of emotions that includes awe and respect for all that transcends the human, then those emotions need to be developed in cultural occasions meant to evoke them. Emotions, like anything else, "arise dependent" upon conditions suited to them, and when those conditions are not mindfully maintained, we cannot expect these feelings to arise. Feelings of reverence are certainly not limited to ritual occasions. Ideally, they emerge on their own whenever an occasion for them arises—looking out over the ocean or a mountain landscape, starring out into the stars at night, contemplating the magnitude of the universe in an observatory, or observing the play of a child. But their origins are nevertheless socially conditioned through ritual and ceremonial occasions, and no culture can afford to forget that.

Although typically what we feel for human beings is respect or admiration rather than reverence, which tends to be directed to what transcends the human, we are capable of feeling reverence for life itself. In fact, in the Buddhist tradition, this is a fundamental principle that is cultivated in ethical training. The contemporary Buddhist leader Thich Nhat Hanh refers to this reverence for life as the "first precept" of Buddhism. Contemplating the sheer fact of life—the miracle that organic life exists, that it has emerged out of nonlife and continues to evolve into higher and more conscious forms—we cannot help but feel amazement, awe, and respect. The Buddhist claim is that compassion for everyone and everything that joins us in this holistic reality is the most worthy response to such reverence and that compassion is the primary aim of ethical development.

Nothing may be more important today than cultivating reverence for life. Buddhist thinkers today join others in warning all of us about the threat to life on the planet earth that human civilization now poses. Reverence for life and wisdom clearly demand that we rapidly alter our habitual modes of living so that the environment that supports life on our planet is wisely maintained. The foolishness of perpetuating current ways of living is now visible for everyone to see. This is a monumental test of human character the proportions of which are historically unique. Do we have the wisdom and the freedom of mind to transform our collective self-understanding in such a way that in profound reverence we nurture the biosphere now placed under our charge? Can we now learn to conceive of ourselves as charged with the responsibility of tending and maintaining the earth and all of its creatures? Can we alter the sense of the biblical charge given millennia ago from "sovereignty over nature" to "humility and reverence within it"? The only form of wisdom worthy of that name today will be one capable of generating a universal reverence for life profound enough to guide us in preserving the fundamental conditions of life itself.

CONCLUSION

Everything you have read in this book has emerged from an effort on my part to pursue ideals, to think idealistically, to be idealistic. For some, this enterprise may still require justification. Some of our contemporaries will claim that they do not believe in ideals. A number of these critics will call themselves "realists" and claim that "idealism" is naïve and unrealistic. Others will call themselves "postmodern ironists" or, without irony, "cynics," and claim that since there are no ideals, being "idealistic" is naïve and deluded. But both of these criticisms miss the mark. Neither can provide a basis for their criticism without invoking the very ideals that they deny, and neither can show how creative effort and movement in life are possible without the cultivation of ideals.

To be "realistic" is simply to be practical, to keep one's focus on the present and our current state of affairs—both legitimate and important concerns. But doing so without also extending one's vision out toward ideals on the horizon and toward the more distant future leaves the mind in confinement and without direction. In fact, "realists" do hold ideals to underwrite their criticisms, but these ideals tend to be near-sighted and short-term. Because "realism" does not encourage thoughtful, imaginative reflection on ideals, the ideals "realists" do nevertheless hold are not developed or extended out very far beyond where they currently stand. These would therefore be ideals in the most minimal sense.

When a recent president of the United States was criticized for lacking a vision for the future of the nation, his response was that he did not really understand "the vision thing." Indeed he did not, and the nation suffered from lack of direction. When ideals have not been cultivated, vision for the future and deliberate direction for change will be lacking. When Martin Luther King Jr. said "I have a dream," "realists" were inclined to scoff at his idealism and opposed his efforts to actualize that dream. They thought he was being naïve and unrealistic. Realists cannot imagine committing themselves to work toward an ideal that cannot be actualized right now. Indeed, that is half the problem. They cannot imagine.

Focused almost exclusively on the present, their vision does not extend much beyond the current situation. Although every society needs to be able to focus on the present in a practical way, it must also produce and maintain ideals to provide vision and direction for these practical efforts.

"Postmodern ironists" are sometimes cynical about ideals. Often historically sophisticated, they have seen how ideals come and go over time and how some have even been employed in the service of oppression and injustice. They understand the contemporary critique of Platonic metaphysics, which undermines the realm of permanent forms in which ideals were thought to be founded. What they have not seen, however, are the ideals hidden in their own critique, because they have not taken the critique far enough to get past the Platonic tendency in Western thought. In effect, they still align themselves with classical metaphysics by accepting its understanding of what ideals are. Without questioning that starting point, they consider themselves to have rejected ideals altogether. So they say, in effect: If you can't be as certain as Plato had hoped that the ideals you propose will withstand the test of time and change, then don't propose any. If you can't hold values that are immune to critique, then don't hold any. From this point of view, only unconditional ideals are regarded as truly ideal and, they conclude, there aren't any.

In response to such a position, we can only concede the initial point. It is true; nothing you can propose will be invulnerable to critical doubt. No value you could hold comes with a guarantee that it will hold its value unconditionally. That just is the human condition. But given that, what is the most appropriate response? Accept the metaphysical terms in which matter has been historically defined and give up on the effort to articulate ideals? That just leaves everyone directionless and without the inspiration and motivation needed for human striving and for deliberate change. Consider instead questioning and altering the metaphysics behind this definition of ideals, and from that vantage point begin to rethink them. Realize that ideals are essential to human minds and culture, and use the critical edge of your irony to deepen the quest for ideals by bringing it to bear on the debate over values that accord with our time.

So anticipating both "realist" and "ironist" doubts about the "six perfections," here for your consideration is a brief account of the understanding of ideals presupposed throughout this book. We have considered six dimensions of human character as classical Buddhist ideals and then as ideals that we might hold today in our own world. That most of us have never known anyone who in every way lives up to even one of these six ideals should not be counted as a mark against the contemplative effort that we have undertaken here, you as engaged reader and I as engaged writer. In fact, if we could point to people around us who have already achieved the most exalted levels of character that we have considered, we would have failed in the representation of ideals. Ideals concern the way the world ought to be, the way it could be, not the way it already is. Although current reality is the ground from which we articulate and project ideals, it is from perspectives offered by ideals that we pass judgment on current reality. Deficiencies in the way the world actually is can only be seen from vantage points afforded by our ideals. Lacking ideals and the mental capacity to be "idealistic," our lives and our communities could only be experienced as just fine the way they are.

That none of us would say that the world is already fine just the way it is shows that all of us are idealists to some extent. We may not be aware of projecting ideals for the world in which we live, but we have and will to the extent that we live a fully human life. Every criticism made presupposes ideals that have already been adopted as standards justifying the criticism. Every exercise of critique assumes an idea of the good in terms of which something can be declared to be not good—bad, wrong, misguided, of poor quality, unfair, naïve, unrealistic, and so forth.

The fact that some people are not conscious of the ideals that form the basis of their criticism just renders the critique insufficiently critical about its own point of view and therefore underdeveloped and immature. But it does not alter the fact that assumed ideals stand at the basis of the critique, regardless of how unintentional and undeveloped they are. Since we inevitably hold ideals as the ground of every criticism, the greater and more profound our awareness of that truth, the more we will self-consciously engage in the cultivation of ideals and, as a consequence, the more seriously our criticisms can be taken. When we articulate, clarify, and refine the ideals that serve as their grounds, our criticisms attain a depth of sophistication that underwrites their prospective value.

Ideals worth their place in our minds will have been articulated there through deliberate critical thinking and a healthy dose of realism. "Realism" here does not mean "devoid of ideals" It means that ideals must be well grounded in the contours of current understanding; it entails understanding clearly that ideals will be unworthy and ineffective if their connection to contemporary life is not clear enough to make it possible for us to understand and admire them. Ideals must accord with actual possibility, since that is what they place before us for the purposes of inspiration and motivation. We could not possibly admire an ideal if, for example, we had never known anyone who approximated that characteristic closely enough for us to identify and praise it. Ideals cannot be arbitrary, any more than we can make ourselves admire something that we simply do not admire. Although the internal criteria determining what we admire are always open to change, at any given time these ideals have a particular form that shapes our judgment. They draw us toward them, whether we make that movement consciously and purposefully or not.

In many ways, ideals resemble horizons that stretch out to the limits of our vision. If an ideal stands out beyond the limits of our current vision, we could not consider it ideal because we cannot see anything beyond the horizon. Conversely, if ideals too closely resemble the actual world in which we reside, they fail as ideals because they do not inspire, they do not motivate and attract our highest admiration. When most effective, ideals *are* the horizon; they are the furthest stretch of current vision, the most impressive ends that can be realistically conceived under current circumstances. Placed out on the horizon of current understanding, ideals motivate us to extend ourselves toward something that exceeds our present condition. They energize effort and striving toward the good that clearly "betters" the selves and worlds that currently define our circumstances. Ideals are a demand placed on us by the weight of our circumstances and the power of our imaginations.

The presence of ideals in our minds and cultures, and the fact that these always develop and evolve, show us that we human beings are a work in progress. The human project, both individually and collectively, is always incomplete. That is what the finitude of humanity means—to be human is to be on a journey toward a wholeness and integrity that is never entirely accomplished. Ideals function as the stimulus and motivation that guide this movement and push us out beyond ourselves. As we move, both individually and communally, so do our ideals, because every accomplishment, every new point of departure, will bring new horizons into view, new images of the good to enlighten and energize our efforts in life.

Lacking a "thought of enlightenment" of this kind, individuals and communities would lack direction, purpose, and motivation. Although they will still change, given changing environments and circumstances, individuals and communities without ideals would not participate in shaping the direction and scope of that change because no admirable ends would stand out ahead of them as the aim and motivation for their efforts. Ideals articulate not just our hope but also the very possibility of human striving. For these reasons, being idealistic is not something we can afford to avoid. Indeed, when we are not idealistic, we have already either accepted the status quo as just fine the way it is or surrendered to hopelessness and fate.

This account of ideals works against the long-standing Platonic tendency in Western culture and analogous tendencies in other traditions to think of ideals as timeless, fixed forms to which human lives must conform. Wherever "human nature" is conceived in static terms, there will be a corresponding fixity in ideals, in ethics, and in conceptions of "enlightenment." In thinking that imagines the ideal structure of the world to be static, the human ethical task is limited to recovery of past values and conformity to norms that are already given and complete. Confining ourselves to the activities of recovering and conforming to the already given, imaginative, creative thinking would have little or no role to play. In this book we have repeatedly taken exception to that understanding of ideals and have attempted to stake out an alternative to it, one that recognizes and welcomes an ongoing human responsibility to renew and recreate the human order. Instead of clinging to past norms, our highest calling is to renew our ideals through imaginative, thoughtful engagement with others in open collaboration, so that we work against and around self-imposed and historically imposed limitations on the quality and character of human life.

Plato was astonishingly insightful in naming "the good, the true, and the beautiful" as the three most prominent dimensions of human striving. We do indeed—all of us—seek in our lives what we take to be good, true, and beautiful. What Plato did not see, or was not able to concede, is that human history is the story of the unfolding of visions of "the good, the true, and the beautiful" as they have come to be experienced throughout the variegated history of human cultures. Rather than being fixed in character and given to us in advance of our quest, these ideals stand out ahead of us as the horizons that inspire our striving and that recede into the future as we approach them. "Enlightenment" and all of its components, from generosity to wisdom, are moving targets. As we move, in whatever direction, our horizons move, always luring us out of complacency and into the quest for richer forms of human excellence. So when Plato saw how coherently "the good, the true, and the beautiful" map the domain of human aspiration, he had no idea how many different ways there might be to fill in the content of that basic structure through human history, nor what thinkers in our era would say about the historical character of the structure itself.

But isn't it entirely traditional—not to mention static—to take the same six "perfections" that Buddhists named centuries ago as the basis for ethical reflection today? How does that basis for this book illustrate the movement of ethical ideals and the role of imagination in creating them? I pose these questions so that in response to them we can propose and clarify a relationship to traditions that would serve us well in our efforts to articulate contemporary ideals.

Traditions are the foundations for any reflective effort. We understand only by virtue of standing within and upon traditions of understanding. Finite human minds never begin at the beginning. Thankfully so, because otherwise they would never attain anything beyond initial levels of understanding. Instead, we begin the effort to understand from particular positions somewhere in the history of human understanding and work forward from there.

The best place to begin reflection on ethical ideals is with the most admirable accomplishments that world cultures have to offer. These can be readily found in two places—in inherited traditions from one's own past and in other cultures. Both of these offer an advanced starting point for reflection and the promise of ethical "difference" as a stimulus to thought. The differences between where we stand right now and standpoints located in either the past or another culture are what motivate and inspire further reflection on ideals. The tension between them is productive in that it opens a vantage point from which we might come to see things differently, a position from which we might change our minds. The role of traditions, therefore, one's own and others, is to provide points of departure for advancing into the future. Creative thinking does not overthrow the past so much as stand upon it and use it for the purposes of renewal, continually amending, rethinking, and reconstituting ideals suitable for current circumstances. The appropriate relationship to traditions before us is neither slavish adherence nor disdainful rejection but rather attentive use, stimulus to thought, and extension of perspective. We transform ourselves and our culture in view of the variety of ideals placed before us by our multiple legacies.

How does this bear on the use of the six perfections in this effort to articulate a contemporary philosophy of self-cultivation? The six perfections are the most accomplished effort at character ethics produced in the long and diverse Buddhist tradition. They offer a sophisticated point of departure for reflections on contemporary ideals and the practices of self-cultivation. But, given that this effort takes place in the English language and in a Western cultural milieu, these are not "our" traditions, or rather they are just now becoming ours. The distance or difference between positions inscribed into our language and culture and others provides the tension necessary to stimulate thought and to inspire the productive questioning and reenvisioning of ideals.

Because the tension between different standpoints is productive, the goal of ethical reflection is not to eliminate that tension but rather to use it in gaining deeper and more comprehensive perspective on the issues we face. New standpoints produced generate new differences and new grounds for insight. For these reasons, one important achievement in the cultivation of character is to learn not to be unnerved and thrown off balance when the tensions inevitably produced by differences arise. As we learn to overcome our discomfort and relax around differences, we place ourselves in a much better position to manage them wisely while putting them to creative use. The goal, therefore, is not to create a world without difference and tension—which would be a lifeless world without movement and stimulation—but rather to understand the place of multiplicity and difference of perspective in our cultural lives to the point that we can live peacefully among them while employing them for enlightening purposes.

One dimension of our initial question remains, however. Although it may be justifiable to begin these reflections with the traditional Buddhist ethic of the six perfections, wouldn't it be less than satisfactory to end there, especially for a book that emphasizes the impermanence of ideals and the importance of imagination in cultivating them? Indeed. If these meditations simply reiterated traditional teachings on the six perfections, they would have failed to work the kinds of mediation necessary to provide a bridge from traditional Buddhist worlds into our time and place. But that is not what these meditations have done or sought to do. The result of these meditations is not a traditional or orthodox rendering of Buddhist teachings on the perfections. Although Buddhists who have learned the six perfections in a traditional Asian context will certainly recognize the general outline of these ideas, they will be surprised to find what they do as they proceed. One hopes that this is a surprise that challenges them to think further about the application of the six perfections to their time and place. New questions posed in new circumstances will have shifted particular aspects of each perfection. New ways of describing them in a new language give different nuance and orientation to them. Critical questioning will have removed certain elements of their traditional form no longer adequate to a new setting. New perspectives will have added new emphases to each of the six—for example, "justice" injected into morality, "mind/body conjunction" into energy, and "imagination" and "judgment" into wisdom. If successful, these meditations both learn from and go beyond traditional conceptions of the six perfections.

This is not a new development. The six perfections have always been a work in progress, changing forms as Buddhism moved through new times and places in Asia. That these six general characteristics have been maintained for this long shows their open character and flexibility in addition to their insight. For centuries they have functioned to invite use and experimentation while providing direction within the overall orientation of character ethics. Although, because of its very different starting point in a non-Asian culture, this rendering of the six perfections may have reenvisioned and revised more than is customary, it is nevertheless true that Asian Buddhists who reflect on the six perfections from their time and place do the same. Invariably something changes. What we hope for is change for the better, a renewal of ideals.

Also there is nothing magical about the number six. Classical Buddhist texts went back and forth between naming six and ten perfections, and often changed which particular ideals were included in these lists. The outcome for us could have just as easily been some other number, depending on the range and breadth of character included within each one. As our rendering of the six unfolds, we see that each perfection incorporates other aspects of ideal character within it. Generosity is structured to include openness, selflessness, compassion, understanding, and gratitude; and, in alternative arrangements, any of these might have been singled out as a separate form of human excellence. Morality encompasses justice, reciprocity, temperance, and trustworthiness. Tolerance includes gentleness, humility, strength, and confidence. Energy encompasses effort, determination, vitality, and courage. Meditation subsumes concentration, deliberation, composure, and self-awareness, while wisdom includes all of the above and more. If it were not for awkwardness and the weight of tradition, we might just as easily have ended up with sixteen rather than six. The rhetorical point here is simply that the traditions of ethical thinking included in the six perfections have provided an excellent point of departure for reflection on human character and ideals even if—no, especially if—we end up extending and stretching these six into somewhat new and interestingly different forms. Their historical success rests on that adaptability to a variety of circumstances.

In our time, one of the strengths of Buddhism as a starting point for reflection on ideals is its commitment to the principle of nondualism. This is a commitment to inclusivity, comprehensiveness, wholeness. Nondualism in Buddhism takes many forms, all worthy of consideration. We have examined the metaphysical principle of "emptiness" in every chapter of this book by developing an understanding of the interdependence of the reality in which we live as its depth dimension. Buddhist "emptiness" is nondualism in the most comprehensive sense—it encompasses everything. The human social dimension included within that has been the focus of the ethical thinking attempted here. Recall that the Buddhist "Mahayana" aspires to be the "great" or "large vehicle" by virtue of its intention to encompass all living beings. In this sense, Buddhists commit themselves to being inclusive in every way possible and to avoiding the religious and cultural exclusivism that has overwhelmed the world's religions with reactionary fundamentalisms of all kinds. The forms of fundamentalism now emerging within virtually every culture are delusional attempts to turn back human history so that the interdependence and unity of human life on the planet need not be either acknowledged or accommodated. That delusion of separation will either fade away or threaten our mutual destruction. Buddhist reflections on inclusivity show us how and why that is so, and the value of this position is becoming more evident daily.

Opting for an ethics of inclusivity indicates a firm resolve to build on our shared humanity, to work with cultural differences and through conflicts peacefully and cooperatively. It indicates a commitment to an ideal of spiritual and cultural endeavor that seeks the common good for everyone rather than a limited good for an exclusivist culture in which differences are disallowed and outsiders shunned. These forms of nondual inclusivity, it seems to me, are the ideal that most closely map our current situation in the world. That situation is one of rapidly unfolding globalism, a recognition of the inevitable oneness of all beings living on this planet that is inescapable at this point in human history. Currently, modern internationalism is giving way to globalism in recognition that nation states are losing their primacy as the driving force behind world affairs. What states and provinces are to nations, nations will soon be to the emerging global reality that is advancing daily. As recent events have shown dramatically, we already live within one global economic system, one global political reality, one global communications network, and one global ecological environment, the one planet we all share.

If we confine ourselves exclusively to the cultural and ethical resources of our own nations, then our culture and ethics will continue to be nationalistic, and the exclusivism that will be required to maintain that nationalism will necessarily be narrow-minded and militant. Although it has evoked currents of reactionary resistance all over the world, the emergence of these historical developments has also provided the basis for the creation of a new world. That newly emerging world already calls out for a new global ethics, and this is the ethical task of our time—the creation of ways of being and living that accord with the reality of the global unity in which we reside. Inclusivity—a patient, open nondualism—will inevitably be a fundamental principle in that global ethics. Since no single philosophy, religion, or culture has a monopoly on wisdom and truth, it will be incumbent upon all participants to join together in this collective effort. Pooling the world's cultural resources and wisdom and working through them toward higher ideals, we commit ourselves to the practice of learning what we can from wherever we can—globally—and putting this learning to use on behalf of everyone. The renewed, regenerated ideals that would arise from this effort and become obvious to new generations born onto this planet will each embody in some way this profound sense of world unity.

Success in this global venture is far from inevitable, however. Our human historical record is uneven at best. Indeed, success in this effort will call on us to practice generosity, morality, tolerance, energy, mindfulness, and wisdom beyond the extent ever demonstrated in any previous culture. It will call on us to rise to levels of maturity and wisdom previously imagined but never actualized in practice. But since pulling back to conserve the past or the present is clearly the path of global failure, we must accept the challenge of change and rise to this occasion by taking responsibility for the emergence of ethical ideals suitable for our unprecedented moment in history. As far as I can see, only a well-grounded, critically honed effort to renew human ideals will put us in a position to actualize the very real possibilities for global enlightenment already there, visible on our horizons.

ACKNOWLEDGMENTS

I begin in gratitude to Occidental College, where for most of my career I have had the privilege to engage in the exchange of ideas with a gifted and diverse group of students and colleagues, and where my personal intellectual energies have received continual encouragement, support, and freedom. On this particular project—*The Six Perfections*—I have received valuable feedback from an engaged and insightful group of Occidental students in a seminar on Buddhist ethics. I thank Nicole Dedic, Kate Fedosova, Nicholas Francis, Jennifer Goth, Philip Grasso, Chelsea Lewkow, Alena Mihas, Mathew Mikuni, Kelli Moriguchi, Lanier Nelson, Phuong Minh Nguyen, Daniel Pappalardo, Caitlin Peel, Alison Reed, Jessica Rutiz, Katrina Senn, Sophie Simonian, Ben Swift, and Mandarin Yan.

Many thanks go to Cynthia Read and her staff at Oxford University Press for the professional expertise and personal care that they have extended to this project. This press has a very long history of redefining excellence in the realm of publishing, and I am honored by their adoption of my work. I have also received technical assistance on this book from Marguerite Dessornes and Shoshone Johnson at Occidental College, and I extend my appreciation to them. A segment of chapter 2 has been developed upon an essay that was published in the *Journal of Buddhist Ethics* (Dale S. Wright, "Critical Questions toward a Naturalized Concept of Karma in Buddhism," volume 11, 2004) and I thank the editors.

I gratefully acknowledge having learned almost everything that appears in this book from a wide spectrum of thinkers, East and West. Although there are certainly others, the most important for helping me shape my thoughts on this project are found in the list of references at the end of this book. Without them, even the idea of writing on these topics would have been absent from my mind; how much more so the book's contents.

Friends have helped me along in thinking through the ideas in this book, some through conversations and some through critical reading of early drafts of these ideas. Sincere appreciation to Maria Antonaccio, Steven Barrie-Anthony, Sylvie Baumgartel, David Eckel, Steven Heine, David James, Karen King, Malek Moazzam-Doulat, Keith Naylor, William Schweiker, Erika Suderburg, and Kristi Upson-Saia.

Two others have been particularly influential on this project, and to them I extend profound gratitude. To David Klemm, who understands more than the rest of us, and to Martha Ronk, whose facility with our shared language far exceeds my own, in appreciation for all that I have learned from them through many years of friendship.

I dedicate this book to my sisters: To Diane, from whom I learned most of the important things in life and whose vibrant life I miss more than I can begin to say. To Janet, whose arrival provided my very first opportunity to take responsibility and to care for someone who occasionally needed me. The fact that I am now the one who needs her is a matter of some joy to me. To my sisters, in appreciation and love.

NOTES

INTRODUCTION

1. Keown, *Nature of Buddhist Ethics*, 130–31.
2. Powers, *Wisdom of Buddha*, 237.
3. Conze, *Large Sutra on Perfect Wisdom*, 617.

CHAPTER 1

1. Conze, *Large Sutra on Perfect Wisdom*, 625.
2. Ibid., 618.
3. Conze, *Perfection of Wisdom in Eight Thousand Lines*, 217.
4. Powers, *Wisdom of Buddha*, 249.
5. Hanh, *Diamond That Cuts through Illusion*, 25.
6. Conze, *Large Sutra on Perfect Wisdom*, 575.
7. Ibid., 488.
8. Ibid., 565.
9. Ibid., 198.
10. Ibid.
11. Ibid., 198–99.
12. Ibid., 199.
13. Ibid., 598–99.
14. Ibid., 576.
15. Ibid., 556.
16. Ibid., 557.
17. Ibid., 614.
18. Ibid.
19. Śāntideva, *Bodhicaryāvatāra*, 34.
20. Thurman, *Holy Teaching of Vimalakīrti*, 41.
21. Cone and Gombrich, *The Perfect Generosity of Prince Vessantara*.
22. Conze, *Perfection of Wisdom in Eight Thousand Lines*, 178.

CHAPTER 2

1. Śāntideva, *Bodhicaryāvatāra*, 34.
2. Ibid., 35.

3. Meadows, *Ārya Śūra's Compendium*, 175.
4. Conze, *Large Sutra on Perfect Wisdom*, 614.
5. This threefold distinction is developed in the *Mahāyāna Samgraha*, the *Bodhisattvabhūmi*, and elsewhere in Mahayana literature. See Keown, *Nature of Buddhist Ethics*, 137–42 for a helpful summary.
6. Meadows, *Arya Śūra's Compendium*, 191.
7. Powers, *Wisdom of Buddha*, 261.
8. The bodhisattva's paradox is first introduced in the *Diamond Sutra*, and amplified in Mahayana texts thereafter. See Hanh, *Diamond That Cuts through Illusion*, 4.
9. Conze, *Large Sutra on Perfect Wisdom*, 197.
10. Ibid., 616.
11. Ibid., 558.
12. Śāntideva, *Bodhicaryāvatāra*, 41.
13. Conze, *Large Sutra on Perfect Wisdom*, 535.
14. MacIntyre, *After Virtue*, 188.
15. Dalai Lama, *Way to Freedom*, 100.
16. Bendall and Rouse, *Śikṣā-samuccaya*, cited in Harvey, *Introduction to Buddhist Ethics*, 28.

CHAPTER 3

1. Śāntideva, *Bodhicaryāvatāra*, 59.
2. Dalai Lama, *Ethics for the New Millennium*, 102–3.
3. This translation is suggested by Gregory Schopen and discussed in Nattier, *A Few Good Men*, 244.
4. Meadows, *Ārya-Śūra's Compendium*, 195.
5. Conze, *Large Sutra on Perfect Wisdom*, 612.
6. Ibid., 559.
7. This threefold division can be found in the *Bodhicaryāvatāra*, *Bodhisattvabhūmi*, *Mahāyānasūtralankāra*, and elsewhere. See Meadows, *Ārya-Śūra's Compendium*, 88.
8. Śāntideva, *Bodhicaryāvatāra*, 50.
9. Ibid.
10. Dalai Lama, *Ethics for a New Millennium*, 104–5.
11. Śāntideva, *Bodhicaryāvatāra*, 51.
12. Skorupski, *Six Perfections*, 55.
13. Ibid., 51.
14. Dalai Lama, *Ethics for a New Millennium*, 105.
15. Rinchen, *Six Perfections*, 59.
16. Ibid., 58–59.
17. Śāntideva, *Bodhicaryāvatāra*, 51.
18. Meadows, *Ārya-Śūra's Compendium*, 90.

19. Conze, *Perfection of Wisdom in Eight Thousand Lines*, 217.
20. Meadows, *Ārya-Śūra's Compendium*, 195.
21. Śāntideva, *Bodhicaryāvatāra*, 50.
22. Ibid., 50.
23. Powers, *Wisdom of Buddha*, 253.
24. Rinchen, *Six Perfections*, 49.
25. Skorupshi, *Six Perfections*, 49.
26. Śāntideva, *Bodhicaryāvatāra*, 99–108.
27. Dalai Lama, *Ethics for a New Millennium*, 107.
28. Meadows, *Ārya-Śūra's Compendium*, 199.
29. Śāntideva, *Bodhicaryāvatāra*, 55.
30. Ibid., 57.
31. Ibid., 52.
32. Ibid., 53.
33. Dalai Lama, *Ethics for a New Millennium*, 106.
34. Skorupski, *Six Perfections*, 58.
35. Lamotte, *Śūramagamasamādhisūtra*, 129.
36. Conze, *Perfection of Wisdom*, 217.
37. Rinchen, *Six Perfections*, 49.
38. Dalai Lama, *Ethics for a New Millennium*, 104.
39. Milarepa, "Song on the Six Perfections," slightly revised, http://lekshe .typepad.com/lekshes_mistake/2004/07/a_song_on_the_s.html.
40. Conze, *Large Sutra on Perfect Wisdom*, 303.
41. Skorupski, *Six Perfections*, 69.
42. Thurman, *Holy Teaching of Vimalakīrti*, 73.
43. Skorupski, *Six Perfections*, 64.
44. Ibid., 70.
45. Meadows, *Ārya-Śūra's Compendium*, 205.
46. Ibid.
47. Śāntideva, *Bodhicaryāvatāra*, 61.
48. Ibid., 56.
49. Conze, *Large Sutra on Perfect Wisdom*, 130.
50. Conze, *Perfection of Wisdom in Eight Thousand Lines*, 217.
51. Dayal, *Bodhisattva Doctrine in Buddhist Sanskrit Literature*, 214.
52. Dalai Lama, *Ethics for a New Millennium*, 104.

CHAPTER 4

1. Meadows, *Ārya Śūra's Compendium*, 64.
2. *Sagaramati Sūtra*, cited in Meadows, *Ārya Śūra's Compendium*, 92.
3. For more variation on the definition of the perfection of energy, see Dayal, *Bodhisattva Doctrine in Buddhist Sanskrit Literature*, 216–21.
4. Śāntideva, *Bodhicaryāvatāra*, 67.

5. Ibid., 67–68.
6. Ibid., 68.
7. Ibid., p. 68.
8. Conze, *Perfection of Wisdom in Eight Thousand Lines*, 217.
9. Meadows, *Ārya Śūra's Compendium*, 215, 211, 213.
10. Ibid., 209.
11. Ibid.
12. Conze, *Large Sutra on Perfect Wisdom*, 500; Meadows, *Ārya Śūra's Compendium*, 217.
13. Śāntideva, *Bodhicaryāvatāra*, 72.
14. Ibid., 69, 71.
15. Meadows, *Ārya Śūra's Compendium*, 209.
16. Ibid., 93.
17. Śāntideva, *Bodhicaryāvatāra*, 69, 70, 71.
18. Ibid., 72–73.
19. Thurman, *Holy Teaching of Vimalakīrti*, 79.
20. Meadows, *Ārya Śūra's Compendium*, 209.
21. Conze, *Large Sutra on Perfect Wisdom*, 561.
22. Meadows, *Ārya Śūra's Compendium*, 217.
23. Ibid., 92.
24. Hanh, *Miracle of Mindfulness*.
25. Śāntideva, *Bodhicaryāvatāra*, 38.
26. Ibid., 70.
27. Thurman, *Holy Teaching of Vimalakīrti*, 60.
28. Meadows, *Ārya Śūra's Compendium*, 235.
29. Thurman, *Holy Teaching of Vimalakīrti*, 59, 57.
30. Ibid., 57.
31. Meadows, *Ārya Śūra's Compendium*, 92.

CHAPTER 5

1. Meadows, *Ārya Śūra's Compendium*, 223.
2. Śāntideva, *Bodhicaryāvatāra*, 37.
3. Ibid., 88.
4. Dayal, *Bodhisattva Doctrine*, 221.
5. Gethen, *Foundations of Buddhism*, 175.
6. Meadows, *Ārya Śūra's Compendium*, 97.
7. Ibid., 221.
8. Conze, *Perfection of Wisdom in Eight Thousand Lines*, 142.
9. Śāntideva, *Bodhicaryāvatāra*, 96.
10. Ibid., 97–99.
11. Ibid., 100.
12. Conze, *Large Sutra on Perfect Wisdom*, 561, 613.

13. Wayman, *Lion's Roar of Queen Śrīmālā*, 72–74.
14. Conze, *Large Sutra on Perfect Wisdom*, 625.
15. Śāntideva, *Bodhicaryāvatāra*, 225.
16. Ibid., 223.
17. Ibid., 227.
18. Conze, *Large Sutra on Perfect Wisdom*, 561.
19. Conze, *Perfection of Wisdom in Eight Thousand Lines*, 276.
20. Sellars, *Science, Perception, and Reality*, 1.
21. *Kalama Sutta, Anguttara Nikaya*, No. 65, http://www.kammatthana.com/anguttara_nikaya_iii.htm.
22. *Majjhima Nikāya*, No. 63, http://www.accesstoinsight.org/tipitaka/mn/mn.063.than.html.

CHAPTER 6

1. Conze, *Large Sutra on Perfect Wisdom*, 256.
2. Conze, *Perfection of Wisdom in Eight Thousand Lines*, 237.
3. Conze, *Large Sutra on Perfect Wisdom*, 456.
4. Ibid., 457.
5. Lopez, *Heart Sutra Explained*, 19.
6. Thurman, *Holy Teaching of Vimalakīrti*, 67.
7. Conze, *Large Sutra on Perfect Wisdom*, 491.
8. Conze, *Perfection of Wisdom in Eight Thousand Lines*, 240.
9. Ibid., 144.
10. Ibid.
11. Conze, *Large Sutra on Perfect Wisdom*, 475.
12. Ibid., 631.
13. Ibid., 311.
14. Ibid., 113.
15. Ibid., 303.
16. Thurman, *Holy Teaching of Vimalakīrti*, 99.
17. Conze, *Large Sutra on Perfect Wisdom*, 193.
18. Conze, *Perfection of Wisdom in Eight Thousand Lines*, 276.
19. Ibid., 142.
20. Conze, *Large Sutra on Perfect Wisdom*, 361, 134.
21. Conze, *Perfection of Wisdom in Eight Thousand Lines*, 149.
22. Conze, *Large Sutra on Perfect Wisdom*, 611.
23. Ibid., 592.
24. Conze, *Perfection of Wisdom in Eight Thousand Lines*, 109.
25. Conze, *Large Sutra on Perfect Wisdom*, 275.
26. Thurman, *Holy Teaching of Vimalakīrti*, 46.
27. Conze, *Large Sutra on Perfect Wisdom*, 470.
28. Conze, *Perfection of Wisdom in Eight Thousand Lines*, 112.

29. Conze, *Large Sutra on Perfect Wisdom*, 476.
30. Ibid., 198–99.
31. Ibid., 199.
32. Meadows, *Ārya Śūra's Compendium*, 60.
33. Conze, *Large Sutra on Perfect Wisdom*, 101.
34. Ibid., 652.
35. Ibid., 229.
36. Ibid.,
37. Ibid., 248.
38. Ibid., 249.
39. Sellars, *Science, Perception, and Reality*, 1.

REFERENCES

Aitken, Robert. *The Mind of Clover: Essays in Zen Buddhist Ethics*. San Francisco: North Point, 1984.

———. *The Practice of Perfection: The Pārāmitas from a Zen Buddhist Perspective*. Washington, D.C.: Counterpoint, 1997.

Almond, Philip. *The British Discovery of Buddhism*. New York: Cambridge University Press, 1988.

Anderson, Carol S. *Pain and Its Ending: The Four Noble Truths in the Theravada Buddhist Canon*. Richmond, England: Curzon, 1999.

Annas, Julia. *The Morality of Happiness*. New York: Oxford University Press, 1993.

Antonaccio, Maria, and William Schweiker. *Iris Murdock and the Search for Human Goodness*. Chicago: University of Chicago Press, 1996.

Arendt, Hannah. *Essays in Understanding*. New York: Schocken Books, 2003.

Aristotle. *Nicomachean Ethics*. Translated by Terence Irwin. Indianapolis: Hackett, 1985.

Arnold, Dan. *Buddhists, Brahmins, and Belief: Epistemology in South Asian Philosophy of Religion*. New York: Columbia University Press, 2005.

Aronson, Harvey B. *Love and Sympathy in Theravāda Buddhism*. Delhi: Motilal Banarsidass, 1980.

Batchelor, Stephen. *Buddhism without Beliefs: A Contemporary Guide to Awakening*. New York: Riverhead, 1997.

Becker, Lawrence C. *Reciprocity*. London: Routledge, 1986.

Bellah, Robert. *Beyond Belief: Essays on Religion in a Post-Traditional World*. Berkeley: University of California Press, 1970/1991.

Bendall, Cecil, and W. H. D. Rouse, trans. *Śikṣā-Samuccaya*. Delhi: Motilal Banarsidass, 1990.

Berlin, Isaiah. *Four Essays on Liberty*. Oxford: Oxford University Press, 1969.

———. *The Sense of Reality: Studies in the Ideas and Their History*. New York: Farrar, Straus and Giroux, 1996.

Berofsky, Bernard. *Liberation from Self*. New York: Cambridge University Press, 1995.

Brandom, Robert. *Articulating Reasons: An Introduction to Inferentialism*. Cambridge: Harvard University Press, 2001.

Bruns, Gerald. *Hermeneutics: Ancient and Modern*. New Haven: Yale University Press, 1995.

Buddhaghosa, Bhadantācariya. *The Path of Purification*. Translated by Bhikkhu Nanamoli. Seattle: Buddhist Publication Society Pariyatti Editions, 1999.

Buswell Jr., Robert E., and Robert M. Gimello, eds. *Paths to Liberation: The Marga and Its Transformations in Buddhist Thought*. Honolulu: University of Hawaii Press, 1992.

Butler, Judith. *Antigone's Claim: Kinship between Life and Death*. New York: Columbia University Press, 2000.

Cabezón, José Ignacio. *A Dose of Emptiness*. Albany: State University of New York Press, 1992.

———. *Buddhism and Language: A Study of Indo-Tibetan Scholasticism*. Albany: State University of New York Press, 1994.

Caputo, John D. *The Weakness of God: A Theology of the Event*. Bloomington: Indiana University Press, 2006.

Chodron, Pema. *No Time to Lose: A Timely Guide to the Way of the Bodhisattva*. Boston: Shambhala, 2007.

Clarke, J. J. *Oriental Enlightenment: The Encounter between Asian and Western Thought*. London: Routledge, 1997.

Clayton, John. *Religions, Reasons, and Gods*. New York: Cambridge University Press, 2006.

Collins, Steven. *Selfless Persons: Imagery and Thought in Theravāda Buddhism*. New York: Cambridge University Press, 1982.

Cone, Margaret, and Richard F. Gombrich, trans. *The Perfect Generosity of Prince Vessantara*. Oxford: Clarendon Press, 1977.

Conze, Edward. *The Prajñāpāramitā Literature*. Gravenhage: Mouton, 1960.

———. *The Perfection of Wisdom in Eight Thousand Lines and Its Verse Summary*. Bolinas, Calif.: Four Seasons Foundation, 1973.

———. *The Large Sutra on Perfect Wisdom*. Berkeley: University of California Press, 1975.

Crosby, Kate, and Andrew Skilton, trans. *Śāntideva: The Bodhicaryāvatāra*. Oxford: Oxford University Press, 1996.

H. H. the Dalai Lama. *Ethics for the New Millennium*. New York: Riverhead, 1999.

———. *The Way to Freedom: Core Teachings of Tibetan Buddhism*. New York: Harper, 1991.

Damasio, Antonio R. *Descartes' Error: Emotion, Reason, and the Human Brain*. London: Penguin, 1994.

———. *The Feeling of What Happens: Body and Emotion in the Making of Consciousness*. New York: Harcourt, 1999.

Davidson, Donald. *Inquiries into Truth and Interpretation*. Oxford: Oxford University Press, 1984.

Dayal, Har. *The Bodhisattva Doctrine in Buddhist Sanskrit Literature*. London: Kegan Paul, Trench, Trübner, 1932.

Dennett, Daniel C. *Darwin's Dangerous Idea: Evolution and the Meanings of Life*. New York: Simon & Schuster, 1995.

Dharmasiri, Gunapala. *The Fundamentals of Buddhist Ethics*. Antioch, Calif.: Golden Leaves, 1989.

Dreyfus, Georges B. J. *Recognizing Reality: Dharmakirti's Philosophy and Its Tibetan Interpretations*. Delhi: Sri Satguru, 1997.

Dunne, John. *Foundations of Dharmakirti's Philosophy*. Boston: Wisdom Publications, 2004.

Eckel, Malcolm David. *To See the Buddha: A Philosopher's Quest for the Meaning of Emptiness*. Princeton: Princeton University Press, 1992.

Faure, Bernard. *Chan Insights and Oversights: An Epistemological Critique of the Chan Tradition*. Princeton: Princeton University Press, 1993.

Flanagan, Owen. *The Problem of the Soul: Two Visions of Mind and How to Reconcile Them*. New York: Basic Books, 2002.

Foucault, Michel. *The Care of the Self: History of Sexuality Vol. 3*. New York: Random House, 1986.

Frankfurt, Harry G. *The Importance of What We Care About*. Cambridge, England: Cambridge University Press, 1988.

———. *The Reasons of Love*. Princeton: Princeton University Press, 2004.

Gadamer, Hans-Georg. *Truth and Method*. Translated by Joel Weinsheimer and Donald G. Marshall. New York: Crossroad, 1989.

———. *Philosophical Hermeneutics*. Berkeley: University of California Press, 1976.

Garfield, Jay L. *The Fundamental Wisdom of the Middle Way: Nāgarjunā's Mūlamadhyamakrārikā*. New York: Oxford University Press, 1995.

———. *Empty Words: Buddhist Philosophy and Cross-Cultural Interpretation*. New York: Oxford University Press, 2002.

Gethen, Rupert. *The Foundations of Buddhism*. Oxford: Oxford University Press, 1998.

Goleman, Daniel, ed. *Healing Emotions: Conversations with the Dalai Lama on Mindfulness, Emotions, and Health*. Boston: Shambhala, 1997.

———. *Destructive Emotions: How Can We Overcome Them? A Scientific Dialogue with the Dalai Lama*. New York: Bantam Books, 2003.

Gombrich, Richard. *How Buddhism Began: The Conditioned Genesis of the Early Teachings*. London: Athlone Press, 1996.

Gregory, Peter N. *Traditions of Meditation in Chinese Buddhism*. Honolulu: University Press of Hawaii, 1987.

Griffiths, Paul J. *On Being Mindless: Buddhist Meditation and the Mind-Body Problem*. Illinois: Open Court, 1986.

———. *On Being Buddha: The Classical Doctrine of Buddhahood*. Albany: State University of New York Press, 1994.

Gyatso, Janet, ed. *In the Mirror of Memory: Reflections on Mindfulness and Remembrance in Indian and Tibetan Buddhism*. Albany: State University of New York Press, 1992.

Hacking, Ian. *The Social Construction of What?* Cambridge: Harvard University Press, 1999.

Hadot, Pierre. *Philosophy as a Way of Life.* Edited by Arnold I. Davidson, translated by Michael Chase. Oxford: Blackwell, 1995.

Hahn, Thich Nhat. *Being Peace.* Berkeley, Calif.: Parallax Press, 1987.

———. *Miracle of Mindfulness.* Boston: Beacon Press, 1999.

———. *The Diamond That Cuts through Illusion: Commentaries on the* Prajña-paramita *Diamond Sutra.* Berkeley, Calif.: Parallax Press, 1992.

Hampshire, Stuart. *Innocence and Experience.* Cambridge: Harvard University Press, 1989.

Harvey, Peter. *The Selfless Mind: Personality, Consciousness and Nirvana in Early Buddhism.* London: Curzon Press, 1987.

———. *An Introduction to Buddhist Ethics.* Cambridge, England: Cambridge University Press, 2000.

Heidegger, Martin. *Basic Writings.* New York: HarperCollins, 1993.

———. *Mindfulness.* New York: Continuum, 2006.

Heine, Steven. *Opening a Mountain: Koans of the Zen Masters.* New York: Oxford University Press, 2002.

Heisig, James W. *Philosophers of Nothingness: An Essay on the Kyoto School.* Honolulu: University Press of Hawaii, 2002.

Heisig, James W., and John C. Maraldo, eds. *Rude Awakenings: Zen, the Kyoto School, and the Question of Nationalism.* Honolulu: University of Hawaii Press, 1995.

Herman, Barbara. *Moral Literacy.* Cambridge: Harvard University Press, 2008.

Hirakawa, Akira. *A History of Indian Buddhism from Śākyamuni to Early Mahā-yāna.* Honolulu: University of Hawaii Press, 1990.

Ives, Christopher. *Zen Awakening and Society.* Honolulu: University Press of Hawaii, 1992.

Kabat-Zinn, Jon. *Wherever You Go, There You Are: Mindfulness Meditation in Everyday Life.* New York: Hyperion, 1994.

Kapstein, Matthew. *Reason's Traces: Identity and Interpretation in Indian and Buddhist Thought.* Somerville, Mass.: Wisdom Publications, 2001.

Katz, Nathan. *Buddhist Images of Human Perfection: The Arahant of the Sutta Pitaka Compared with the Bodhisattva and Mahāsiddha.* Delhi: Motilal Banarsidass, 1982.

Kekes, John. *Moral Wisdom and Good Lives.* Ithaca, N.Y.: Cornell University Press, 1995.

———. *The Art of Life.* Ithaca, N.Y.: Cornell University Press, 2002.

Keown, Damien. *The Nature of Buddhist Ethics.* Basingstoke: Macmillan, 1992.

Kierkegaard, Søren. *The Concept of Irony, with Continual Reference to Socrates.* Translated by H. V. Hong and E. H. Hong. Princeton: Princeton University Press, 1992.

King, Karen L. *What Is Gnosticism?* Cambridge: Harvard University Press, 2003.

King, Richard. *Indian Philosophy: An Introduction to Hindu and Buddhist Thought*. Washington, D.C.: Georgetown Press, 1999.

Klein, Anne C. *Path to the Middle: Oral Madhyamika Philosophy in Tibet*. Albany: State University of New York Press, 1994.

Klemm, David E. *Hermeneutical Inquiry*. 2 vols. Atlanta: Scholars Press, 1986.

———. *The Hermeneutical Theory of Paul Ricoeur*. Lewisburg, Pa.: Bucknell University Press, 1983.

Klemm, David E., and William Schweiker. *Religion and the Human Future: An Essay on Theological Humanism*. London: Wiley-Blackwell, 2008.

Kraft, Kenneth, ed. *Inner Peace, World Peace: Essays on Buddhism and Nonviolence*. Albany: State University of New York Press, 1992.

Kuhn, Thomas S. *The Structure of Scientific Revolutions*. 2nd ed. Chicago: University of Chicago Press, 1970.

Kupperman, Joel J. *Character*. New York: Oxford University Press, 1991.

———. *Learning from Asian Philosophy*. New York: Oxford University Press, 1999.

———. *Value . . . and What Follows*. New York: Oxford University Press, 1999.

LaFleur, William. *Liquid Life: Abortion and Buddhism in Japan*. Princeton: Princeton University Press, 1994.

Lakoff, George, and Mark Johnson. *Philosophy in the Flesh: The Embodied Mind and Its Challenge to Western Thought*. New York: Basic Books, 1999.

Lamotte, Etienne. *Śūramagamasamādhisūtra*. Delhi: Motilal Banarsidass, 2003.

Lamrimpa, Gen. *Realizing Emptiness: Madhyamaka Insight Meditation*. Translated by B. Alan Wallace. Ithaca, N.Y.: Snow Lion, 2002.

Little, David, and S. B. Twiss. *Comparative Religious Ethics: A New Method*. New York: Harper & Row, 1978.

Lopez, Donald S., Jr. *The Heart Sūtra Explained*. Albany: State University of New York Press, 1987.

———. *Elaborations on Emptiness: Uses of the Heart Sūtra*. Princeton: Princeton University Press, 1996.

———. *The Story of Buddhism: A Concise Guide to Its History and Teachings*. New York: HarperCollins, 2001.

Loy, David. *The Great Awakening: A Buddhist Social Theory*. Somerville, Mass.: Wisdom Publications, 2003.

MacIntyre, Alasdair. *After Virtue*. Notre Dame, Ind.: University of Notre Dame Press, 1983.

———. *Whose Justice? What Rationality?* Notre Dame, Ind.: University of Notre Dame Press, 1988.

———. *Three Rival Versions of the Moral Enquiry*. Notre Dame, Ind.: University of Notre Dame Press, 1990.

Mahasi Sayadaw. *Sallekha Sutta: A Discourse on the Refinement of Character*. Hinsdale, Ill.: Buddhadharma Meditation Center, 1981.

Makransky, John J. *Buddhahood Emboddied: Sources of Controversy in India and Tibet*. Albany: State University of New York Press, 1997.

Marion, Jean-Luc. *Being Given: Toward a Phenomenology of Givenness*. Translated by Jeffrey L. Kosky. Stanford, Calif.: Stanford University Press, 2002.

McDowell, John. *Mind and Reality*. Cambridge: Harvard University Press, 1996.

McGinn, Collin. *The Mysterious Flame: Conscious Minds in a Material World*. New York: Basic Books, 1999.

McRae, John R. *Seeing through Zen: Encounter, Transformation, and Genealogy in Chinese Chan Buddhism*. Berkeley: University of California Press, 2003.

Meadows, Carol. *Ārya-Śūra's Compendium of Perfections: Text, Translation, and Analysis of the Pāramitāsamāsa*. Bonn: Indica et Tibertica Verlag, 1986.

Misra, G. S. P. *Development of Buddhist Ethics*. New Delhi: Munshiram Manoharlal, 1984.

Mohanty, Jitendra Nath. *Classical Indian Philosophy*. Lanham, Md.: Rowman & Littlefield, 2000.

Murdoch, Iris. *The Sovereignty of Good*. London: Routledge, 1970.

Nagel, Thomas. *The View from Nowhere*. New York: Oxford University Press, 1986.

Nakasone, R. Y. *Ethics of Enlightenment: Essays and Sermons in Search of a Buddhist Ethic*. Fremont, Calif.: Dharma Cloud, 1990.

Nattier, Jan. *Once upon a Future Time: Studies in a Buddhist Prophecy of Decline*. Berkeley, Calif.: Asian Humanities Press, 1991.

———. *A Few Good Men: The Bodhisattva Path According to the Inquiry of Ugra*. Honolulu: University Press of Hawaii, 2003.

Nehamas, Alexander. *The Art of Living*. Berkeley: University of California Press, 1998.

Neiman, Susan. *Evil in Modern Thought: An Alternative History of Philosophy*. Princeton: Princeton University Press, 2004.

Nietzsche, Friedrich. *On the Genealogy of Morality*. Translated by M. Clark and A. Swensen. Indianapolis: Hackett, 1998.

Nishitani, Keiji. *Religion and Nothingness*. Berkeley: University of California Press, 1992.

Nussbaum, Martha C. *The Fragility of Goodness*. New York: Cambridge University Press, 1986.

———. *The Therapy of Desire*. Princeton: Princeton University Press, 1986.

Oakeshott, Michael. *On Human Conduct*. Oxford: Clarendon Press, 1975.

Obeyesekere, Gananath. *Imagining Karma: Ethical Transformation in Amerindian, Buddhist, and Greek Rebirth*. Berkeley: University of California Press, 2002.

O'Flaherty, Wendy Doniger, ed. *Karma and Rebirth in Classical Indian Traditions*. Delhi: Motilal Banarsidass, 1983.

Pagel, Ulrich. *The Bodhisattvapitaka: Its Doctrines, Practices and Their Position in Mahayana Literature*. Tring, England: Institute of Buddhist Studies, 1995.

Parks, Graham, ed. *Heidegger and Asian Thought*. Honolulu: University of Hawaii Press, 1987.

Powers, John, trans. *Wisdom of Buddha: The Samdhinirmochana Sutra*. Berkeley, Calif.: Dharma Publishing, 1995.

Prebish, Charles S. *Buddhist Discipline: The Sanskrit Prātimokṣa Sūtras of the Mahāsāmghikas and Mūlasarvāstivādins*. University Park: Pennsylvania State University Press, 1975.

Pye, Michael. *Skilful Means: A Concept in Mahayana Buddhism*. London: Duckworth, 1978.

Queen, C. S., and S. B. King, eds. *Engaged Buddhism: Buddhist Liberation Movements in Asia*. Albany: State University of New York Press, 1996.

Rawls, John. *Theory of Justice*. Cambridge: Harvard University Press, 1971.

Ray, Reginald A. *Buddhist Saints in India: A Study in Buddhist Values and Orientations*. New York: Oxford University Press, 1994.

Ricard, Matthieu. *Happiness: A Guide to Developing Life's Most Important Skill*. Translated by Jesse Browner. New York: Little, Brown, 2006.

Ricoeur, Paul. *Memory, History, Forgetting*. Translated by Kathleen Blamey and David Pellauer. Chicago: University of Chicago Press, 2004.

———. *Oneself as Another*. Translated by Kathleen Blamey. Chicago: University of Chicago Press, 1992.

———. *The Just*. Translated by David Pellauer. Chicago: University of Chicago Press, 2000.

Rinchen, Geshe. *The Six Perfections*. Ithaca, N.Y.: Snow Lion, 1998.

Rorty, Richard. *Philosophy and the Mirror of Nature*. Princeton: Princeton University Press, 1979.

———. *Philosophy and Social Hope*. New York: Penguin, 1999.

Saddhatissa, H. *Buddhist Ethics: Essence of Buddhism*. London: George Allen & Unwin, 1970. Śāntideva. *See* Crosby and Skilton.

Scharlemann, Robert P. *The Being of God: Theology and the Experience of Truth*. New York: Seaburg, 1981.

———. *Inscriptions and Reflections: Essays in Philosophical Theology*. Charlottesville: University of Virginia Press, 1989.

Schopen, Gregory. *Bones, Stones, and Buddhist Monks: Collected Papers on the Archaeology, Epigraphy, and Texts of Monastic Buddhism in India*. Honolulu: University of Hawaii Press, 1997.

Schweiker, William. *Theological Ethics and Global Dynamics: In the Time of Many Worlds*. London: Wiley-Blackwell, 2004.

Sellars, Wilfred. *Science, Perception, and Reality*. New York: Humanities Press, 1963.

Sharf, Robert. *Coming to Terms with Chinese Buddhism*. Honolulu: University Press of Hawaii, 2003.

Shklar, Judith N. *Ordinary Vices*. Cambridge: Belknap Press of Harvard University Press, 1984.

Shusterman, Richard. *Practicing Philosophy*. New York: Routledge, 1997.

Siderits, Mark. *Personal Identity and Buddhist Philosophy: Empty Persons*. Aldershot, England: Ashgate, 2003.

Singer, Peter. *Writings on an Ethical Life*. New York: HarperCollins, 2000.

Skorupski, Tadeusz. *The Six Perfections*. Tring, England: Institute of Buddhist Studies, 2002.

Slingerland, Edward. *Effortless Action: Wu Wei as Conceptual Metaphor and Spiritual Ideal in Early China*. New York: Oxford University Press, 2003.

Stout, Jeffrey. *Democracy and Tradition*. Princeton: Princeton University Press, 2004.

———. *Ethics after Babel*. Boston: Beacon, 1988.

Tatz, Mark, trans. *Asanga's Chapter on Ethics, with the Commentary of Tsong-Kha-Pa; The Basic Path to Awakening, the Complete Boddhisattva*. Lewiston, N.Y.: Edwin Mellen Press, 1986.

Taylor, Charles. *Sources of Self: The Making of the Modern Identity*. Cambridge: Harvard University Press, 1985.

———. *The Ethics of Authenticity*. Cambridge: Harvard University Press, 1991.

Taylor, Mark C. *After God*. Chicago: University of Chicago Press, 2007.

Thannissaro, Bhikkhu. *The Buddhist Monastic Code*. Valley Centre, Calif.: Metta Forest Monastery, 1994.

Thera, Nyanaponika. *The Heart of Buddhist Meditation*. New York: Samuel Weiser, 1973.

Thurman, Robert A. F., trans. *The Holy Teaching of Vimalarkīrti: A Mahāyāna Scripture*. University Park: Pennsylvania State University Press, 1976.

———. *Infinite Life: Awakening the Bliss Within*. New York: Riverhead, 2005.

Tillemans, Tom. *Scripture, Logic, Language: Essays on Dharmakīrti and His Tibetan Successors*. Boston: Wisdom, 1999.

Wallace, B. Alan. *The Taboo of Subjectivity: Toward a New Science of Consciousness*. New York: Oxford University Press, 2000.

———. *Balancing the Mind: A Tibetan Buddhist Approach to Refining Attention*. Ithaca, N.Y.: Snow Lion, 2005.

Walzer, Michael. *On Toleration*. New Haven: Yale University Press, 1997.

Wayman, Alex, and Hideko Wayman, trans. *The Lion's Roar of Queen Śrīmālā*. Delhi: Motilal Benarsidass, 1974.

Williams, Bernard. *Moral Luck*. New York: Cambridge University Press, 1981.

———. *Ethics and the Limits of Philosophy*. London: Collins, 1985.

Williams, Paul. *Mahāyāna Buddhism: The Doctrinal Foundations*. London: Routledge, 1989.

———. *Altruism and Reality: Studies in the Philosophy of the Bodhicaryāvatāra*. Richmond, England: Curzon, 1998.

———. *The Reflexive Nature of Awareness: A Tibetan Madhyamaka Defense*. Surrey, England: Curzon, 1998.

Willis, Janice Dean, trans. *On Knowing Reality: The Tattvārtha Chapter of Asanga's Bodhisattvabhūmi*. New York: Columbia University Press, 1979.

Woodruff, Paul. *Reverence: Renewing a Forgotten Virtue*. Oxford: Oxford University Press, 2001.

Wright, Dale S. *Philosophical Meditations on Zen Buddhism*. New York: Cambridge University Press, 1998.

CPSIA information can be obtained at www.ICGtesting.com
Printed in the USA
BVOW04s0325150813

328566BV00001B/2/P

9 780199 895799